Transactions
of the
AMERICAN PHILOSOPHICAL SOCIETY
Held at Philadelphia
For Promoting Useful Knowledge
Volume 94, Pt. I

STUDIES ON THE NEOPLATONIST HIEROCLES

Ilsetraut Hadot

Translated from the French by Michael Chase

American Philosophical Society
Philadelphia ■ 2004

ISBN: 0-87169-941-9
US ISSN: 0065-9746

Library of Congress Cataloging-in-Publication Data

Hadot, Ilsetraut.
    [Selections. English. 2004]
    Studies on the Neoplatonist Hierocles / Ilsetraut Hadot ; translated from
the French by Michael Chase.
        p. cm. — (Transactions of the American Philosophical Society, ISSN
    0065-9746 ; v. 94, pt. 1)
    Includes bibliographical references (p.) and index.
    ISBN 0-87169-941-9 (pbk.)
    1. Hierocles, of Alexandria, fl. 430. I. Title. II. Series.

BJ214.H8H33 2004
186'.4—dc22
                                                                2004054780

Contents

Contents

Preface

The Neoplatonist Hierocles, who lived in the fifth century A.D. and taught at Alexandria, has not yet received his due place in the history of Neoplatonic philosophy; or, rather, he has not found any place at all. Most modern works that try to sketch an overview of the history of one or all of the Neoplatonic doctrines leap from Porphyry and Iamblichus to Syrianus and Proclus, without mentioning Hierocles. However, the attentive study of the fragments of his treatise in seven books *On Providence* and of his commentary on the Pythagorean *Carmen aureum* provides us with many important details on the development of Neoplatonic doctrines between Iamblichus and Syrianus-Proclus, knowledge of which would have spared some scholars some rather considerable errors. For instance, there is the fairly recent affirmation that a characteristic of the so-called Athenian Neoplatonism consisted of the tendency to wish to harmonize the various theological traditions with each other, whereas we can plainly read in the extracts that Photius has preserved for us of the *De providentia* that the fourth book of this treatise "wishes to harmonize with the doctrines of Plato what is called the Oracles [*scil.* the *Chaldaean Oracles*] and the hieratic institutions," and that the fifth book "attributes to Orpheus and to Homer and to all those who were famous before Plato appeared, the philosophical theory of Plato on the subjects dealt with above."[1] The texts from Hierocles thus show that this harmonizing tendency existed before the Neoplatonists taught at Athens, and goes back, in all probability, already to Iamblichus.

I therefore think it is useful to publish an updated and slightly abridged English translation of my previous work on Hierocles, published in various places,* which allows Hierocles' median position in the history of Neoplatonic philosophy, between Iamblichus and Syrianus-Proclus, to emerge.

The notes contained in this book are rather numerous, which is nowadays frowned upon by editors. Nevertheless, they are indispensable. They enable the quotation and translation of most of the principal texts

---

* I. Hadot 1978; 1979; 1990b; 1993; 2002, especially pp. 325–327.
[1] Photius, *Library,* cod. 214, p. 173a Bekker, vol. III, pp. 128ff. Henry.

of Hierocles, and especially of other authors, which are necessary in order to situate Hierocles at a precise point in the history of Neo-platonism. If these important texts are placed in footnotes, it is with a view to the clarity of my exposition; in this way, the continuity of the exposition is not interrupted, and the material necessary to back it up is not lacking.

I thank with all my heart my colleague and friend Michael Chase, who has carried out the translation with all his competence as a translator and a scholar.

CHAPTER I

Biographical Elements

Few details of the life of the philosopher Hierocles are known to us. In his treatise *On Providence,* Hierocles introduces himself[2] as the faithful disciple of Plutarch of Athens, the Platonic, or, as we are now accustomed to say, Neoplatonic philosopher. The Platonic diadoch Plutarch of Athens died in A.D. 431 or 432 at a very advanced age,[3] approximately two years after the young Proclus arrived in his school. This date supplies us with a *terminus ante quem* for dating Hierocles' studies under Plutarch. In addition, Damascius, in his biography of his master Isidorus, the Platonic diadoch who succeeded Marinus, speaks of Hierocles as someone no longer alive. Now, the *Life of Isidorus* was written at the time of the reign of Theodoric the Great in Italy,[4] and therefore between 497 and his death in 526.[5] Here is the extract concerning Hierocles from Damascius' *Life of Isidorus* as preserved by Photius:[6]

> <He says> that Hierocles, who adorned studies at Alexandria with his elevated mind and sublime language, possessed, together with his confidence and magnificence of diction, an extreme abundance of thought. As he was distinguished by his facility of speech and the abundance of the prettiest nouns and verbs, he always struck his auditors with admiration, constantly vying with the beauty of language and the wealth of thought of Plato. This Hierocles was once explaining Plato's *Gorgias* to the members of his school, and Theose-

[2] Photius, *Library,* cod. 214, p. 173a37 Bekker, vol. III, p. 130 Henry: cf. below, the text cited at p. 7.

[3] Marinus, *Vita Procli,* 12: cf. H. D. Saffrey and L. G. Westerink, (1968–1997), xii–xiii.

[4] Damascius, *Vita Isidori,* 64, p. 94, 10–11 Zintzen; Photius, *Library,* cod. 242, 340a15–18 Bekker, vol. VI, p. 21 Henry, fr. 51A Athanassiadi.

[5] This margin may be reduced if we suppose that Damascius wrote this work while he was already diadoch of the School of Athens, and thus probably after 515. On this date, cf. P. Hoffmann, 1994.

[6] Damascius, *Vita Isidori,* 54, p. 80 Zintzen, in Photius, *Library,* cod. 242, 338b28–339a7 Bekker, vol. VI, p. 18 Henry, fr. 45A Athanassiadi.

bius, one of his auditors, wrote down his explanation. When, as is normal, after some time, Hierocles came to explain the *Gorgias* for the second time, the same disciple wrote it down, and when he compared the first comments with the second, he found as it were nothing identical in them, although—and this seems incredible—each one followed Plato's intention as closely as possible. This, then, indicates how immense was the ocean of this man's intelligence.

From this passage, then, we learn that Hierocles taught at Alexandria at some point in time, and that he taught there long enough to be able to take up a second series of explanations of a part or of all the dialogues of Plato contained in the Neoplatonists' program of study.[7] We should also note the laudatory tone of the entire passage.[8] This does not prevent Damascius from situating Hierocles at a fairly low level in the hierarchy of the various Neoplatonic virtues: Hierocles, like Aristotle and Chrysippus, did not achieve a result of great importance with regard to the great wisdom that is worthy of a god, so preoccupied was he with the problems situated in the domain of that which is mortal and human.[9] In other words, Hierocles, like Aristotle, Chrysippus, and other philosophers of the same tendency, remained at the level of civic virtues.[10] The *Suda* transmits another passage about Hierocles, taken from the same work by Damascius; it must have followed Photius' summary, which we have just quoted, fairly closely:

> Hierocles' courage and magnanimous character was demonstrated by the misfortune that happened to him. For when he went up to Byzantium, he offended the party in power, was dragged into court, and was beaten up by the blows of men [cf. Aeschines, *In Timarchum*, 59]. Covered with blood, he plunged the cup of his hand into his own blood and sprinkled the judge with it, saying: "Here, Cyclops, drink this wine now that you have eaten human flesh" [= Homer, *Od.*, 9, 347]. Condemned to exile, he later returned to Alexandria, where

[7] Cf. I. Hadot, 1990a, pp. 44–46; 80–93; A. J. Festugière, 1969.

[8] One can well understand Damascius' judgment by reading Hierocles' commentary on the *Carmen aureum*, especially if one has previously read a comparable commentary, such as that of Simplicius on the *Manual* of Epictetus. Both commentaries are intended for beginners (cf. chap. III, sec. 11, p. 62), and they therefore strive to furnish an initial introduction to Neoplatonic philosophy. Hierocles succeeds admirably in giving a simple, clear, and brief overview of this highly complex system, while managing to avoid the risk of deformation. Simplicius, on the contrary, finds it much more difficult to make his explanation conform to the demands of this kind of commentary, and he succeeds only at the cost of sacrificing concision.

[9] Damascius, *Vita Isidori*, 36, p. 62 Zintzen = fr. 39 Athanassiadi, in Photius, *Library*, cod. 242, vol. VI, p. 15 Henry.

[10] On the Neoplatonic virtues, cf. I. Hadot, 2001, pp. LXXVII–C.

he studied traditional matters with his disciples."[11]

This text shows us the attitude of the pagan philosopher Hierocles during the persecution led by the Christians at Constantinople, a situation in which he kept his cool in a way Damascius found admirable. Damascius also notes with satisfaction that Hierocles, even after these bitter experiences, continued imperturbably to teach traditional—that is to say, pagan—philosophy at Alexandria, without compromising. The *Suda* text on Hierocles ends as follows:

> One may get an idea of the magnanimous wisdom of Hierocles by reading the treatises he wrote on the *Golden Verses* of the Pythagoreans and by numerous other books on providence. In these works the man appears, with regard to his "form of life,"[12] as of elevated character; but lacking precision with regard to philosophical notions.[13]

Damascius thus enumerates as Hierocles' written work the two treatises we still know today: the commentary on the *Carmen aureum*, which we possess in its entirety, and the treatise *On Providence,* of which we have a few traces in two summaries by Photius.[14] We will see in subsequent chapters that these two treatises, as far as their doctrinal content is concerned, are consistent with the trend of post-Iamblichean Neoplatonism, but they do not yet contain all the refinements that characterize Neoplatonism under Proclus, and even later under Damascius. This is what Damascius means when he says that Hierocles was not exact with regard to philosophical notions.

R. Henry[15] mistakenly attributes to our Hierocles a work on Apollonius of Tyana, but the author in question is another Hierocles, also a pagan, who lived two centuries earlier, under the reign of Diocletian, and whose work is known to us through the polemics of Eusebius of Caesarea. In his dialogue *Theophrastus,* Aeneas of Gaza[16] distinguishes two Hierocles: one of them, the pagan philosopher who taught at Alexandria, is presented in it as the professor of two of the three char-

---

[11] Damascius, *Vita Isidori,* fr. 106, p. 83, 5–11 Zintzen = fr. 45B Athanassiadi.

[12] Ζωή is a Neoplatonic technical term that designates the vivifying aspect of the soul, or, in the words of Hermias, *In Phaedr.,* p. 110, 7 Couvreur, the soul under the aspect of motion. This term is thus applied to the rational soul as much as to the irrational and vegetative souls. For this reason, ζωή is almost interchangeable with "soul" (ψυχή) in cases where the term "soul" is used in a wide sense and according to common usage.

[13] Damascius, *Vita Isidori,* fr. 106, p. 83, 12–15 Zintzen = fr. 45B Athanassiadi.

[14] Photius, *Library,* cod. 214, vol. III, pp. 125–130 Henry; ibid., cod. 251, vol. VII, pp. 189–206 Henry.

[15] Photius, *Library,* vol. III, p. 125 Henry, note 1.

[16] On this work, cf. A. Segonds, 1989, 1994².

acters of the dialogue, and he is to be identified with our philosopher. He is called Hierocles the professor (ὁ διδάσκαλος), to distinguish him from an author of marvelous stories,[17] about whom it is difficult to say if he is the same as the Hierocles mentioned by Eusebius. Hierocles does not appear in this dialogue by chance, for it is indeed against him, or rather against his treatise *On Providence*, that the *Theophrastus* seems to be directed. However, since Hierocles was already dead at the time,[18] and philosophical instruction in Alexandria was on the decline,[19] the principal pagan interlocutor is a certain Theophrastus, probably a fictitious personage, depicted as one of the last pagan philosophers who are condemned to wander alone, with no school or fellow students, seeking out a limited, strictly private audience here and there. In any case, Aeneas of Gaza refutes the principal arguments of Hierocles' treatise *On Providence* point by point, at the same time as he makes a clear distinction between the various stages Platonic doctrine went through down to Syrianus and Proclus.

The treatise *On Providence* was dedicated to a certain Olympiodorus, who distinguished himself in Roman embassies and had "brought many very mighty barbarian nations under obedience to the Romans."[20] The identification of this Olympiodorus has been a frequent topic of modern study, without any certain results having been achieved.[21]

---

[17] Aeneas of Gaza, *Theophrastus,* p. 18, 13ff. Colonna.
[18] Ibid., p. 2, 20 Colonna.
[19] Ibid., p. 3, 4–8 Colonna.
[20] Photius, *Library,* cod. 214, p. 171b22 Bekker, vol. III, p. 125 Henry.
[21] On the hypothetical identification with Olympiodorus of Thebes, cf. I. Hadot, 2000.

CHAPTER II

Hierocles' Ideas on the History of Platonic Philosophy

I hope to have demonstrated elsewhere,[22] while refuting the views of Praechter,[23] that in the commentary on Epictetus' *Manual,* Simplicius' theology, or his doctrine of first principles, by no means corresponds to a doctrinal tendency peculiar to the school of Alexandria, but rather reflects the doctrines of the school of Athens; in particular those of Proclus and Damascius. In this same commentary by Simplicius, we find a theory of providence that is very close to that of Hierocles. Following Praechter, could we not recognize in Hierocles' doctrines on providence a typically Alexandrian doctrinal tendency that was then taken over by Simplicius?[24] On this view, Hierocles, in his doctrines concerning the creation of the world, providence, and the destiny of the soul, departs from the tendency of the Neoplatonic philosophy of his time, and takes up the theses of Middle Platonism, which are even tinged with Christianity.

However, if we submit Hierocles' doctrines on the history of Platonic philosophy, on matter, the Demiurge, the soul, and providence, to careful analysis, we shall discover that these theories are not, any more than the theology of Simplicius, evidence of the anachronistic survival of the theories of Middle Platonism or of Ammonius Saccas, and that they do not depart from the overall evolution of Neoplatonism.

1. *Photius' Summaries of Hierocles' Treatise* On Providence

Let us begin with the careful examination of the two summaries of Hierocles' seven books *On Providence,* which we owe to the zeal of Photius. We can leave aside the beginning of the first summary (codex

---

[22] In I. Hadot, 1978, chaps. III and VII, reprinted in I. Hadot, 2001a, pp. XLV–C.
[23] K. Praechter, 1913.
[24] K. Praechter, 1927.

214), in which Photius is only concerned with the personality of the treatise's addressee, and read the text starting from 171b33:[25]

> The declared goal of the present investigation is to deal with providence, by combining the doctrine of Plato with that of Aristotle. The author wishes to bring the two thinkers together, not only in their theories on providence, but also on all the points on which they conceive of the soul as immortal, and in which they have philosophized on the heavens and on the world. As far as all those are concerned who have set these authors at odds with one another, he explains at length that they have been gravely mistaken, and that they have departed as much from the intention of the two thinkers as from the truth: some willingly, because they have offered themselves up as sacrifices to their quarrelsome temperament and their foolishness; others, because they were the slaves of a preconceived opinion and of their ignorance. He adds that previous authors formed an imposing chorus, until there shone forth the wisdom of Ammonius, who, he recalls emphatically, was nicknamed "the pupil of the gods." It was he, he says, who restored the doctrines of these two ancient philosophers to their purity, abolished the foolishness that had accumulated on both sides, and showed the agreement between the thought of Plato and that of Aristotle concerning the important and most necessary doctrinal questions.

Let us note two important points. First, Hierocles adopts the hypothesis of doctrinal agreement between Plato and Aristotle, a hypothesis that was almost universally accepted in the Neoplatonic school after Porphyry. Secondly, Hierocles designates a certain Ammonius as the restorer of this agreement. We learn which Ammonius is meant at the end of Photius' first summary, where he gives a glimpse of the structure of Hierocles' treatise. Let us continue to follow Photius' account in due order:

> His work is divided into seven books. The first consists in the exposition (εἰς ἔκθεσιν διατυποῦται) of the exercises and investigations he has carried out on providence, justice, and the judgement that will descend upon us according to the merits of our actions; the second, in gathering together the Platonic opinions (τὰς πλατωνικὰς δόξας), seeks to confirm them on the basis of Plato's very writings; the third

---

[25] For passages from codices 214 and 251, the translation is based on that by R. Henry, vol. III, p. 125ff., and vol. VII, pp. 189ff. This translation has sometimes been modified.

presents the objections that could be used to contest these opinions, and seeks to refute their intention; the fourth wishes to set what are called the *Oracles,* and the hieratic institutions, in agreement with Plato's doctrines; the fifth attributes Plato's philosophical theory on the above subjects to Orpheus, Homer, and all those who were famous before the appearance of Plato; the sixth takes up all the philosophers after Plato, taking Aristotle himself as the most eminent, until Ammonius of Alexandria, whose most remarkable disciples were Origen and Plotinus. After Plato, then, and up until the men we have just mentioned, he takes up all those who have made a name for themselves in philosophy, and he shows that they all agree with the doctrine of Plato. All those who have tried to break the unity of views between Plato and Aristotle, he ranges among the mediocre, and those who should be considered with horror: they have altered many aspects of Plato's works, even as they proclaimed him to be their master. The same is true of the works of Aristotle, on the part of those who identify themselves with his school. All their maneuvers have had no other goal than to find a way to set the Stagirite and the son of Aristo at odds with one another. The seventh book starts from a different angle, as it deals with the doctrine professed by Ammonius, Plotinus and Origen, and also Porphyry and Iamblichus, as well as their successors—all those who, according to him, are born of sacred stock—as far as Plutarch the Athenian, who he says was the Master who taught him these doctrines; all these concur with the philosophy of Plato in its pure state.

We can thus see that this work was a treatise on providence, which could claim to give a complete outline of the question, from both the dogmatic and the historical points of view. With regard to the first phrase: it cannot be decided with certainty whether the phrase εἰς ἔκθεσιν διατυποῦται ought to be understood as meaning a complete exposition of Hierocles' doctrines, or merely a "prototheory," or preliminary overview of the contents of the entire treatise, as I would tend to understand it in the light of the analyses that A. Elter[26] carried out on codices 214 and 251 of Photius' *Library.*

As a function of these two interpretative possibilities, we may imagine that the second book set forth the Platonic doctrines in detail, or else demonstrated them, in both cases based on texts by Plato. Needless to say, we must understand by "Platonic doctrines" the theses elab-

---

[26] A. Elter, 1910. According to this author, the structure of the first book of Hierocles' treatise was the following: dedication to Olympiodorus; preliminary overview of the contents of the entire treatise; consolations to Olympiodorus; and brief summary of the various books.

orated by the Platonic school, in its uninterrupted exegesis of Plato's writings. More precisely, thanks to what Photius tells us of the seventh book of Hierocles' treatise *On Providence,* we can affirm that, for Hierocles, these "Platonic doctrines" corresponded to the contemporary trend represented for him by Plutarch of Athens. These were the theses that Hierocles sought to corroborate by citing the works of Plato. For an example of this type of procedure, which the Neoplatonists used very often, it suffices to read, for example, chapter four of book two of Proclus' *Platonic Theology,* where the author confirms his thesis that the One is the first principle beyond the Intellect by citations with commentary from Plato's *Republic, Sophist,* and *Philebus.* The few extracts that Photius gives us from the second book of Hierocles' treatise (codex 251) also allow us to recognize the procedure in question, but in a highly abbreviated and mutilated form.

After setting forth the Platonic theses on providence, and demonstrating their conformity with the teaching of Plato, there followed, in the third book, the refutation of his adversaries. Needless to say, such a refutation once more implied setting forth and confirming Hierocles' own doctrines. Thus, Photius' summary (codex 251) has preserved for us extracts from Hierocles' response to those who deny the existence of free will in man. In this response Hierocles sets forth all his arguments in favor of his own thesis, most of which had already been collected in the *De fato* of Alexander of Aphrodisias.

The description of the contents of the fourth book contributes a very important element: What Photius calls τὰ λεγόμενα λόγια are nothing other than the famous *Chaldaean Oracles,*[27] and the expression ἱερατικοὺς θεσμούς designates the hieratic institutions—in other words, theurgy, a method of access to the divine that included ritual and mystical practices. If Photius had wished to speak of the oracles of Delphi, or of other such prophecies, he would not, it seems to me, have used the phrase τὰ λεγόμενα λόγια, but would have written simply τὰ λόγια. In any case, the presence of the two terms together in the expressions: τὰ λεγόμενα λόγια and ἱερατικοὶ θεσμοί, which were so characteristic of the Neoplatonism of Hierocles' time, excludes, in my opinion, any possibility of giving another meaning to the phrase. We know that the Neoplatonists from Iamblichus on attached a great deal of importance to proving the conformity of the theological system of the *Chaldaean Oracles* with the system of Plato. We also know that Porphyry still

---

[27] The most frequent designation of the *Chaldaean Oracles* among the Neoplatonists was τὸ λόγιον or τὰ λόγια. Cf. H. Lewy, 1978, Excursus I, p. 443. According to the same author (p. 3ff.), the *Chaldaean Oracles* were written in the second half of the second century of our era.

maintained a fairly reserved attitude toward the cult practices linked with the *Chaldaean Oracles,* and that it was under the influence of Iamblichus that theurgy, as well as the term ἱερατικὴ τέχνη, were introduced into the tradition of the Neoplatonic school.[28] If, therefore, Hierocles, in the fourth book of his treatise *On Providence,* tried to prove Plato's agreement with the *Chaldaean Oracles* and with theurgical practice, then he is to be ranged among the partisans of Iamblichus, and he uses a procedure that he could not have found among the exponents of Middle Platonism. This is amply confirmed, moreover, in the commentary on the *Carmen aureum,* verses 67–69, where Hierocles declares that the ἱερατικὴ ἀναγωγή is an indispensable complement to theoretical philosophy.[29]

The fifth book, Photius tells us, dates Platonic philosophy as far back as Orpheus, Homer, and others who were famous before Plato. We encounter this systematic effort at assimilation in the commentaries of Proclus, but also, very clearly, in the commentary by Hermias[30] on Plato's *Phaedrus.* We shall discuss an example of this later on. As far as the *Chaldaean Oracles,* the *Orphica,* and Neoplatonic doctrine are concerned, Proclus had elaborated a concordance between these three systems, a synopsis of which we may find in H. Lewy's book on the *Chaldaean Oracles.*[31] Proclus may have been the first Neoplatonist to

---

[28] Cf. Lewy, 1978, p. 464. Cf. Damascius, *In Phaed.*¹ § 172, p. 105 Westerink: "Some place philosophy above all other things, as do Porphyry, Plotinus, and many other philosophers; others place the hieratic art in the first position, as do Iamblichus, Syrianus, Proclus, and all the hieratics."

[29] Hierocles, *In Carmen aureum,* XXVI, p. 116, 20–117, 2 Köhler. Hierocles affirms that the rational soul must be purified by philosophy, but that the soul's immortal vehicle, the αὐγοειδὲς σῶμα, must be purified by hieratics and telestics, and that it would be of no use to purify one without the other. Following Iamblichus, this is clearly directed against Porphyry, who, in the *De regressu animae,* did admit that the pneumatic soul can be purified by theurgy, but who affirms at the same time that the philosopher is not to concern himself with theurgy, which has no usefulness for the rational soul, the only one that counts. Theurgy will thus be useful only for people who are not capable of leading the life of a philosopher (Porphyry, *De regr. an.,* fr. 287–288 Smith). Cf. Iamblichus, *De myst.,* I, 12 (41, 12), p. 62 des Places: "It is clear that the salvation of the soul of which we speak is also (καὶ) ensured by the theurgical practices themselves (ἀπ'αὐτῶν τῶν ἔργων)." The καὶ is directed against Porphyry. Cf. F. W. Cremer 1969, p. 95. Cremer's book not only helps us directly to understand the extent of the influence of the *Chaldaean Oracles* on Iamblichus' *De myst.,* but also, indirectly, to see the impact that the *Chaldaean Oracles* and Iamblichus had on Hierocles. Cf. below, chap. III, sec. 8: "Theurgy."

[30] According to Zintzen (in P. Couvreur, 1971, p. 299), Hermias in his commentary followed rather faithfully the course of his master Syrianus, which he attended together with Proclus (but cf. H. Bernard 1997, pp. 10ff.; 18ff.). Syrianus himself was the disciple of Plutarch of Athens. We know from the *Suda,* IV, p. 479, 1 Adler, s.v. Συριανός, that he had written ten books on the doctrinal agreement between Orpheus, Pythagoras, Plato, and the *Chaldaean Oracles.*

[31] Lewy, 1978, Excursus VII, pp. 481–485.

furnish a wealth of material on this subject, but neither he nor his master Syrianus was the first to make such an exhaustive attempt at harmonization; this is proved by the commentary of Hermias and Hierocles' treatise *De providentia*. Nevertheless, it is unlikely that a systematization of such breadth could have been carried out before Iamblichus.

The sixth book reviewed all the philosophers who came after Plato, starting with Aristotle, the agreement of whose thought with that of Plato was also demonstrated. The result of this investigation was that all the partisans of the Platonic and Aristotelian schools who had believed they saw doctrinal differences between Plato and Aristotle—and there were many until the time of Ammonius[32]—had to be either declared to be forgers or else dismissed as merely envious. This Ammonius, says Hierocles, had as his most famous disciples Plotinus and Origen, and it was thanks to his influence that the truth was definitively victorious. Obviously, the person in question was Ammonius Saccas.

With the doctrines of this Ammonius, Photius tells us, Hierocles made a new departure in his seventh book, and he asserted that the philosophical tendency in the Platonic school, which took as the basis of its interpretation the agreement in thought between Plato and Aristotle, flourished up until his master Plutarch of Athens, passing through Plotinus, Origen,[33] Porphyry, and Iamblichus. With regard to Plutarch of Athens, Hierocles tells us explicitly that it was he who taught him these Platonic doctrines in their purified form, which was due to the reforming genius of Ammonius of Alexandria. The role of Ammonius Saccas is also mentioned in another passage from Photius' second summary.[34]

---

[32] See above, p. 6, the translation of the first passage from Photius.

[33] K.-O. Weber's book (1962), gave definitive proof—despite the objections of P. F. Beatrice (1992)—that we must distinguish between the Christian and the Pagan Origen, although his work is open to criticisms on several points with regard to Ammonius (cf. P. Hadot, 1963). The Origen mentioned by Hierocles is the Pagan.

[34] Photius, *Library*, cod. 251, pp. 461a24ff. Bekker, vol. VII, p. 191 Henry: "Many Platonists and Aristotelians devoted a great deal of labor and work to setting their respective masters in contradiction with one another, with regard to their principal dogmas. They carried their love of dispute and their audacity to such an extreme that they even falsified the doctrines of their own masters in order better to demonstrate that the two men did not agree. And this disturbance that had struck philosophical teachings lasted until Ammonius, the pupil of the gods. For he, filled with enthusiasm for the philosophical truth, and despising the opinions of the masses, who were inflicting the greatest dishonor upon philosophy, was the first adequately to understand the thought of the two philosophers, and to make it unanimous. And he transmitted philosophy, untroubled by factions, to all his disciples, but first and foremost to Plotinus and Origen, the best of his familiars, and to all their successors."

2. *The Development of Platonic Philosophy According to Hierocles*

This brief summary of the seven books of Hierocles' *On Providence* informs us that Hierocles had a specific historical view of the development of Platonic philosophy. Plato's philosophy, itself interpreted as a revelation, was understood as a meeting point, and at the same time the first culminating point between the revelations prior to Plato's time (traces of which are found in the *Orphica,* in the philosophy of Pythagoras, and in the poetry of Homer and Hesiod, with the totality being identical to the later revelations, the *Chaldaean Oracles*), and later philosophy up until Ammonius, represented exclusively by the disciples of Plato, that is, the Platonists together with Aristotle and his school. The philosophies of Plato and Aristotle were considered as concordant in everything having to do with the doctrines on the soul, the heavens and the earth, and providence. After Aristotle, there began a period of decadence in the interpretation of Plato and of Aristotle: a good number of the philosophers of both schools denied the agreement in the thought of their respective masters. Yet Ammonius succeeded in putting a definitive end to all these false interpretations and to the arbitrary falsifications of the two works, so that after him the true Platonic philosophy was restored to its state of purity until the days of Hierocles, and no one doubted the agreement between the thought of Plato and of Aristotle any longer.

On the subject of this history of Platonic philosophy, we may start by making the following two observations.

First, the historical overview that Hierocles gives of the development of the Platonic school implies Hierocles' adherence to a philosophical system that is typically Neoplatonic, and even late Neoplatonic. The contents of books four and five, with their systematic incorporation of the *Chaldaean Oracles,* theurgy, the *Orphica,* and such divinely inspired poets as Homer, presuppose a degree of development of the Neoplatonic system that was reached only between Iamblichus and Proclus, and thus corresponds perfectly to the philosophy of Hierocles' time.

So far, consequently, the summary has not contributed any elements that allow us to doubt, as Praechter nevertheless does,[35] the truth of

---

[35] Praechter, 1913, col. 1481–1482: "When, according to Phot. 173a32ff., Hierocles claims the authority of Plotinus, Origen, Porphyry, Iamblichus, and the other Neoplatonists as far down as Plutarch, from whom he claims to have taken over his theory, for his doctrine of providence and retribution, this proves nothing with regard to any genuine dependency. Obviously, the only thing that matters to Hierocles is to be able to support himself by the authority of these famous leaders of his philosophical school. No doubt, in the part of his work which is lost, he brought the agreement of his theory with theirs into existence in the usual way: through artificial interpretation." Praechter is followed by R. Beutler, 1951, col. 962.

Hierocles' affirmation that he adheres to the Platonic doctrines which his master Plutarch of Athens had taught him.

The doctrine of Plutarch of Athens, who was also the master of Syrianus and—albeit briefly—of Proclus, is virtually unknown to us from elsewhere. Beutler[36] and especially Évrard[37] have tried to detach him from the evolutionary direction that Neoplatonism had taken with Iamblichus, and they have brought him closer to Porphyry, by attributing to Plutarch—hesitantly, to be sure—the *Anonymus Turinensis,* which has since been attributed to Porphyry himself by P. Hadot.[38] Of all the other arguments that Évrard brings up to prove that Plutarch was not influenced by Iamblichus, but rather adhered to the theological system of Plotinus and Porphyry, none seems valid to me. Moreover, we know today, thanks to the work of H. D. Saffrey and L. G. Westerink,[39] that the Neoplatonism of Iamblichus may have become established within the Athenian schools in the mid-fourth century. Here I will limit myself to giving the conclusion at which Saffrey and Westerink arrive after a meticulous examination of the historical details: "Plutarch of Athens, these authors tell us, no doubt initiated by Priscus and Iamblichus II, and drawing directly at the very source of the works of the 'divine Iamblichus,' was the first scholarch resolutely to enter into the Neoplatonic current. Thus, together with his disciple and successor Syrianus, he was worthy of being considered as the founder of Neoplatonism at Athens."[40] It is therefore not surprising to find traces of the doctrine of Iamblichus in Hierocles' historical overview. We will see later on if the examination of the various doctrines on providence that Photius attributes to Hierocles leads to the same results.

Before that, however, we must deal with some difficulties raised by Hierocles' presentation of the history of Academic thought. It might be thought surprising that, for Hierocles, the renewal of Platonic philosophy coincides with the general and henceforth uncontested acknowledgment of the agreement between the thought of Plato and of Aristotle, and that this phenomenon should be linked to the name of Ammonius rather than to that of Antiochus of Ascalon or of Porphyry. Of Anti-

[36] Beutler, "Plutarchos von Athen," col. 962–975, especially col. 963, 18ff.

[37] É. Évrard, 1960.

[38] P. Hadot 1968, 1: 102–143; for the text, 2: 61–113. Victorinus' sources have been further discussed by, among others, M. Tardieu 1996, P. Hadot 1996. G. Bechtle (1999) has attributed the anonymous commentary to second-century Middle Platonist circles, but see now M. Zambon 2002, who returns to P. Hadot's attribution to Porphyry.

[39] H. D. Saffrey and L. G. Westerink (1968–1997) 1: "L'École d'Athènes au IVᵉ siècle."

[40] H. D. Saffrey and L. G. Westerink 1968–1997, 1: p. XLVII. D. P. Taormina (1989, pp. 54–55) reaches the same conclusion, after reviewing and analysing scholarly opinion on the philosophical tendencies of Plutarch of Athens (*ibid.,* pp. 26–54).

ochus of Ascalon, we know from Cicero that he was the first Academic resolutely to affirm the unity of doctrine between Plato and Aristotle. As for Porphyry, he is known for having written a treatise in seven books entitled *On the Unity of the Doctrine of Plato and of Aristotle*,[41] and we know that after him, and only after him,[42] this conception became traditional in the Neoplatonic school. Why does Hierocles mention the name of Ammonius in this context? First of all, if Hierocles names Ammonius, that does not necessarily imply, as Theiler would have it, a personal knowledge of Ammonius' teaching, which knowledge would have come down to him through intermediary sources.[43] We can just as well, and with still greater likelihood, propose other hypotheses. For instance, the following, which is perhaps not the only probable one, but which is one of the possible explanations: in his historical account, might not Hierocles simply be following Porphyry's treatise *On the Unity of the Doctrine of Plato and Aristotle?* Might it not be Porphyry himself who designated Ammonius Saccas as the first upholder of this thesis, in the same way as he had elsewhere mentioned this same Ammonius, the master of Plotinus, as the author of a very important dogma concerning the soul's union with the body?[44] In addition, Plotinus himself, according to Porphyry,[45] took the teaching of Ammonius as the foundation of his philosophy. It would have been difficult for Porphyry to attribute to Plotinus himself a doctrine according to which the teachings of Plato and of Aristotle were identical; for Plotinus' *Enneads*, which Porphyry himself had edited, contained sharp criticisms by Plotinus against Aristotle. Porphyry must therefore have restricted himself to pointing out a *de facto* agreement between the philosophical systems of Plotinus and of Aristotle,[46] and to defending by this means his thesis of the unity of the Platonic and

[41] Sudas, s.v. *"Porphyrios"*; cf. R. Beutler, 1953, col. 285.

[42] In the second half of the second century, the Middle Platonist Atticus was still hostile to this tendency toward harmonization. Cf. Ph. Merlan, 1969. Numenius was also far from admitting the unity of thought between Plato and Aristotle: cf. fr. 24 des Places. Similarly, Plotinus criticizes Aristotle several times, for instance on the subject of the category of essence (οὐσία); cf. *Enn.*, VI, 1, 2, 1ff. Atticus wrote a treatise "Against those who profess the doctrines of Plato while relying on the doctrines of Aristotle" (Πρὸς τοὺς διὰ τῶν Ἀριστοτέλους τὰ Πλάτωνος ὑπισχνουμένους), cited at length by Eusebius in his *Evangelical Preparation*; cf. *Praep. Evang.*, XI, 1, 2, vol. II, p. 6, 21 Mras.

[43] W. Theiler, 1966, p. 37, thinks that Hierocles could have used the *collectio Ammonii scholarum* mentioned by Priscian in his *Solutiones ad Chosroem* (*Comment. in Arist. Graeca, Suppl. Arist.*, I, 2, p. 42, 15 Bywater), which, according to Theiler, were written by Theodotus, a professor of Platonic philosophy at Athens, mentioned by Longinus in Porphyry's *Vita Plotini*, 20, 39 Henry-Schwyzer.

[44] Cf. H. Dörrie, 1959, pp. 54–55.

[45] Cf. Porphyry, *Vita Plotini*, 3, 32–34; 14–16 Henry-Schwyzer.

[46] Cf. P. Hadot, 1974. [See the English version in R. Sorabji, ed., *Aristotle Transformed* (London, 1990), pp. 125–140—Trans.]

Aristotelian doctrines. Yet he could not have attributed to Plotinus an active role in the tendency toward harmonizing the Aristotelian and Platonic doctrines; apparently, therefore, Ammonius was more suitable for such an interpretation.

As far as Antiochus of Ascalon is concerned, he no longer counted for much among the Neoplatonists. A comparison between the descriptions of the history of the Academy found in the fragments of Numenius' treatise *On the Academy's Deviation from Plato* and in Augustine's *Contra Academicos* reveals the purely negative role that the tradition of the Platonic school attributed to Antiochus of Ascalon: he was considered a traitor, because he had dared to introduce Stoic dogmas into the teachings of the Academy.[47]

Thus, Hierocles is, it seems, a witness to a period of Neoplatonism (Porphyry, Iamblichus, Plutarch of Athens), in which the unity of the doctrines of Plato and of Aristotle was an article of faith, and in which the paternity of this rediscovery was attributed to Ammonius. As we have seen, other features of his account of the history of Platonism allow us to situate Hierocles still more precisely: they presuppose a degree in the development of Neoplatonism that was achieved only between Iamblichus and Proclus. This will be confirmed by the following chapter.

[47] Numenius, fr. 28 des Places. Augustine, *Contra Academicos,* III, 18, 41.

CHAPTER III

Hierocles' Philosophical Ideas on Matter, the Demiurge, and the Soul

1. Photius' Summaries Concerning the Demiurge and Matter

We now move on to examine the various doctrines of Hierocles himself, as reported by Photius, following as much as possible the order observed by Photius in his summaries. Photius tells us:

> In conformity with Plato, his research establishes the previous existence of a god who is the demiurge of the entire cosmic order (διακόσμησις), both visible and invisible, which the artisan, he says, produces without any substrate (μηδενὸς ὑποκειμένου): his will alone was enough to bring beings into existence. From corporeal substantialization (οὐσίωσις) united to incorporeal creation: from these two he constituted a perfect world (κόσμος), which is at the same time double and one.[48]

With this text, we must compare the following extract, which Photius gives us in his second summary, and which is textually almost identical:[49]

> Plato, he says, establishes the previous existence of a demiurgic god (δημιουργὸς θεός) who governs the entire cosmic order (διακόσμησις), both visible and invisible, which is not produced from any pre-existing substrate (μηδενὸς προϋποκειμένου): his will sufficed for him to bring beings into existence. From corporeal nature (φύσις) united with incorporeal creation, out of these two a perfect world (κόσμος) is constituted, which is at the same time double and one.[50]

---

[48] Photius, *Library*, cod. 214, 172a22ff. Bekker, vol. III, p. 126 Henry.

[49] Photius, *Library*, cod. 251, 461b7ff. Bekker, vol. VII, p. 192 Henry.

[50] The last phrase of this and of the preceding quotation is based on an interpretation of Plato, *Tim.*, 47c: "Indeed, the birth of this World took place through a mixture of the two orders of reality, necessity and intelligence (ἐξ ἀνάγκης τε καὶ νοῦ συστάσεως). However, intelligence dominated necessity. . . ." Necessity was already identified with

Finally, we quote a third parallel text:[51]

> Why, he says, do I enumerate these ones (probably Peripatetics) for you, when there are even Platonists who have conserved a false opinion on the creator god? For they did not think him capable of bringing the world into existence by himself alone, thanks to his own power and wisdom, acting from all eternity (ἐξ ἀϊδίου). But they thought he could only create with the help of an unengendered matter (ἀγενήτου ὕλης), by utilizing that nature (φύσις) which had not been brought into existence by him: all things were pre-existent potentially in this so-called matter (πάντων μὲν δυνάμει προϋποκειμένων ἐν τῇ λεγομένῃ ὕλῃ), whereas he, so to speak, only painted them in different colors, placed them in order, and separated them from their hylic form.

2. Matter Engendered Outside of Time: A Neoplatonic Doctrine Since Porphyry

With these passages, clearly directed against Middle Platonists like Plutarch of Chaeronea and Atticus,[52] we are in the presence of a doctrine according to which matter is engendered (γενητή). Among the Neoplatonists, the word γεηντός may take on a twofold meaning: first of all, it can signify that something is caused, by a superior principle, outside of time; second, that it is caused and participates in time, that is, that it belongs to the world of becoming. We see from the distinction made by Hierocles a bit later between the two parallel senses of the

---

matter by Calcidius, *In Tim.*, cap. 269, p. 274 Waszink, who was probably following Numenius on this point (cf. Van Winden, 1965², pp. 33ff.). Proclus, for his part, identifies it with *Heimarmenê: De prov.*, 13, 14ff. (H. Boese, 1960), p. 121. For the end of the phrase, cf. Hermias, *In Phaedr.*, p. 45, 11 Couvreur: "Thus, we must say that creation is double; one is invisible, the other visible. . . ."

[51] Photius, *Library*, cod. 251, p. 460b22 Bekker, vol. VII, p. 189f. Henry.

[52] Cf. Plutarch, *De an. procr.*, 1014a: "It is thus better to let ourselves be persuaded by Plato, and to say that the world was engendered by a god—and to sing: 'This is the best of engendered things, and that is the best of causes,'—whereas substance or matter, from which it was engendered, not having been engendered but having always been at the disposition of the demiurge (οὐ γενομένην ἀλλὰ ὑποκειμένην ἀεὶ τῷ δημιουργῷ), offered itself up to be disposed, set in order, and assimilated to him in so far as was possible. For creation did not take place from that which does not exist (οὐ γὰρ ἐκ τοῦ μὴ ὄντος ἡ γένεσις), but from that which was not in a good enough state and in sufficient quality as in the case of a house, a cloak, or a statue." Cf. Atticus, according to Proclus, *In Tim.*, vol. I, p. 283, 27 Diehl, quoted after the translation of A.-J. Festugière, 1966–1968, 2: 131: "However, let us pursue once again the extraordinary hypotheses of Atticus, according to whom the mass moved by irregular and disorderly movements is unengendered, but the World is engendered at a moment of time. . . ." Cf. the refutation of this theory in Proclus, *In Tim.*, vol. I, p. 383, 23ff. Diehl.

word ἀγένητος,[53] which refer to matter (for him, matter is "unengendered" with regard to time, but "engendered" with regard to its cause), that these two interpretative possibilities were known to him, and that he approved of them. This detail is not unimportant, but Praechter neglects it completely. He thinks that Hierocles abandons the doctrine, universally accepted in Platonism, affirming the coexistence of two principles (God, Matter) or three principles (Ideas, God, Matter)—a doctrine that Neoplatonism conserved while admitting, in the form of an opposition between the demiurge and matter, a certain dualism beneath the One.[54]

In fact, however, Praechter confused two different problematics. It is true that Neoplatonism contains a kind of dualism that opposes the demiurge and matter, but this dualism is inscribed within a monism that is more fundamental, since all the Neoplatonists since Porphyry admit that matter proceeds from the One. In his commentary on Plotinus' treatise Πόθεν τὰ κακά, Porphyry had drawn the final consequences

---

[53] Photius, *Library,* cod. 251, p. 460b39–41 Bekker, vol. VII, p. 190 Henry: ". . . so that, for the matter which is at issue here, if it were unengendered not only outside of time, but also outside of a cause in the sense in which we say that god is unengendered, to find itself set in order would not be a good thing." This distinction appears for the first time, to my knowledge, in Taurus, a Platonist of the second century of our era; it was then taken up by Porphyry and Proclus, as is affirmed by Philoponus (*De aeternit. mundi,* p. 145, 1ff. Rabe): "Some of Plato's exegetes, like the Platonist Taurus and Porphyry the Phoenician, and following them Proclus, admit that according to Plato, the world is engendered; but it is not engendered in the sense in which it began from a certain beginning of its being (ἀπό τινος ἀρχῆς τοῦ εἶναι ἀρξάμενον), but according to another mode of generation: for they say that what is 'engendered' is said in several different ways." Philoponus, who may have still been able to read Taurus' commentary on the *Timaeus,* then cites Taurus word for word, concerning these different interpretations of the word "engendered" (op. cit., p. 147, 5ff. Rabe): "The world must, therefore, be said to be engendered, because its being comes to it from elsewhere, and because it comes to it from the god in conformity with whom it was set in order. Likewise also for those according to whom the world is eternal, the moon possesses a light which is engendered by the sun, although there was no moment in which it was not illuminated by it. In this sense, then, if someone wishes to say that the world is engendered according to Plato, let him say so; but if he wishes to imply something temporal by this, and the fact that, whereas it did not exist before, it was engendered later: this can no longer be accepted." This twofold interpretation of the word γενητός, which also favors the harmonizing exegesis of Plato and of Aristotle (cf. Simplicius, *In Phys.,* p. 256, 14ff.; 1154, 3ff. Diels), allows an escape from the alternative: the cosmos must be either engendered and corruptible, or unengendered and incorruptible; an alternative which caused problems for the ancient interpreters of Plato's *Timaeus.* On this subject, cf. C. Andresen, 1955, chap. 3, "Zeit und Ewigkeit," pp. 276ff., with the review by H. Dörrie, *Gnomon,* 29 (1957), pp. 185ff. Cf. J. W. Waszink 1955, and 1965, p. 129 ff.; also J. Pépin, 1964, pp. 38ff.; 86ff. The texts that refer to the Platonic doctrine on the genesis of the cosmos are conveniently collected and commented in H. Dörrie and M. Baltes 1998, vol. 5, Bausteine 136–145. Cf. also ibid., vol. 4 (Stuttgart, 1996), Baustein 124b. These texts deny that matter is a principle; but the relevant texts from Hierocles are lacking.

[54] Praechter, "Hierokles," col. 1482.

from the monistic system of Plotinus, by making matter a hypostasis of the One.[55] Plotinus himself, to judge by his writings, had not given as clear a solution to this problem. It was probably under the joint influence of the *Chaldaean Oracles*,[56] which called matter πατρογενής,[57] that Porphyry reached this interpretation. But the *Chaldaean Oracles* were not the only authority to which Porphyry referred. We know from the testimony of Simplicius that Porphyry also relied upon the Pythagoreans to justify his doctrine. According to Porphyry, Moderatus the Pythagorean reported that the Pythagoreans, followed by Plato, were the first of the Hellenes to conceive of matter as engendered.[58] Simplicius cites Moderatus, through the intermediary of Porphyry, as follows:

> And here is what Porphyry writes in the second book of the treatise *On Matter*, citing in his favor the words of Moderatus: "The Unifying proportion [ὁ ἑνιαῖος λόγος = the One that functions as a proportion, λόγος] wished, as Plato says somewhere, to constitute the generation of beings from itself, detached quantity from itself by privation, after having deprived it of all the proportions and forms which are proper to it. This was called quantity without form, without division, and without figure, but which nevertheless receives form, figure, division, quality, and all analogous things."[59]

It is interesting, as A.-J. Festugière remarks,[60] that Iamblichus refers in his treatise *De mysteriis* to the same doctrine of Moderatus, while

---

[55] Cf. Aeneas of Gaza, *Theophrastus*, p. 45, 4ff., Colonna, 51 Boissonade (the speaker is the Christian Euxitheos): "Matter is thus neither unengendered nor without a beginning (ἄναρχος); this is what the *Chaldaean Oracles* and Porphyry teach you. He entitles 'On the Descent of the Soul' the book which makes public the *Chaldaean Oracles*, in which the fact that matter is engendered is strongly defended, and while interpreting Plotinus' book entitled 'On the origin of evils,' he says somewhere that matter is not unengendered, and that the affirmation that it must be counted among the principles must be rejected as atheistic." With regard to the title "On the descent of the soul," my translation follows the correction by H. Lewy, 1978, p. 450. For a parallel passage that probably comes from Porphyry, cf. Johannes Lydus, *De mensibus*, iv, 159, p. 175, 5ff. Wünsch, cited by W. Theiler, 1933, p. 17.

[56] Cf. preceding note.

[57] Cf. Johannes Lydus, *De mensibus*, iv, 159, p. 175, 9 Wünsch, and Psellus, *Hypotyp.*, 27, in É. des Places, ed., *Oracles Chaldaïques*, p. 201.

[58] Simplicius, *In Phys.*, p. 230, 34ff. Diels; cf. the commentary by P. Hadot, 1968, I, p. 166.

[59] Simplicius, *In Phys.*, p. 231, 5ff. Diels, translation based on that by A.-J. Festugière, 1944–1954, 4:38. In the same chapter, entitled "The One which transcends the Dyad-matter," A.-J. Festugière comments on other Pythagorean attestations of this same doctrine (pp. 36–40). Cf. Simplicius, *op. cit.*, p. 181, 7ff., where he presents the same doctrine of the Pythagoreans, according to Eudoros.

[60] Festugière, 1944–1954, 4:39–40.

attributing it to the Egyptians. The two texts resemble one another down to the Greek terms which Festugière has carefully compared. Here is the text:

> Thus, from on high until the ultimate things, the doctrine concerning the principles, for the Egyptians, begins from the One, and proceeds to multiplicity, and the many, again, are governed by the One, and everywhere the indeterminate nature is mastered by some determinate measure, and the highest, unitary cause of all things. As for matter: God produced it from substantiality by separating the materiality off from below. The Demiurge took this matter, which is vivifying, in hand, and from it he fashioned the simple, incorruptible spheres, and with the extreme residue that remained, he fabricated engendered and corruptible bodies.[61]

Later on, we shall have to specify the meaning of the last lines of this text, which allude to the role of substrate played by matter in the work of the demiurge. For the moment, let us say that this doctrine of engendered matter, of which we possess the first traces within Platonism in Eudorus of Alexandria[62] (first century B.C.) but which was vigorously attacked by Numenius[63] and Atticus,[64] remained in effect until the end

---

[61] Iamblichus, *De myst.*, VIII, 3 (264, 14), p. 197 des Places, translation based on that by Festugière, 1944–1954, 4:39. Cf. Proclus, *In Tim.*, vol. I, p. 386, 9 Diehl, where he refers to this passage of the *De myst*. Cf. Iamblichus, *In Tim.*, fr. 38 Dillon, quoted in the translation by Dillon, 1973, fr. 38: "And indeed the tradition of the Egyptians has the same account of it [i.e. matter]: at least, the divine Iamblichus relates that Hermes wishes materiality to be created out of substantiality (ἐκ τῆς οὐσιότητος τὴν ὑλότητα παράγεσθαι); and indeed it is likely from this source that Plato derived such a doctrine of Matter."

[62] Cf. H. Dörrie, 1944.

[63] Numenius, *Test.* 30 Leemans = fr. 52 des Places (= Calcidius, *In Tim.*, cap. 295–299, p. 297, 7ff. Waszink), translation based on that by É. des Places: "Let us now examine the Pythagorean doctrine. Numenius, who was of the school of Pythagoras, has recourse, in order to refute this Stoic doctrine of the principles, to the doctrine of Pythagoras, with which he says that of Plato is in agreement. According to him, Pythagoras gave to God the name of monad, and to matter that of dyad; this dyad, according to him, when it is indeterminate, has no generation, but when it is determined, it is engendered. In other words, before it is adorned and receives form and order, it is without birth nor generation, but when it is adorned and embellished by the demiurgic God, it is engendered, and thus, since generation is a later event, this totality without order nor generation must be understood as being as old as the God who brings order to it. Some Pythagoreans, however, have not grasped the point of this theory; for them, this indeterminate and measureless dyad is also produced by the unique monad, when this monad leaves off its nature to take on the appearance of the dyad; with the paradoxical result that the monad, which existed, disappears, and the dyad, although non-existent, comes into being, and that a transformation makes matter out of God, and the measureless, limitless dyad out of the monad: an opinion unacceptable even to people of inferior culture."

[64] Cf. Proclus, *In Tim.*, I, 283, 28ff. Diehl = above, n. 52, second quotation.

of the Neoplatonic school.[65] Proclus, in his *Commentary on the Timaeus,* not only maintains this doctrine personally, but he transmits to us, in great detail, the arguments by which Porphyry defended this thesis, confirmed it by Platonic texts, and refuted the contrary opinions of the Middle Platonist Atticus.[66] We are justified in supposing that Hierocles also ranged Atticus among the Platonists who had maintained a false doctrine about the creator god, and whom Photius' report leaves anonymous.

The difference between the doctrines of the Middle Platonists Plutarch of Chaeronea, Numenius, and Atticus, on the one hand, and those of the Neoplatonists beginning with Porphyry, on the other—for the moment, we leave Hierocles outside the discussion—is as follows. The two groups distinguish two matters, or rather two states of the same matter: a state in which it is largely or completely indeterminate, and another state in which it is set in order by the demiurge.[67] For the Middle Platonists Plutarch, Numenius, and Atticus, by contrast, indeterminate matter is unengendered in both senses of the word: both outside of a cause and outside of time, it is "as old as the demiurge." In other words, it is not engendered (γενητή), but is a substrate (ὑποκείμενον) for the work of the demiurge.[68] Moreover, it is the cause of evil, either in itself,[69] or by virtue of the evil soul that moves it.[70] At most, they admit that *de-*

---

[65] Cf. Simplicius, *In Phys.,* p. 256, 14–257, 4 Diels.

[66] Proclus, *In Tim.,* vol. I, p. 391, 4ff. Diehl; French translation in Festugière, 1966–1968, 2:258ff.

[67] In a logical context, Porphyry designated these two states of matter by the terms πρῶτον ὑποκείμενον or πρώτη ὕλη and δεύτερον ὑποκείμενον; cf. Simplicius, *In Cat.,* p. 48, 6–21 Kalbfleisch.

For the later Neoplatonists, things become even more complicated. Proclus distinguishes a state of matter in which it is completely indefinite, incorporeal, and invisible; an intermediary state, corresponding to the matter that Plato describes as moved by an irregular movement, and visible (= *Timaeus,* 30a2–6), which is matter already provided with forms by the Model, prior to the work of the demiurge; and then a final state, in which it is completely qualified. This last state results from the action of the demiurge, who is responsible for setting in order the forms inherent in matter (Proclus, *In Tim.,* vol. I, p. 387, 5ff. Diehl; French trans. in A.-J. Festugière 1966–1968, 2:252ff. Proclus calls matter in its first state πρῶτον ὑποκείμενον or πρώτη ὕλη, and matter in its third state δεύτερον ὑποκείμενον; cf. Festugière, op. cit., p. 252, n. 1; Proclus, *In Tim.,* p. 388, 20ff. Diehl. Between the πρῶτον ὑποκείμενον and the δεύτερον ὑποκείμενον comes the ὁρατὸν πλημμελῶς καὶ ἀτάκτως κινούμενον. This terminology appears already in Porphyry's lost commentary on the *Categories,* addressed to Gedalios, cf. fr. 55, p. 45, 17ff. Smith (= Simplicius, *In Cat.,* p. 48, 1ff. Kalbfleisch).

[68] Cf. the quotation from Plutarch, above, p. 16 n. 52. For Numenius, cf. the text cited at n. 63. For Atticus, cf. Proclus, *In Tim.,* vol. I, p. 381, 26ff. Diehl; French translation in A.-J. Festugière, 1966–1968, 2:244ff.

[69] This is the view of Numenius; cf. Test. 30 Leemans = fr. 52 des Places (= Calcidius, *In Tim.,* cap. 295–299, p. 297, 7–302, 20 Waszink). Cf. F. P. Hager, 1962.

[70] This is the doctrine of Plutarch of Chaeronea and of Atticus, according to Proclus, *In Tim.,* vol. I, p. 391, 10 Diehl.

terminate matter may be said to be engendered,[71] because it has a beginning. For the Neoplatonists beginning with Porphyry, by contrast, even indeterminate matter is engendered, by a cause superior to the demiurge, but outside of time. This allows Proclus to say that this indeterminate matter is just as much engendered (γενητή) as it is the first substrate (πρῶτον ὑποκείμενον) relative to the work of the demiurge.[72] Thus, for the Neoplatonists, the demiurge merely receives, as it were, a matter that has already been provided for him; but since this matter derives ultimately from the same cause as the demiurge himself, it cannot be opposed to the demiurge as good is to evil. Matter is not foreign to the demiurge, but is in a certain sense immanent within him. Besides, since the demiurge is the closest cause, as far as the creation of the cosmos is concerned, the Neoplatonists may speak of the demiurge in terms that may give someone unfamiliar with the entire ontological background of their philosophy the impression that, for them, the demiurge was the one and only cause of the universe, and of its constituent elements.[73] Their system allows them just as much to say that the One produces matter as that the demiurge produces it, and the only difference between these two generative causes—which they often do not bother to explain—consists in this: the One produces matter in a primordial sense, and the demiurge produces matter in a derived sense.[74]

3. Two Texts by Porphyry on the Fact That Matter Does Not Preexist

We have seen that both a Neoplatonist like Proclus, and the Middle Platonists we mentioned, could conceive of matter as a substrate (ὑποκείμενον) for the work of the demiurge, albeit in a different way.

---

[71] Cf. the quotation from Numenius, above, p. 19 n. 63.

[72] Cf. n. 67.

[73] For instance, Proclus calls him "the unique and universal demiurge of the entire world" (*In Tim.*, vol. I, p. 314, 25f. Diehl).

[74] Cf. Proclus, *El. Theol.*, prop. 56, translation Dodds: "All that is produced by secondary beings is in a greater measure produced from those prior and more determinative principles from which the secondary were themselves derived. . . . For if the superior principle has conferred on the secondary being the causality which enabled it to produce, it must itself have possessed this causality primitively (prop. 18), and it is in virtue of this that the secondary being generates, having derived from its prior the capacity of secondary generation. . . ." Cf. Proclus, *In Tim.*, vol. I, p. 386, 13ff. Diehl (trans. based on A.-J. Festugière, 1966–1968, 2:250f: "First of all, then, it is from those principles that Matter receives being; then it is produced by the secondary and tertiary, intelligible, intellective, supracelestial, and encosmic causes. But why speak only of the gods? It is also universal Nature that brings Matter into being, in so far as it is a cause, and according to its own mode of being; for it is through Nature that Matter participates in the very first Cause. . . . According to the Henad that is in him, by virtue of which he is also God, the Demiurge is the cause of Matter, even in its lowest degree."

For the latter, matter is a substrate in the sense of a thing that exists by itself, and it preexists the work of the demiurge; whereas for the Neoplatonists beginning with Porphyry, matter is a substrate that has neither existence nor preexistence, but only potential existence. I quote Simplicius, who cites Porphyry:[75]

> Porphyry says that Plato affirms that the non-existent (μὴ ὄν) also exists, but that nevertheless it exists *qua* not-being; that truly existent being (τὸ ὄντως ὄν) is the Idea, and that the latter is the true essence (οὐσία), but that the highest and primordial matter (τὴν δὲ ἀνωτάτω πρώτην ὕλην), which is amorphous and without form (ἄμορφον καὶ ἀνείδεον), from which everything exists, certainly exists, but does not belong in any way among beings. Considered in itself, it is all things potentially, but nothing in actuality (δυνάμει μὲν πάντα ἐστίν, ἐνεργείᾳ δὲ οὐδέν).

Another difference between the Middle Platonists enumerated above and the Neoplatonists beginning with Porphyry—for the moment, we shall continue to leave Hierocles out of the debate—consists in the fact that the former understand the cosmogonic story of the *Timaeus* as expressing a temporal succession, so that it was at a certain moment that the work of the demiurge, the cosmos, was created.[76] The Neoplatonists, by contrast, understand it as a discourse "that theoretically separates the work produced from productive agent, and that makes a totality which necessarily co-exists, come into being successively and within time . . . since all that is created forms a well-linked system."[77] I quote Porphyry again, after an Arabic source:

> Porphyry says in his *Letter to Anebo*[78] with regard to what Plato is accused of by you—that is, that he attributed to the world a begin-

---

[75] Simplicius, *In Phys.*, I, 3, p. 135, 1–5 Diels = Porphyry, fr. 134, p. 139, 7–140, 13 Smith.

[76] For Plutarch of Chaeronea and Atticus, cf. Proclus, *In Tim.*, I, p. 381, 26, with the refutation by Porphyry and Iamblichus. For Numenius, cf. the text cited above, p.19, n. 63 and Beutler, "Numenios," in *R.E.*, Suppl. vol. VII, col. 673, 18–19. For other Middle Platonists, like Alcinoos (*Didasc.*, 14 (169, 32–35), p. 32 Whittaker), however, the *Timaeus* story did not express a beginning of the cosmos at a given moment.

[77] Cf. Proclus, *In Tim.*, vol. I, p. 382, 30ff. Diehl, quoted after the translation of Festugière. Proclus approves of this refutation of the ideas of Plutarch and of Atticus by Porphyry and Iamblichus.

[78] Porphyry, in al-Šahrastānī, *De sectis*, vol. II, pp. 357–358 Gimaret-Jolivet-Monnot. Despite the testimony of this Arabic source, A. R. Sodano (1964, p. 119) attributes the passage to Porphyry's commentary on the *Timaeus*. I see no reason to doubt this source's explicit statement; Iamblichus (*De myst.*, VIII, 2, p. 260, 9 Parthey = p. 195 des Places) attests the fact that such subjects were dealt with in Porphyry's *Letter to Anebo*.

ning within time—that is a lie. For Plato did not think the world had a temporal beginning, but a beginning with regard to a cause, and he also affirms that the cause of its existence is its beginning. He also thought that those who conceive suspicions against Plato when he said that the world was created, that it came into being out of nothing, and that it passed from disorder to order—they are in error; for it is not always true that every kind of not-being precedes being, in the case of those beings which have the cause of their being in something other than themselves; nor that all forms of disorder precede order. Plato merely means that the Creator caused the world to appear out of not-being, and that he brought it into existence, if it is obvious that it does not exist by itself, but that the cause of its existence comes from the Creator.[79]

The second part of Porphyry's argument thus refutes those among Plato's interpreters (Christians?) who upheld something equivalent to the Christian thesis of creation *ex nihilo*. For Porphyry, there can be no question of the world being born from not-being. The world, in so far as it is engendered and has the cause of its existence outside itself, belongs itself to a certain form of not-being. By contrast, the demiurge, or cause that engendered it, belongs to the class of beings that are truly beings, because they contain the cause of their existence within themselves. According to the point of view of a Neoplatonist, then, the creation of the world does not take place from not-being but, on the contrary, from those things that are truly beings, among which is the immediate cause, the demiurge. However, when they referred to the One, the supreme cause, which is not-being above being and which precedes the true beings in the order of causality, the Neoplatonists could also say that the world derives from not-being, albeit indirectly, through intermediary causes. If, with regard to the parts of the corporeal creation of the sublunary world, which is no longer the direct work of the demiurge, a Neoplatonist could speak in a certain sense of creation from not-being, because the matter from which these corporeal parts originate itself represents a possible existence, or a certain category of not-being, this has once again nothing to do with the creation *ex nihilo* of the Christians. These elements are eternal, for they "continually change into one another around the matter that is their substrate," and the corruption of one signifies the birth of the other.[80] This is the doctrinal background of the phrase "for it is not always true that every kind of not-being precedes being

---

[79] Porphyry, in al-Šahrastānī, *De sectis*, vol. II, p. 359, 12ff. Gimaret-Jolivet-Monnot.
[80] Cf. Simplicius, *In Phys.*, vol. II, pp. 1330, 34–1331, 7; p. 1177, 26–37 Diels.

in the case of those beings that have the cause of their being in something other than themselves."[81]

The two texts from Porphyry on which I have just commented show clearly that, with regard to the doctrines on the creation of the world, the Neoplatonists from Porphyry on were as clearly distinct from Middle Platonists like Plutarch, Atticus, and Numenius as they were from the Christians.

4. For Hierocles, as for the Neoplatonists, the Demiurge Creates Without Preexisting Matter, from All Eternity, by His Being and His Will Alone

Where can we situate Hierocles with regard to the problem of the creation of the world? We have seen that he sharply criticizes the doctrine of unengendered matter, which had been upheld by some Platonists[82] whom Photius does not name, but whose teaching is, in its broad outlines, identifiable with that of Plutarch, Atticus, and Numenius. Hierocles describes matter according to these Platonists as being unengendered in both senses of the term: that is, outside of a cause, and outside of time. It is unengendered in the same sense as the demiurge; it preexists the work of the demiurge in a disorderly state, and is set in order by the demiurge at a moment of time. Matter as Hierocles conceives it, on the contrary, is engendered outside of time, by a cause. It does not preexist[83] prior to the demiurge's work, either in the temporal sense or in the ontological sense. This becomes clear from Hierocles' polemics against the theses of the Middle Platonists, where, moreover, he utilizes elements of arguments that had been developed by Porphyry, and that were later constantly reused.[84] It is true that most Christians also denied the

---

[81] For a complete exposition of Porphyry's doctrine on the modes of beings and of not-beings, cf. P. Hadot, 1968, 1:147–178.

[82] Photius, *Library*, cod. 251, p. 460b22 Bekker, vol. VII, pp. 189ff. Henry, text quoted above, p. 16.

[83] In the strict Platonic sense, only beings that are truly beings *exist*; cf. the first text quoted above, p. 22. Matter therefore does not *exist* before the Demiurge, although some Neoplatonic texts feature a certain logical priority of matter with regard to the Demiurge (cf. above p. 20, n. 67). Cf. Photius, *Library*, cod. 251, p. 460b25–461a23 Bekker, vol. VII, p. 190f. Henry.

[84] See Porphyry's refutation of Atticus' theses, in Proclus, *In Tim.*, vol. I, p. 391, 4ff. Diehl. Cf. in particular the text by Hierocles cited below at n. 86, with the following text by Porphyry as reported by Proclus (*In Tim.*, vol. I, p. 394, 12, trans. based on Festugière, 1966–1968, 2:263): "Let us suppose that God wants to lead all things into order: how does he want this? Always, or at a given moment? If it is at a given moment, it is either because of himself, or because of Matter. Is it because of himself? This is absurd, for God is always good, and that which is always good always also does good." See also the par-

preexistence of matter, and that they considered matter to be engendered. If, like Augustine, they distinguish a disorderly state of engendered matter before the creation, this occurs under the influence of Platonism, as it does in the case of Philo.[85] In general, however, matter for the Christians is not created outside of time. For them, the Platonic distinction between two senses of the word γενητός has no meaning as far as the created universe is concerned. Moreover, the fact that Hierocles, like all Neoplatonists, conceives of the demiurge's creative act as eternal (ἐξ ἀϊδίου)[86]—that is, as dating from all eternity and having neither beginning nor end—is contrary to orthodox Christianity.[87] Christians laid particular emphasis on the fact that God creates the cosmos at a moment in time, from nothing, as something that did not exist previously and that must eventually disappear into nothingness. Thus, we see that creation ἐκ μηδενός προϋποκειμένου, which Hierocles defended against the Middle Platonists' thesis of creation ἐκ προϋποκειμένου, is not the same thing as the Christians' creation ἐξ οὐκ ὄντων. Praechter was a bit over-hasty when he identified them.

Hierocles' argument that the creator of the world did not work like a human artisan—an argument that also appears in the pseudo-Aristotelian *De mundo*[88]—was once again utilized by both Neopla-

---

allel text by Proclus (translation based on Festugière): "Moreover, if the Demiurge is of the number of the Beings that always exist, it cannot be that sometimes he creates and sometimes he abandons the rudder. In this case, he would possess neither identity nor immutability. But if he is always creating, his creation lasts for ever. For indeed, with what purpose, whereas he has remained inactive for an infinity of time, would he suddenly shift to the creative act? Was it because the idea came to him that this would be better? But was he previously unaware of this better thing, or not? If he was unaware of it, he who is Intellect, then this is strange: in this case, there would sometimes be ignorance within him, and sometimes knowledge. If he knew it, why did he not begin to create and produce a world earlier?—'No,' someone will reply, 'it is not better to create.'—Why, then, did he not remain inactive, if it is licit to speak in this way?" (Proclus, *In Tim.*, vol. I, p. 288, 14ff. Diehl; Festugière, 1966–1968, 2:137).

[85] Augustine, *Confessions*, XII, 3, 3–9, 9. Cf. Philo, *De providentia*, I, § 6–8; § 22 and H. A. Wolfson, 1962, 1:304–312. Cf. also the introduction by M. Hadas-Lebel to her *Philon d'Alexandrie, De providentia* (Paris, 1973), pp. 68–70.

[86] Cf. the text quoted above at p. 16, and Photius, *Library,* cod. 251, 461a8 Bekker, vol. VII, p. 190 Henry: "We would be even farther from the truth if, in addition to the need he would have of the cooperation of matter, God began to set matter in order at a moment of time; this behavior takes away from him the possibility of remaining constant in his own nature (οὐκ ἐᾷ μένειν αὐτὸν ἐν τῷ αὐτοῦ ἤθει = an allusion to Plato, *Timaeus*, 42e: ἔμενεν ἐν τῷ ἑαυτοῦ κατὰ τρόπον ἤθει). For if it were better not to act, how did he come to act? And if it were better to act, why didn't he do it from all eternity, if, that is, even acting from all eternity seemed indifferent to him?" (text based on the trans. by Henry).

[87] Hermogenes, the contemporary of Tertullian and heterodox Christian, accepts the theories of Plutarch and Atticus on unengendered matter; cf. J. H. Waszink, 1955.

[88] Pseudo-Aristotle, *De mundo,* 398b10–23 Lorimer.

tonists and Christians against the Middle Platonists.[89] Yet Hierocles' argumentation is clearly situated within the Neoplatonic context. I quote Photius:[90]

> The author writes: those things of which it is said that they act according to their essence (κατ' οὐσίαν) are those that remain immutable in their own essence and in their activity, without detaching[91] anything from themselves, without setting themselves in motion in order to bring about the existence of engendered beings, but which, merely according to the very being which they are,[92] bring about the generation of secondary things (τῶν δευτέρων). It follows that they do not utilize matter in addition, that they do not act from a moment in time, that they do not cease to act at a moment of time, and that that which is born does not exist outside the activity of what produces it. Indeed, all things of this kind accompany the activity that is accidental, as in the case of an architect and in other similar cases.

This text presents us with one of the fundamental theorems of Neoplatonism: the distinction between the immobile mode of creation of the hypostases above the soul, and the mode of creation of the soul, which is characterized by movement.[93] The Neoplatonists gave partic-

[89] Atticus, for instance, sees in the demiurge "the best of artisans" (cf. Atticus in Eusebius, *Praep. evang.*, XV, 6, 12, vol. II, p. 362, 7 Mras). For the Christians, cf. the testimonies collected in French translation by C. Tresmontant, 1961 chap. II: Création divine et fabrication humaine. Le problème de la matière," pp. 114ff.

[90] Photius, *Library*, cod. 251, p. 463b30ff. Bekker, vol. VII, p. 198 Henry.

[91] μηδὲν ἑαυτῶν ἀπομερίζοντα. Speaking of the mode of creation of the demiurge, Proclus employs almost the same expression: "In fact, if he creates by his mere existence—and this is necessary, to avoid attributing previous choice and inclination in one or the other direction to him—either he creates by the fact that something is detached from him, and there is diminution of his powers, as in the case of fire (κατὰ ἀπομερισμὸν καὶ ἐλάττωσιν ποιεῖ τῶν ἑαυτοῦ δυνάμεων), or else he produces what comes after him by his mere existence, while remaining what he is" (= Proclus, *In Tim.*, I, 390, 10ff. Diehl, cited after the trans. by Festugière, 1966–1968, 2:256f.).

[92] κατ' αὐτὸ μόνον τὸ εἶναι ὅ ἐστι [ἐστι refers to the neuter plural subject]. This turn of phrase is intended to indicate that being that remains purely being. For the expression, cf. Proclus, *El. Theol.*, prop. 174, quoted below, n. 101.

[93] Cf. Plotinus, *Enn.*, III, 4, 1, 1: "The productions of the higher principles take place while they remain immobile; only the soul, as has been said, moves in order to engender." Cf. Marius Victorinus, *Adv. Arium*, IV, 21, 19–25, following Porphyry: "First of all, among eternal, divine, and absolutely primary things, it is while remaining at rest, and contenting themselves with being where they are, and without experiencing change of themselves in movement, that first God, then *Noûs* have engendered. For only the soul moves in order to engender." Cf. Porphyry, *Sent.*, 24, p. 14, 5ff. Lamberz; Iamblichus, in Proclus, *In Tim.*, vol. I, p. 398, 26 Diehl. For an ample commentary on this doctrine, cf. P. Hadot, 1968, 1:432–451, *Génération, Manifestation, Formation*, and *La génération de la pensée*, pp. 432–451.

ular emphasis to the fact that the demiurge creates by his being alone, in order to oppose the mode of action of their demiurge to that of the demiurge of the Gnostics and of the God of the Jews and the Christians, who creates by reflective will.[94] The Neoplatonic demiurge creates eternally, and as Hierocles says, the world does not exist "outside of the activity of that which produces it." In order to create, the demiurge has no need whatsoever of a matter existing beside him in a self-produced way. For all these reasons, the Neoplatonic demiurge does not resemble human artisans, who cannot do without matter or without instruments, and whose activity is only accidental (κατὰ συμβεβηκός).

Let us note above all that Hierocles formulates this theorem like a true Neoplatonist: he uses the plural to speak of *causes* which act by their very being. If, as Praechter would have it, Hierocles' system was unaware of a hypostasis higher than the demiurge = Noûs, which would thus be the only hypercosmic divinity,[95] we should expect Hierocles to speak in this context of one single cause, the demiurge, instead of describing the mode of action of an entire class of beings in which the demiurge is included. Moreover, Hierocles' formulation, as reported by Photius, makes room for the Neoplatonists' habitual distinction between the primary beings (τὰ πρῶτα) and the secondary beings (τὰ δεύτερα).[96] In this context, the term τὰ δεύτερα designates all the degrees of being from the hypostasis of the soul on down, and the term τὰ πρῶτα, understood but not stated in our text, therefore includes the hypostasis or, more likely, the hypostases above the soul. If Photius does not give us precise information on the hierarchy of the hypostases above the Noûs, or the hierarchy inside the Noûs, this is probably to be ex-

---

[94] Cf. the citation at n. 91. Cf. also Porphyry, in Proclus, *In Tim.*, I, 395, 10ff. and 396, 5ff. Diehl (trans. based on Festugière, 1966–1968, 2:265–266): "The fourth point of Porphyry's arguments, besides what has been said, is that in which he shows that the Divine Intellect carries out the particular manner in which it creates by its very being. . . . [W]hat is surprising about the fact that the Demiurge, by the mere fact that he thinks the Universe, gives substantial existence to sensible reality, immaterially creating the material, impalpably the palpable, and indivisibly distending the spatial? And there is nothing to be surprised about, if something incorporeal and non-spatial is the cause of the existence of this visible Universe. For if it is true that human sperm, which in so little volume contains all reasons within itself, is the cause of so many differences . . . how much more must we believe that the Reason in the Demiurge can produce all things, without having any need of matter in order that things should exist, as does that reason that is innate within sperm; for this reason is not outside of matter, whereas the Reason that causes all beings to exist is eternally fixed within itself, and it causes the whole Universe to be born from it without leaving its state of rest."

[95] Praechter, "Hierokles," col. 1482.

[96] These technical terms, proper to the doctrine of emanation, designate in a narrow sense the first terms of each series, and the beings derived from these primary terms. In a wider sense, however, they can also designate classes of beings. In the latter case, the secondary beings are often divided in turn into τὰ μέσα and τὰ ἔσχατα.

plained by Photius' lack of interest in such questions, and is not a confirmation of Praechter's hypothesis. We shall return to this problem later.

If Hierocles affirms that the class of beings in which the demiurge is included acts by its mere being, this does not contradict what he said earlier: that the demiurge's will is sufficient for him to bring beings into existence.[97] We have already seen in a previous quotation[98] that Porphyry unites within the same text the affirmation that the demiurge creates by his mere being and the affirmation that he creates by his mere thought. Iamblichus does the same.[99] As Proclus explains in a proposition of his *Elements of Theology,* at the ontological level of the *Noûs*—to which, following Plato, the demiurge generally belongs[100]—to act by being and to act by thought are one and the same.[101] In contrast to the Christians, however, the Neoplatonists would not say that the demiurge creates with the help of deliberative reflection.[102] As Dodds correctly explains, the Neoplatonic demiurge creates because he thinks, but he does not think in order to create.[103] The same holds true of the demiurge's will:

[97] Cf. the first text cited at p. 15 = Photius, *Library,* cod. 214 p. 172a22ff. Bekker, vol. III, p. 126 Henry.

[98] Cf. the quotation at n. 94.

[99] Cf. Iamblichus, *De myst.,* III, 28 (168, 19), p. 139 des Places, where the demiurge is said to create (τοὺς κόσμους) ταῖς ἐννοίαις καὶ βουλήσεσι καὶ τοῖς ἀύλοις εἴδεσι. Cf. J. M. Dillon, 1973, the commentary on fr. 39, p. 313.

[100] Porphyry's attitude concerning the ontological position of the demiurge seems, however, to have been ambiguous. We have testimonies proving that Porphyry's demiurge was an intelligence (*Noûs*)—all the quotations in the present chapter belong to this category (cf. the quotations nn. 94 and 104)—and testimonies affirming that Porphyry considered the hypercosmic soul to be the demiurge (cf. Proclus, *In Tim.,* vol. I, p. 307, 1ff.; p. 322, 1ff.; 431, 22ff. Diehl). Yet this contradiction is not as important as might appear at first glance; for Plotinus and Porphyry, the borders between these two hypostases still remained fluid, and overlaps of one upon the other were possible.

[101] Proclus, *El. Theol.,* prop. 174, trans. Dodds: "Every intelligence gives rise to its consequents by the act of intellection: its creative activity is thinking, and its thought is creation.—For if intelligence is identical with its object (prop. 167), and the existence of each intelligence with its thought (prop. 169), and if further it creates by existing all that it creates, and produces by virtue of being what it is [παράγει κατὰ τὸ εἶναι ὅ ἐστι; prop. 26], then it must constitute its products by the act of thought. For its existence and its intellection are one thing, since intelligence is identical with the being which is its content. If, then, it creates by existing, and its existence is thought, it creates by the act of thinking.—Again, its thought is actualized in the act of thinking, which is identical with its existence; and its existence is creation (for all which creates without movement has its existence perpetually in the creative act): therefore its thought too is creation."

[102] Cf. Proclus, *In Tim.,* vol. I, p. 321, 19ff. Diehl, trans. based on Festugière, vol. II, p. 179: "Besides, since the Demiurge is an Intellect (*Noûs*), if he creates by his very being, he creates an object completely similar to himself; that is, he creates a copy of himself. If, however, we suppose that he creates with deliberation, this is, first of all, something completely and absolutely unworthy of the Demiurgic Cause."

[103] E. R. Dodds, 1963², p. 290, note to prop. 174.

> In so far as the Demiurge is Intellect, he produces all things by his intellections; in so far as he is an Intelligible, he creates by his existence alone; in so far as he is a god, he creates by his will alone.[104]

Once again, however, the will of the Christian God and the will of the Neoplatonic demiurge are not the same thing; their wills are distinguished in the same way as their thoughts. In any event, each of Plato's exegetes was obliged to attribute a will to the creator of the universe because of the following passage from Plato's *Timaeus,* which concerns the demiurge:[105]

> He was good; but since he was good, he never conceived a feeling of envy towards anyone. Being exempt from such a feeling, he willed (ἐβουλήθη) that all things, in so far as was possible, should become similar to him . . . indeed, having willed (βουληθείς) that all things should be good, and that there should be nothing vile, in so far as was possible. . . .

Proclus provides the following commentary:[106]

> For, if the Father was good, he wished to create all things as good, and if he willed this, then he did it; and he brought the Universe to order. For providence depends on will, and will on goodness.

This commentary gives us a good idea of how, for the Neoplatonists, providence was intimately linked to the goodness and the will of God. If, therefore, Hierocles in his treatise on providence mentions the will of the demiurge, this, like his thesis of creation without preexisting matter, is easy to explain within the system of post-Porphyrian Neoplatonism

---

[104] Proclus, *In Tim.,* vol. I, p. 362, 2 Diehl (trans. Festugière, 1966–1968, 2:221). Cf. the Arabic text (*Epistle of the Divine Science,* attributed to al-Fārābī, in A. Badawi, 1955, 174), which Pinès considered to be Porphyrian. I quote after the French translation of the Arabic text by S. Pinès in his article (1971, p. 308): "Between Intelligence and its act, there is volition, for it wills (first) and then acts. Indeed, it does not act by its being, but by the fact of being an Intelligence. But the Intelligence knows, and he who knows, wills; for he wills a thing, and consequently aspires to know it. If the Intelligence has this character, it is necessarily multiple, and not one. It is therefore not the First Agent. Indeed, the act of the First Agent is not preceded by volition, for it acts only by its being." It goes without saying that Porphyry did not mean that the will of *Noûs* temporally precedes its act; nor did he want to deny that the *Noûs* acts by its very being (cf. the quotation n. 94). It is rather a matter of distinguishing the act of the One, which Porphyry identifies with pure Being, from the act of the *Noûs,* which acts in accordance with its own being; that is, in accordance with the fact of being a *Noûs;* for the being of *Noûs* already contains a certain multiplicity. Cf. Proclus, *In Tim.,* II, p. 70, 27–31 Diehl.

[105] Plato, *Timaeus,* 29e-f.

[106] Proclus, *In Tim.,* vol. I, p. 371, 4 Diehl, trans. based on Festugière, 1966–1968, 2:231.

itself, and there is no need whatsoever to look for Christian or Judaic influence coming from outside.

5. Hierocles' Demiurge Has a Ternary Structure Reflected in the Three Classes of Souls

In the continuation of the first text quoted on page 15,[107] it is said of this demiurge that he created this world, the visible and invisible universe, by the unification of the incorporeal and the corporeal natures, and that

> in this universe the wisdom that created the world distinguished, in conformity with their nature, beings which occupy the top, the center, and the bottom. The first of these rational beings are called celestial and gods; those rational beings that have been allotted to the space following this group he calls ethereal[108] and good demons: they have become the interpreters and messengers (ἄγγελοι) of the things it is useful for men to know.[109] The tribe of men occupies the last rank; they are called terrestrial beings, human souls, and—as Plato would say—immortal men. These three kinds are attached to one another as if in a single living being, or in a chorus and a harmony, but their distinction in accordance with their nature is preserved unmixed with regard to their unity and their mutual connection. And those that are placed in the superior rank command the lower ones, but the god who is their father and demiurge reigns as king over them all.

Throughout this text and the parallel text from codex 251,[110] there is nothing that differs from the traditional conceptions of the Neoplatonists. First, however, let us explain what "creative wisdom" (ἡ κοσμοποιὸς σοφία) means for Hierocles. A parallel text from Hierocles' commentary on the *Carmen aureum* can enlighten us with regard to this question:[111]

---

[107] Hierocles, in Photius, *Library*, cod. 214, p. 172a30ff. Bekker, vol. III, p. 126f. Henry. Cf. the parallel text from cod. 251 (p. 461b12ff. Bekker, vol. VII, p. 192 Henry): "In it (that is, the universe) there are beings which occupy the top, the center, and the bottom, of which he names the first: celestial beings and gods, the rational beings of the center: ethereal beings and good demons, who have become interpreters and messengers of the things that are useful for men, and the last rational beings: terrestrial, human souls and immortal men. And the beings of the higher category always command those of the category beneath, but the god who is their creator (ποιητής) and father reigns as king over them all."

[108] This division of regions is probably of Pythagorean provenance. In this case, αἰθέρια signifies the beings who inhabit the region of the air; cf. Proclus, *In Tim.*, vol. I, p. 136, 29ff. Diehl and the trans. by Festugière, 1966–1968, 1:185 with n. 1.

[109] For the gist of these remarks, cf. Iamblichus, *De myst.*, I, 5 (16, 13ff.), p. 47 des Places.

[110] Text cited n. 107.

[111] Hierocles, *In Carmen aureum*, I, p. 10, 2–21 Köhler.

30

God the demiurge produced the first, second, and third things different from one another by their nature, without them being confused with one another, and without them changing their rank (τάξις)[112] as a function of their virtue or their vice. For the things which by essence are set in place for eternity have been distinguished according to kind, by the order (τάξει) that proceeds forth with them, and they have been disposed in a manner analogous to the demiurgic causes. In the same way as above [that is, on the ontological level of the demiurgic causes], the order (τάξις) of perfect wisdom includes things of the first rank, of the intermediary rank, and of the last rank—for it, being wisdom consists in producing creation in order (ἐν τάξει) and perfection, so that wisdom, order (τάξιν), and perfection go together—in the same way, in the whole that is down here below, the things produced according to the god's first thought will be the first in the world; those conceived in accordance with intermediary thought will themselves be intermediary, and those that resemble the lowest limit of his thoughts will also be last among rational beings. For the whole of the plane of rational beings, with the incorruptible body that is connatural to it, is the image of the demiurgic god as a whole. Of the summit above, the first things that are in the world are the pure image; and the things that in this world have an intermediary rank are the middle image of the mean above; and the things that come in the third and last rank among rational beings are the image of the lowest limit of the divinity above, coming in the last rank.

The "creative wisdom" of the universe is thus nothing other than the thought of the demiurge taken separately, as the cause of the differentiation of the beings of his creation. Proclus identifies it with Athena.[113]

---

[112] The meanings of the term τάξις are twofold. It can designate the rank that each being occupies in the cosmos, both visible and invisible, which, as Hierocles says, corresponds to the quality of its essence. This order is immutable. Yet rational human souls may acquire an individual value for which they are wholly responsible and which can be greater or less. This depends on the kind of life they lead, whether virtuous or vicious, and it may change with the various ethical dispositions the souls adopt during their incorporations. We have accordingly translated τάξις by "order," "rank," or "value."

[113] Cf. Proclus, *In Tim.*, vol. I, p. 166, 2–17 Diehl, (trans. after Festugière, 1966–1968, 1:220): "In the Father and Demiurge of the whole Cosmos, no doubt the individual divine classes—gods that are guardians, creators, elevators, maintainers, perfecters—appear to be multiple, yet unique is the divine essence (θεότης) itself, unpolluted and indomitable, of the intellective and primary henads that are in the Father; divine essence according to which both the Demiurge himself remains inflexible (ἀκλινής) and immutable, and all the beings that proceed from him participate in an inexorable power, according to which the Demiurge also thinks all things, although he is separated from and transcendent of the totality of the real. All the *Theologians* name

In the text by Hierocles we have just cited, one notes, on the one hand, the very precise allusions to the ternary structure of the demiurge. The plural "demiurgic causes," used to describe the demiurge's action, is already significant: it is an expression typical of late Neoplatonism, which we encounter very frequently in Proclus' commentary on the *Timaeus*. Above all, however, we here see Hierocles attributing to demiurgic reality a ternary structure that is just as much horizontal (wisdom, order [τάξις], and perfection) as it is vertical (primary thought, secondary thought, and ultimate thought; or summit, mean, and lower limit). This representation of a hierarchy inherent in the demiurge is, in different forms, constant within Neoplatonism, since Amelius and Iamblichus. It is clearly expressed in the following text by Proclus:

> The Demiurge contains within himself a hierarchy of different ranks, of the first, the middle, and the last.[114]

---

this divine essence Athena, in so far as it bursts forth from the head of the Father, and remains in him, since it is the separate and immaterial demiurgic Thought—this is why Socrates in the *Cratylus* (407*b*5) sang of it under the name of Theonoe—and in so far as she surges forth fully armed, she who, without suffering any stain, organizes the Universe with the unique Demiurge and, together with the Father, ranges all things in battle order (τάττουσαν). . . . Since the Goddess unitively contains all the wisdom of the Father, she is the 'friend of wisdom.'" Cf. also Proclus, *In Tim.*, vol. I, p. 168, 8f. (1:223 Festugière): "The Goddess is the 'friend of wisdom' as the demiurgic Thought and as separate and immaterial Wisdom."—For the Jews and the Christians, the wisdom of their God plays a role in the creation of the cosmos similar to the wisdom of the Neoplatonic demiurge: for their interpretation, they base themselves on *Prov.* 8, 22–25 (cf. Calcidius, *In Tim.*, cap. 276, p. 281, 6ff. Waszink, with the commentary of J. M. C. Van Winden, 1965², 55–57).

[114] 1° For the use of the expression "demiurgic causes" cf. Proclus, *In Tim.*, vol. I, p. 67, 25; 75, 13; 118, 12; 145, 3. For an analogous plural, cf. above, p. 26 (the text of Hierocles).

2° Horizontal ternary structure: wisdom, order, perfection; this was already noted by W. Theiler, 1933, p. 32 n. 2.

3° Vertical ternary structure. This problematic derives from *Timaeus* 41d7, where souls of the second and third degree are mentioned: Proclus (*In Tim.*, vol. III, p. 245, 19 Diehl; trans. Festugière, 1966–1968, 5:112), very probably following Iamblichus, considered that the production of these inferior souls—that is to say, demonic and human (as we can see by the continuation of Proclus' text) corresponded to a second (and probably to a third) thought of the demiurge. The consequences for the theory of the soul were crucially important. As is underlined by Proclus, in the same passage, and by Iamblichus (*De anima*, in Stobaeus, *Eclog.*, I, 49, 37, p. 372, 26 Wachsmuth), the classes of souls are not, as Plotinus had held, distinguished as a function of their acts, but as a function of their essences, which are the results of different demiurgic acts: "It is by a series of primary, secondary, and tertiary processions that the various essences of souls advance ever further," says Iamblichus.

4° Hierarchy inherent in the demiurge. The text by Proclus is taken from *In Tim.*, vol. I, p. 161, 21 Diehl, trans. Festugière, 1966–1968, 1:214. On the Neoplatonic conception of the demiurge, cf. Proclus, op. cit., vol. I, p. 303, 24ff. Diehl.

In these texts, on the other hand, we can easily recognize a Neoplatonic classification of souls, and in particular of encosmic souls,[115] of which Hierocles names the principal groups: the primary rational souls (τὰ πρῶτα λογικά), which inhabit the supralunary region (constituted in particular by the Soul of the world, the souls of the planets and of the fixed stars); the intermediate rational souls (τὰ μέσα λογικά), demons, angels, or heroes,[116] placed between the moon and the earth in the space of the air; and the last rational souls (τὰ τελευταῖα λογικά) or human souls incorporated on earth. The triadic structure of the class of rational souls is the image of the triadic structure of the demiurge-*Noûs,* which thinks itself as it creates. It seems that the creation of the class of rational souls according to a series of primary, secondary, and tertiary processions comes from Iamblichus.[117] It goes without saying, and Hierocles states as much explicitly in his interpretation of the *Carmen aureum,*[118] that there are many other subdivisions within this triadic division of the class of rational souls, especially among the gods; they are, of course, always a faithful reflection of the structure of the demiurge-*Noûs.* Such a structured and complex demiurgic entity is characteristic of a Neoplatonic system that has already reached an advanced developmental stage, and it always supposes another simple cause that precedes it in the order of the hierarchy. With regard to these three classes of souls, Hierocles specifies that they form a unity, although each maintains its distinctness. The expression ἀσύγχυτος ἕνωσις had been a key term in Neoplatonism since Porphyry,[119] which, among other things, was used to explain the birth of the multitude of sensible forms from the pure unity of the One. In the first hypostasis after the One, alterity is almost nonexistent, and the unity of all the beings it contains is therefore far superior to their mutual distinction, which nevertheless already exists. From hypostasis to hypostasis, unity

---

[115] On the Neoplatonic classification of souls, cf. Proclus, *El. Theol.,* prop. 184: "Every soul is either divine [= soul of the stars] or else subject to oscillation between thought and unconsciousness [= soul of men] or else in an intermediate condition; that is, always thinking, but inferior to the divine souls [= the demonic souls]." Cf. n. 114, 3°. Hierocles himself, a little later, designates the three classes of souls as encosmic; cf. the text cited below, p. 43.

[116] Hierocles (cf. *In Carmen aureum,* III, p. 19, 9–27 Köhler) bears witness to the fact that usage fluctuated considerably as far as the appellation of the class of intermediary souls is concerned. It was either designated as a whole by the name of heroes, of demons, or of angels; or else the whole of this class of souls was divided into three, by means of these names. In this case, the order from top to bottom was: angels, demons, heroes. Cf. also Proclus, *In Tim.,* vol. III, p. 165, 6–22 Diehl.

[117] Cf. Iamblichus, *De anima,* in Stobaeus, *Eclog.,* I, 49, 37, p. 372, 26 Wachsmuth. Cf. n. 114, 3°.

[118] Hierocles, *In Carmen aureum,* I, p. 10, 26–11, 5 Köhler.

[119] Cf. H. Dörrie, 1958, p. 173.

becomes weaker and distinction increases. The last hypostasis that still maintains its unity, although it contains distinctions that are already fairly pronounced, is the hypostasis of the soul. Porphyry explains this as follows:[120]

> We must not believe that the multitude of souls results from the multitude of bodies, but, on the contrary, that before bodies there are both multiple souls and one single soul. The soul that is both one and universal does not prevent the multiple souls from being within it, and the multiple souls do not divide between them the soul that is one; for they have been distinguished without being cut off from one another and without breaking the universal soul into their different individualities, and they are present to one another without being confused with one another, and without constituting the universal soul by their addition. For they are not separated by limits, nor are they confused within one another, in the same way as the sciences, which are multiple, are not confused within one single soul, nor are they inserted within the soul as if within a body, that is, as an essence different from the soul; but they are the qualifying acts of the soul. . . .

From Porphyry to Iamblichus, the meaning of the expression "universal soul" (ἡ ὅλη ψυχή) underwent an evolution: the former understands it as the World Soul, the latter as an unparticipated and hypercosmic soul. Moreover, the difference within the totality of souls became more and more clearly marked. It was apparently Iamblichus who introduced the classification of souls by kind, such as is set forth by Hierocles.[121] Nevertheless, the dogma of *henosis* was maintained in its full value, and without change.[122] What constitutes the unity of its essence is the fact that the soul, according to Iamblichus,[123] is defined as "the middle term between the divisible and indivisible kinds, <and between the corporeal kinds and the in> corporeal kinds," but this does not exclude that between the three classes of souls there may exist differences of kind and of nature, as Hierocles specifies.[124] Hierocles will explain what these differences are a little further on.

[120] Porphyry, *Sent.*, 37, p. 42, 13–43, 8 Lamberz.

[121] Cf. Iamblichus, *De anima*, in Stobaeus, *Eclog.*, I, 49, 37, p. 372, 15ff.; p. 372, 26ff. Wachsmuth, and J. M. Dillon, 1973, pp. 43–45.

[122] On the *henosis* of the various parts of the incorporated human soul, cf. Simplicius, *In De anima*, p. 76, 14–77, 37, and especially p. 77, 11–15 Hayduck.

[123] Cf. Iamblichus, *De anima*, in Stobaeus, *Eclog.*, I, 49, 32, p. 365, 27ff. Wachsmuth. Cf. also Plato, *Timaeus*, 35a1–b1.

[124] Cf. the end of the text cited on p. 30, and the text cited on p. 31.

As Hierocles emphasizes by his repeated addition of the adjective λογικά, the souls in the three groups enumerated are rational souls only. He thus adheres to the doctrine of late Neoplatonists like Hermias, Syrianus, Proclus, and their successors, who understand by "soul" in the strict sense only the rational soul, even when it is the human soul that is under consideration. For them, the principles of animal and vegetable life, considered as mere reflections or traces of the rational soul in the body, do not fall within the class of truly self-moving souls.[125] Yet this does not prevent them from occasionally accepting, especially when interpreting Aristotle, the broad habitual concept of "human soul." The irrational soul is no longer the work of the demiurge himself. Hierocles explains this as follows:[126]

> that which is deprived by nature of intellect is in no way capable of participating in the truth and in virtue; for this reason it cannot be the work of the demiurge. How, indeed, could the irrational and that which is deprived of intellect, be an image of the intelligible god? Each image of him is provided with intellect and with reason, and is capable of knowing itself and of knowing its creator.

Obviously, as in the text cited on page 31, what is at issue is the Neoplatonic thesis according to which each hypostasis is the image of the cause that precedes it. Thus, Proclus can say that "every soul is . . . the intelligibles in the mode of an image (εἰκονικῶς)."[127] The hypostasis at two removes from a cause is no longer the image of this cause but an image of the image. The Neoplatonic doctrine to which Hierocles alludes developed from the passage of the *Timaeus*, where Plato says that the demiurge "wanted all things, as far as was possible, to become similar to him," (29e) and from another passage of the *Timaeus* (42dff.)

---

[125] Hermias, *In Phaedrum*, 102, 19ff. Couvreur, tells us that the ancient philosophers were accustomed to call simply "soul" that which in his time was called "rational soul": ". . . so that the present discourse (= *Phaedrus*, 245c) refers to the rational soul. Besides, the ancients are accustomed to calling the rational soul 'soul' in the proper sense. They call 'intelligence (*Noûs*)' that which is above it, and they call what is beneath it not simply 'soul,' but 'irrational soul' and 'mortal kind of soul' and 'second trace of the form of life (δεύτερον ἴχνος ζωῆς)' and 'irrational form of life,' or again 'animation of the pneuma' and 'form of life within bodies,' etc.; but that which they call 'soul' in the proper and essential sense is the rational soul. And he [*scil.* Plato] calls man in the proper sense 'rational soul.'"—Cf. also Hermias, *op. cit.*, p. 111, 27ff. Couvreur and E. R. Dodds, 1963² commentary on prop. 184, p. 296. Cf. Simplicius, *In Phys.*, vol. II, p. 1248, 6ff. Diels. This same doctrine seems to be already present in Calcidius, *In Tim.*, cap. 188, p. 213, 3 Waszink, where the class of rational souls is discussed.

[126] Hierocles, in Photius, *Library*, cod. 251, p. 462a24 Bekker, vol. VII, p. 194 Henry. Cf. Hierocles, *In Carmen aureum*, XI, p. 52, 26ff. Köhler, cited n. 128.

[127] Proclus, *El. Theol.*, prop. 195, p. 170, 4-5 Dodds.

from which the Neoplatonists deduced that the last work of the demi-urge himself was the rational human soul.[128]

As is shown by the text of Hierocles that has just been cited,[129] the affirmation that the rational human soul was the demiurge's last work must be understood in the sense that it was the last work to come directly from the demiurge. For it is obvious that, in a certain sense, the demiurge also creates mortal beings. On this subject, too, Proclus shares Hierocles' opinion; I quote from his *Commentary on the Timaeus*:[130]

> But let us not say that the Demiurge does not also create mortal beings. He does create them, but by means of the recent gods. For before they create, he created by the mere fact of thinking.

Thus the irrational soul is not, properly speaking, the work of the demiurge, but of the recent gods of Plato's *Timaeus*, or of nature (φύ-σις);[131] and according to Hierocles it is blown into the material or "shell-like"[132] body by the luminous, immaterial body.

6. Hierocles' Doctrine of the Vehicle of the Soul Is Post-Iamblichean

Since the doctrine concerning the various souls and the luminous body allows us to situate Hierocles in a quite determinate place within the history of Neoplatonism, it may be useful to study it with some care.

---

[128] Cf. Hierocles, *In Carmen aureum*, XI, p. 52, 26ff. Köhler: "He [*scil.* the demi-urge] seems to have brought into existence each of the human souls himself, but only the kinds among the irrational souls, offering them to nature to be moulded, as is the view of Plato and Timaeus the Pythagorean, who believe that nothing among mortal things is an immediate product of the divine, but that human souls are engendered from the same *crater* as the encosmic gods, the demons, or the noble heroes." According to Needham (in *Hierocles, In Carmen aureum*, ed. Gaisford, Oxford, 1850, p. 80, n. 3), Hierocles seems to be referring to the treatise falsified under the name of Timaeus of Locri (*De natura mundi et animae*, 217, 25ff., p. 138 Marg.): ... τὰν μὲν ὦν ἀνθρωπί-ναν ψυχὰν ἐκ τῶν αὐτῶν λόγων καὶ δυναμίων συγκερασάμενος καὶ μερίξας διένειμε τᾷ φύσει τᾷ ἀλλοιωτικᾷ παραδούς· διαδεξαμένα δ' αὐτὸν ἐν τῷ <γεννᾶν> ἀπεργάζετο θνατά τε καὶ ἐφαμέρια ζῷα· ὦν τὰς ψυχὰς ἐπιρρύτως ἐνάγαγε, τὰς μὲν ἀπὸ σελάνας, τὰς δ' ἀπ' ἀλίω, τὰς δὲ ἀπὸ τῶν ἄλλων τῶν πλαζομένων ἐν τᾷ τῶ ἑτέρῳ μοίρᾳ. ... Cf. Proclus, *In Tim.*, vol. III, p. 199, 15–29 Diehl.

[129] Cf. preceding note.

[130] Proclus, *In Tim.*, vol. III, p. 228, 25ff. Diehl, quoted after the trans. by Festugière, 1966–1968, 5:91ff.

[131] Cf. Iamblichus, *De myst.*, VIII, 6 (269, 1), p. 199 des Places.

[132] "Shell-like body" translates ὀστρεῶδες or ὀστρέϊνον σῶμα. The image comes from Plato, *Phaedrus*, 250c6: "exempt from the mark imprinted by this tomb which, under the name of body, we carry with us, attached to it like an oyster to his shell."

As Hierocles explains in his commentary on the *Carmen aureum,*[133] the rational human soul possesses a vehicle, the luminous body (αὐγοειδὲς σῶμα), which is congenital to it, sempiternal, and which, like it, is the work of the demiurge.[134] This luminous or pneumatic immaterial body,[135] which is a kind of life, ensures the junction of the rational human soul with its mortal body. At the time of the rational soul's incorporation, the luminous body is placed within the still-inanimate mortal body, and it breathes into it the life that is active within matter (ζωὴ ἔνυλος); that is, irrational life or soul. Our animate mortal body or mortal animal, since it is made up of the irrational soul and the material body, is a mere image of the human being constituted by the rational soul and the immaterial body.[136] We thus obtain the following schema:

$$\left.\begin{array}{l}\text{rational soul} \\ \text{immaterial body}\end{array}\right\} = \left.\begin{array}{l}\text{created by} \\ \text{the demiurge}\end{array}\right\} = \text{immortal} \Big\} = \text{human being}$$

$$\left.\begin{array}{l}\text{irrational soul} \\ \text{material body}\end{array}\right\} = \left.\begin{array}{l}\text{created by} \\ \text{the recent or} \\ \text{encosmic gods}\end{array}\right\} = \text{mortal} \Big\} = \begin{array}{l}\text{image of the} \\ \text{human being}\end{array}$$

Hierocles thus knows of two bodies, one that is congenital (συμφυές)[137] to the rational soul, immortal like it, and immaterial; this is the luminous or pneumatic body. The other body is adventitious

---

[133] Hierocles, *In Carmen aureum,* XXVI, p. 112, 5–17 Köhler: "Here is the teaching that he who is not deaf to the Pythagorean symbols may derive from these verses: at the same time as the exercise of virtue and the acquisition of truth, we must take care of the purity relating to our luminous body, which the *Oracles* call 'the light vehicle of the soul' [= frag. 120 des Places]. Such purity extends to our food, our drink, and to the entire regimen of our mortal body, in which the luminous body resides, breathing life into the inanimate body and maintaining its harmony. For the immaterial body is a kind of life, which also engenders life within matter; it is thanks to this last life that that part of myself that is the living mortal being is made complete, being composed of irrational life and of the material body, being the image of man, who is made up of the rational essence and of the immaterial body."

[134] Hierocles, *In Carmen aureum,* XXVI, p. 110, 22–111, 2 Köhler.

[135] It is formed of a material so subtle (αἰθερῶδες: cf. Iamblichus, *De myst.,* III, 14 (132, 12), p. 117 des Places) that it can be said to be immaterial in comparison with the visible and material body. Cf. also Iamblichus, in Proclus, *In Tim.,* III, p. 266, 25 Diehl (trans. based on Festugière, 1966–1968, 5:141): "We must consider, as the great Iamblichus is accustomed to say, that the psychic vehicles are born and are constituted from the whole of the ether (ἀπὸ παντὸς τοῦ αἰθέρος), which possesses a generative power. . . ." The expression ψυχικὸν σῶμα or ὄχημα = psychic vehicle is also used by Hierocles, *In Carmen aureum,* XXVI, p. 113, 6 Köhler.

[136] Cf. the definition of man at *In Carmen aureum,* XXVI, p. 111, 11–13 Köhler: "in the same way (*scil.* as the heroes) man is a rational soul with a congenital and immortal body." Cf. the entire text, quoted pp. 38–39.

[137] *In Carmen aureum,* XXVI, p. 110, 22 Köhler.

(προσφυές)[138] to the first body, material, and mortal; this is the human body, composed by the four elements, earth, water, air, and fire.

The pneumatic body itself is described by Hierocles as a "kind of life (ζωή τις)" that is obviously neither a rational soul nor an irrational soul,[139] but is associated with the former, although it is inferior to it because of its very function as vehicle or body.[140] However, it is the creator of the irrational soul, and therefore superior to it.[141] Hierocles indicates, moreover, that it is immortal, and that it is the work of the demiurge, for these two characteristics are said of the luminous vehicle. Hierocles[142] explains the relation of the rational human soul to its luminous body as follows:

> The rational essence came into being, having received from the demiurge a body that is congenital (συμφυές) to it, so that it is neither a body, nor without a body: it is incorporeal itself, but its entire species terminates in a body. It is as with the stars: the upper part of the stars is an incorporeal essence, the part below is corporeal; and the sun in its totality is what results from the incorporeal and the body, without there being any moment in which these parts are distinguished and are then put back together (for they would thus be separated again), but they are produced together and are co-engendered according to a hierarchical order, so that one commands and the other obeys. The same holds true of the rational kinds that come later, that is, the heroic kind[143] and the human kind: each hero is a rational soul with a luminous body. In the same way, man is a rational soul with a congenital, immortal body. This was the doctrine of the Pythagoreans which Plato revealed subsequently, com-

---

[138] *In Carmen aureum,* XXIV, p. 98, 24–26 Köhler, following Plato, *Tim.,* 42c4–d2; XXVI, p. 113, 3–4 Köhler.

[139] *In Carmen aureum,* XXVI, p. 112, 13f. The terms ψυχή and ζωή are virtually interchangeable; cf. Proclus, *El. Theol.,* prop. 188, p. 165 Dodds. More specifically, ζωή designates the soul from the point of view of movement; for instance in Hermias, *In Phaedr.,* p. 110, 7 Couvreur.

[140] In Neoplatonic language, to be a body or a vehicle means only for a given level of reality to become matter or body for a level that is ontologically superior. Cf. P. Hadot, 1968, 1:340; 342: "From this viewpoint, no reality 'descends.' The 'fall' consists essentially in the act of taking an inferior reality as its 'body' or instrument; that is, ultimately, to allow a derivative act after the act that is interior to the essence . . . The fall of particular souls consists only in the fact that they 'pay attention' to the things they have taken as their body or instrument, and therefore that they turn towards inferior things."

[141] Cf. *In Carmen aureum,* XXVI, p. 112, 13f. Köhler: "The immaterial body is a kind of life that also engenders life within matter," that is to say, irrational life.

[142] Hierocles, *In Carmen aureum,* XXVI, p. 110, 22–111, 16 Köhler.

[143] In the context of the commentary on the *Carmen aureum,* the "heroes," because of the text to be interpreted, designate the entire tripartite and intermediate class of demonic souls, of which the heroic souls normally form the third part, which is the part closest to human souls; cf. Hierocles, *In Carmen aureum,* III, p. 17, 24–19, 27 Köhler.

paring every divine and human soul "with the coordinate power of the winged chariot and its driver" [= *Phaedrus* 246a].[144]

The human soul's pneumatic body will thus return with the rational soul to the ethereal region (ὁ αἰθέριος τόπος) whence it came.[145] This region is situated beneath the moon.[146]

Although Hierocles agrees with Iamblichus with regard to the immortality of the pneumatic or luminous vehicle, he departs from the latter's doctrine of the creator of the vehicle and the irrational soul: for Hierocles the creator of the vehicle is the demiurge, whereas for Iamblichus it is the recent gods. For Hierocles, the irrational soul is mortal, whereas Iamblichus, like Plutarch of Athens, conceives of it as immortal.[147] This is shown by the following text of Proclus:[148]

> In the third place come those who remove all kinds of destruction both from the vehicle and from the irrational, who reduce both the permanence of the vehicle and that of the irrational to the same thing, who explain what is mortal within it as being the corporiform that is subject to the desire of matter, and which cares for mortal things. Such is the opinion of Iamblichus and of all those who think it good to agree with him, who do not make the existence of the vehicle and of the irrational derive purely and simply from the divine bodies, so that, having issued forth from moved causes, they should also be mutable by their own nature; but from the gods themselves who direct the World and fabricate all things eternally.[149]

Proclus' declaration is corroborated by two texts from Iamblichus' *De anima* collected by Stobaeus, in which Iamblichus expresses his own opinion, which is generally identical to the view of those he calls the "Ancients" or the "ancient priests." In the first, he says:

---

[144] For an in-depth study of this *Phaedrus* text, cf. Hermias, *In Phaedr.*, p. 122, 10ff.; p. 192, 28–193, 29 Couvreur.

[145] Cf. Hierocles, *In Carmen aureum*, XXVI, p. 113, 9–13 Köhler.

[146] Cf. Hierocles, *In Carmen aureum*, XXVII, p. 120, 2–7 Köhler: "but since it [*scil.* the rational human soul] possesses a congenital body, it needs a place in order to be ranged similar to the stars, since it seeks a position. For such a body, the appropriate place is that which is situated immediately beneath the moon, for such a place is superior to mortal bodies, but is beneath the heavenly bodies: this place is called 'free ether' by the Pythagoreans. . . ."

[147] Cf. Damascius, *In Phaed.*, I, § 177, p. 107f. Westerink, and Olympiodorus, *In Phaed.*, 10, § 7, p. 145 Westerink.

[148] Proclus, *In Tim.*, III, p. 234, 32ff. Diehl, trans. based on that of Festugière, 1966–1968, 5:99ff.

[149] Cf. W. Deuse, 1987, p. 409.

. . . or else, the entire irrational life, separated from the Intelligence, subsists as well, and is conserved in the cosmos, as the most ancient Priests declare.

In the second, he adds:

> But perhaps one could formulate the new and quite plausible conjecture that these lives too continue to exist within the All, and that they are not destroyed.[150]

On the other hand, with regard to the doctrine of the vehicle of the soul, Hierocles differs from Proclus and from Syrianus on other points than that concerning immortality. Proclus attributes to his master Syrianus the following doctrine, which was maintained, broadly speaking, until Damascius, and which appears as a combination of preceding systems. The rational soul, produced by the demiurge, receives from him a vehicle that is eternal and immortal, like the soul is (συμφυές, ἄϋλον or αὐγοειδὲς ὄχημα), and that always remains attached to the same soul.[151] At each new series of incarnations of a rational soul, before the visible body that is created together with vegetative life at each individual incorporation, the recent gods of Plato's *Timaeus,* who are the encosmic gods, produce the irrational soul, and another vehicle, this one pneumatic, composed of the four elements (ὄχημα προσφυέν), which is attached to the irrational soul.[152] This vehicle, with its irrational soul, enters and leaves the visible or "shell-like" body together with the rational soul and its vehicle; that is to say, together with its soul, it survives an entire series of reincorporations. Ultimately, however, it is destroyed, together with its soul on the occasion of the complete purification of the rational soul.[153] The vegetative soul, by contrast, dies immediately along with the visible body, which is sometimes called "the third vehicle."[154] As Proclus says:[155]

> Threefold is thus the vehicle, either simple and immaterial, or simple and material, or composite and material. And the lives of these ve-

---

[150] Iamblichus, *De anima,* in Stobaeus, *Eclog.,* I, 49, 43, p. 384, 26; I, 49, 35, p. 370, 11ff. Wachsmuth, cited after the trans. of A.-J. Festugière, 1944–1954, 3:236; 195f.

[151] Cf. Proclus, *In Tim.,* vol. III, p. 232, 1ff.; p. 267, 25ff. Diehl.

[152] Cf. Proclus, *In Tim.,* vol. III, p. 238, 18ff.; 297, 26ff.; 298, 2–300, 5 Diehl.

[153] Cf. Proclus, *In Tim.,* vol. III, p. 238, 18ff; 298, 2–300, 5 Diehl; cf. Damascius, *In Phaed.* I, § 239, p. 143 Westerink. Yet Damascius even seems to admit the disappearance of the first vehicle, for those souls that have completed an entire series of incorporations by the acquisition of the cathartic virtues; cf. Damascius, *In Phaed.* I, § 551, p. 283 Westerink. See also Olympiodorus, *In Phaed.* 10, § 5, p. 143 Westerink.

[154] Cf. Proclus, *In Tim.,* vol. III, p. 299, 22ff. Diehl; Olympiodorus, *In Phaed.* 9, § 3, p. 131; 13, § 3, 8ff., p. 173 Westerink.

[155] Proclus, *In Tim.,* vol. III, p. 285, 12ff. Diehl.

hicles are three: one immortal, the other of longer duration than the body, the third perishing with the body.

This increase in the number of vehicles[156] is important, not only in the case of human souls, but also within the entire hierarchy of the psychic class. According to Proclus,[157] the divine souls possess only the luminous vehicle, whereas the mediate class of the demons, in addition to the luminous vehicle, also uses the pneumatic vehicle; and the human souls have, over and above these two vehicles, the mortal body as third vehicle. For Hierocles, on the contrary, as we have seen,[158] the three classes of souls all possess one unique vehicle, which is at the same time luminous and pneumatic. Human souls, however, possess the mortal body in addition.

In Hermias, we find the same system as in Hierocles. In his commentary on Plato's *Phaedrus,* he too is aware of only one vehicle of the soul besides the visible body: a vehicle which is at the same time luminous and pneumatic, conceived of as eternal and immaterial,[159] the purification of which takes place by the telestic art.[160] We also find in him

---

[156] I do not think that H. Bernard (1997) is correct in attributing already to Porphyry (p. 64 n. 131) and to Hermeias (pp. 68ff.) the distinction between two bodies or vehicles of the human soul, the luminous vehicle and the pneumatic vehicle. As far as Porphyry is concerned, she relies on *Sentence* 29, which, in her view, contains such a distinction. Yet I agree with W. Deuse (1983, pp. 219–222), who understands this *Sentence* in the following way. Throughout the text, one and the same pneumatic body is under discussion; it is made up of various bodies, which correspond to the various stages of the soul's descent through the spheres. At each stage of this descent, the body corresponding to one of the various spheres dominates within the pneumatic body. By comparing *Sentence* 29 with a text from Proclus (*In Tim.,* I, 147, 6ff.), Deuse arrives at the conclusion that the first component of the pneuma, the αἰθέριον σῶμα, comes from the totality of the first five spheres; whereas the second and third components, the σῶμα ἡλιοειδές and the σῶμα σεληνοειδές, come from the spheres of the sun and the moon. The fourth component, which renders the pneuma heavy and moist, comes from the sphere beneath the moon.

[157] Proclus, *Theol. Plat.,* III, 5, p. 18, 23–19, 5 Saffrey and Westerink.

[158] Cf. above, the quotation on pp. 38–39.

[159] Hermias, *In Phaedr.,* p. 130, 25ff. Couvreur (with regard to Plato, *Phaedrus,* 246b): "It is obvious that, by calling what is enmattered 'a solid' [*stereon*], he does not see fit to call the soul's perpetual vehicle 'a solid,' since it is not extended in three dimensions, but it is a plane (*epipedon*), in so far as it is subtle and immaterial. It is for this reason that it is recommended *not to extend in depth that which is a plane,* and not to make it earthlike and moist through a form of life full of stains." The words in italics are a quotation of a *Chaldaean Oracle* (fr. 104 des Places). In his commentary on the *Oracles* (1137c, p. 176 des Places), Psellus interprets this same verse from the *Oracles* on the basis of the Neoplatonic doctrine that was in vigor from Proclus on. He no longer identifies the *pneuma* with the plane surface, as Hermias does, but he defines the bidimensional vehicle as the first vehicle of the soul, and the pneuma as the second. Cf. O. Geudtner, 1971, p. 23, n. 104. As Geudtner remarks, the *Chaldaean Oracles* know of only one soul vehicle.

[160] Hermias, *In Phaedr.,* p. 73, 27–74, 9 Couvreur. With regard to the rational soul, Hierocles recommends mathematics as καθαρμοί, by analogy with the τελεστικοὶ καθαρμοί and the ἱερατικὴ τέχνη, and dialectics as ἀναγωγὸς λύσις (*In Carmen aureum,* XXVI, 116, 21ff. Köhler; cf. below, pp. 47–48). Proclus also attributes to mathematics and to geometry a cathartic influence on the rational soul, which leads to cathartic virtue;

the same distinction between man and the living being,[161] all of which is combined with the thesis of the mortality of the irrational soul.[162] This system avoids the alternative Proclus thinks is inevitable for all those who admit the existence of only one vehicle of the soul:

> Of these people, he says,[163] some, after having destroyed the vehicle, are forced to represent the soul as being at a certain moment outside of all bodies. Others, who preserve the vehicle, are obliged to render irrational life immortal as well. This results from the fact that neither group has made a distinction between the congenital vehicle (συμφυὲς ὄχημα) and that which is adventitious (τὸ προσφυέν), between the first and the second, the one fabricated by the one and only Demiurge and that which has been "woven together with the soul" by the multiple demiurges; although Plato clearly distinguished between these vehicles.

According to Proclus, then, Plato's phrase in the *Timaeus* (42c) "τὸν πολὺν ὄχλον καὶ ὕστερον προσφύντα ἐκ πυρὸς καὶ ὕδατος καὶ ἀέρος καὶ γῆς, θορυβώδη καὶ ἄλογον ὄντα" thus relates to the pneumatic vehicle with the irrational soul; whereas for Hierocles and Hermias, it designates the visible human body together with the irrational soul. Hierocles and Hermias therefore do not yield to Proclus' alternative; they consider the irrational soul to be mortal, whereas they attribute immortality to the one and only vehicle of the soul. For them, the irrational soul is not linked to the vehicle at all, but to the body. Nevertheless, nothing in Proclus' brief historical exposition allows us to glimpse the existence of a doctrine like the one we find in Hermias and Hierocles, although it is hard to imagine he did not know it. The alternative that Proclus' own system inspires makes him exclude a priori the existence of such a doctrine.

This brief survey of the various Neoplatonic doctrines on the pneumatic vehicle and the irrational soul lets us see that the doctrine presented by Hierocles corresponds exactly to a stage of development that the theory of the pneumatic vehicle attained between Iamblichus and Syrianus[164] or Proclus.

---

and he calls dialectics an ἀναγωγὸς νόησις which leads to theoretical virtue (*De prov.*, 18, 9ff., p. 126; 49, 1–50, 14, p. 158ff. Boese).

[161] Hermias, *In Phaedr.*, p. 131, 15–17 Couvreur.

[162] For instance, Hermias, *In Phaedr.*, p. 125, 8–15 Couvreur.

[163] Proclus, *In Tim.*, vol. III, p. 299, 16–23 Diehl.

[164] If we consider Hermias' commentary on the *Phaedrus* as simply a record of the classes of Syrianus, as is generally done (but H. Bernard, 1997, is of a different opinion), we are obliged to think either that Syrianus, at this time, had not yet developed the whole of his own doctrine concerning the soul's vehicles, or else that the conception of the soul's two vehicles, instead of one, is due to Proclus.

7. Hierocles' Doctrine of the Three Classes of Souls Is Post-Iamblichean

Although we cannot fix a *terminus ante quem* this time, it is again a post-Iamblichean doctrine we encounter in the description that Hierocles now proposes of the three classes of souls. After insisting that only rational souls are under discussion, and that these three classes of souls form a unity, although each maintains is distinctiveness, Hierocles now specifies how they differ from one another:[165]

> Since there are three encosmic intellective kinds, the first and highest of the demiurge's productions which has received unchangeably and invariably (ἀτρέπτως καὶ ἀμεταβλήτως) its resemblance (ὁμοίωσις) to him, is in all godlike good order, as we said of the kind of the heavenly beings. The second <kind>, which receives the divine order in a secondary and degraded way, does not share in the demiurgic resemblance unchangeably and indivisibly (οὐκ ἀτρέπτως . . . οὐδ' ἀμερίστως), but is unerringly and unafflictedly turned towards the paternal laws, which <characteristic> we attributed to the ethereal beings. The third, as the last of the divine kinds, is not only inferior to the excellence of the heavenly beings by the fact that it is to some extent subject to alteration (τῷ ὁποσοῦν τρέπεσθαι), but because of the fact that it can sometimes be worsened (τῷ ποτε κακύνεσθαι)[166] it is situated below the worth (ἀξίαν) of the ethereal beings. For the fact of always intelligizing the god, and of possessing knowledge of him in unified form (ἡνωμένως), pertains to the heavenly beings, whereas <intelligizing him> always, but discursively (διεξοδικῶς), belongs by essence to the ethereal beings. But the fact of not always intelligizing, and of intelligizing in a partial way (μεμερισμένως), in the very act of intelligizing, has been attributed as a proper characteristic to human souls, which by nature fall short of the undivided intellection (ἀμέριστος νόησις) of the heavenly beings and the knowledge, plurified in an orderly way, of the ethereal beings, since these souls do not intelligize either in a unified way (ἑνιαίως) or perpetually (ἀϊδίως); but even when they are raised up to the worth of intelligizing, they imitate the knowledge of the ethereal beings, and by following them thus they reap the fruit of the vision of the intelligibles.

[165] Hierocles, in Photius, *Library*, cod. 251, 461b37 Bekker, vol. VII, p. 193 Henry.

[166] In this context, the infinitives τρέπεσθαι and κακύνεσθαι have the meaning "to be capable" or "to be subject to": "to be subject in a certain way to change"; "to be subject to sometimes becoming bad." For the Neoplatonists, it is obvious that the nature of souls of the third class does not constrain them to undergo change and to become evil, but that this depends only on themselves. A similar case is found in Simplicius, *In Ench. Epict.*, XXXV 245–273 Hadot (1996). With regard to this text, Schweighäuser had already argued (J. Schweighäuser, 1799–1800, 5:368), that all the participles in this section (XXXV 259 γινόμενα καὶ φθειρόμενα; XXXV 260 αἱ παρατρεπόμεναι ψυχαί; XXXV 266 γινομένων καὶ φθειρομένων; XXXV 267 τὰ γινόμενα καὶ φθειρόμενα) mean "to be capable of."

We can easily recognize the broad outlines of the doctrine that developed[167] from Plato's *Phaedrus* (248a), to which all the late Neoplatonists subscribe, and which Proclus condensed as follows in propositions 184 and 185 of the *Elements of Theology:*[168]

> Every soul is either divine, or else subject to passing from thought to ignorance, or else intermediary between these two; that is, it intelligizes always, but is inferior to the divine souls . . .”; and “All the divine souls are gods at the level of the soul, whereas all souls which participate in the intellective intellect always belong to the cortege of the gods, and all souls subject to change belong to the cortege of the gods only intermittently. . . .

It seems to have been Iamblichus[169] who introduced this doctrine of the three classes of souls, which differ from one another by the degree of their participation in ἑτερότης and ταυτότης.

The most important element of the text we have cited from Hierocles is the last sentence, where he implies that human souls do not participate directly in the intellect but require the mediation of intermediary souls.[170] Proclus explains this in his *Commentary on the Timaeus:*[171]

---

[167] Cf. the citation from Proclus, below, p. 46.

[168] Proclus, *El. Theol.*, prop. 184; 185, pp. 160–161 Dodds. Cf. Proclus, *In Tim.*, vol. III, p. 218, 3; 246, 19ff. Diehl.

[169] See above, n. 114, 3°.

[170] Cf. Hierocles, *In Carmen aureum*, XXVII, p. 120, 22ff. Köhler, where the three classes of souls, and the degree of resemblance to the demiurge that each can attain, are discussed. The human soul cannot attain resemblance with the demiurge and resemblance with the first class of souls either by nature (φύσει) or by essence (κατ᾽ οὐσίαν), but only by relation (κατὰ σχέσιν), and by imitating the intermediary class: “To be sure, the third kind, once it has become perfect, will not become superior to the intermediary kind or equal to the first, but while remaining in the third rank, it becomes assimilated (ὁμοιοῦται) to the first kind, although it is subordinate to the middle kind. For the similarity with the heavenly beings which we see in men—a similarity which is situated only in the order of relation (κατὰ σχέσιν)—already pre-exists in a more perfect and connatural mode in the heroic and intermediary genera. Similarity to the demiurgic god may be considered as one common and unique similitude to all the rational genera. It belongs always and in the same mode (ὡσαύτως) to the heavenly beings. It belongs always, but not always in the same mode, to the stable beings of the ether; and neither always nor in the same mode to the changeable beings of the ether who can also live on earth. If one were to take the first and perfect similitude to God as the model of the second and the third resemblance, or again the second as model of the third, he would express himself correctly.” On the origin of the expression κατὰ σχέσιν in Porphyry, cf. H. Dörrie, 1959, 87. According to Dörrie, Porphyry was the first to oppose the soul's mode of existence καθ᾽ ἑαυτὴν to its mode of existence κατὰ σχέσιν. For the opposition between demons κατὰ σχέσιν (= human souls that have attained the rank of demons) and demons κατ᾽ οὐσίαν, cf. Proclus, *In Tim.*, vol. III, p. 219, 8–17, where the text reveals that this distinction was already known to and defended by Iamblichus.

[171] Proclus, *In Tim.*, vol. II, p. 143, 31–144, 22 Diehl (trans. based on Festugière, 1966–1968, 3:184–185).

Indeed, each of these [that is, of human souls] has a body attached to it, through which it is encosmic. However, there is no peculiar intellect established above it, and this is why it does not always think. For all the intermediary souls,[172] however, there is, on the one hand, a body attached to them, and this is why they are encosmic, exceeding hypercosmics <souls> by their union with the body; and there is a peculiar intellect, on which they depend, and this is why they are always in the Intelligible . . . And we will say that, in human souls, the Indivisible is what is indivisible in the souls above them—these souls which are always in intellection, on which they depend, and in which they participate in so far as is possible; for it is thanks to these intermediary souls that they are also linked to the intellects superior to the intermediary ones, and they become intellective by means of these intermediary souls. Since, then, the extremes are as we have described them, all intermediary souls have their own forms of the indivisible and of the divisible, whether they are of divine rank, or of the demonic rank of demons endowed with reason.[173]

According to Hierocles and Proclus, the human soul, unlike the other souls, does not participate directly in the Intellect. It can therefore know the Forms only in an indirect and very imperfect way. This rather low status given to the rational human soul by no means dates from Middle Platonism, but reveals the influence of Iamblichus. We know that Iamblichus objected against the doctrine of the ancients—Plotinus and Porphyry, among others—who maintained the existence within us of something impassive and always in the act of thinking, and who declared that the soul is consubstantial with the intellect.[174] According to Proclus, Iamblichus' argument against such theories ran as follows:

[172] Proclus here designates as "intermediary" the souls situated between hypercosmic souls and human souls; that is, the divine and demonic souls.

[173] Cf. also Proclus, *In Tim.,* vol. I, p. 245, 17 Diehl (trans. based on Festugière, 1966–1968, 2:81): "Now, what this particular Intellect is, and that it is not distributively one for each individual soul, and that it is not participated directly by individual souls, but by the intermediary of the angelic and demonic souls, which act continuously according to this Intellect, and by virtue of which individual souls also sometimes participate in the Intellective Light, we have explained at length elsewhere."

[174] Iamblichus, *De anima,* in Stobaeus, *Eclog.,* I, 49, 32, pp. 365, 5ff. Wachsmuth; cf. Iamblichus in Proclus, *In Tim.,* vol. III, p. 334, 3 Diehl. As far as Porphyry is concerned, this presentation of his doctrine is not quite correct. According to P. Hadot, 1968, 1:340, Porphyry only attributes consubstantiality to the soul in its state of preexistence: "In fact, there are two states of the soul. In its state of preexistence and its pure being, the soul is an idea, and is itself in a transcendent mode; it is then merged with the Intellect, and consubstantial with it. In its state of self-definition, which is at the same time the result of a derivative act of the Intellect, the soul is distinguished from the Intellect; it becomes its 'matter,' and descends to the purely intellectual plane."

What is it that sins in us, when, under the impulse of the irrational part, we hasten towards an impure imagination? Is it not our free choice (προαίρεσις)? How could it be anything else? For it is by this that we overcome the precipitous floods of the imagination. But if free choice may sin, how can the soul be without sin?—Moreover, what is it that makes our entire life happy? Is it not the fact that reason possesses its own virtue? This, at any rate, is what we shall say. But if it is when the dominant part within us is perfect that our entire being is also happy, then what would prevent all human beings from being happy now as well, if the highest part within us is always thinking, and always among the divine beings? If this part is the intellect, then it has nothing to do with the soul. But if it is a part of the soul, then all the rest of the soul is also happy.—Besides, who is the soul's charioteer? Is it not what is most beautiful in our being, and which is, so to speak, its head to the greatest degree? How can we avoid saying this, if it is true that this charioteer is he who governs our entire substance; he who, with his head, sees the supracelestial place and becomes similar to the "Great Leader" of the gods; this charioteer who drives a winged chariot and is the first to advance in heaven? But if the highest part within us is the charioteer, and if, as is said in the *Phaedrus* (248a1ff.), this charioteer sometimes travels above the heights of the heavens and raises his head towards the place beyond, and sometimes plunges and <befouls his carriage> by his lameness and the shedding of wings . . . the conclusion is evident, that the highest part within us is necessarily sometimes in one state, and sometimes in another.[175]

We must also situate the following testimony of Photius on Hierocles within the same context:

It is good to know, says the author, that the soul, when it is turned towards the intellect, is not rid of that weakness that sometimes makes it unreasonable; conversely, in the most abominable vice, it has not lost the ability to return to thought and to repeat in a healthy way. For the human soul, having been created thus by its nature, has the capacity to participate simultaneously in divine happiness and in mortal destiny.[176]

---

[175] Proclus, *In Tim.,* vol. III, p. 334, 4ff. Diehl (trans. based on Festugière, 1966–1968, 5:216). Cf. Simplicius, *In de anima,* p. 240, 33 Hayduck; *ibid.,* pp. 5, 39; 89, 33; 313, 1; 237, 37; Priscian, *Metaphr. in Theophr.,* p. 32, 13 Bywater. All these texts are translated by Festugière 1944–54, 3:253ff.

[176] Hierocles, in Photius, *Library,* cod. 251, 463b14 Bekker, vol. VII, p. 198 Henry.

This natural defectiveness of the rational human soul explains the importance of theurgy for its salvation. As we have briefly had occasion to mention,[177] theurgy, in a process that began with Iamblichus, occupies a considerable place in Hierocles' commentary on the *Carmen aureum,* as we will now see in more detail.

8. Theurgy

The extracts that Photius took from Hierocles' treatise *On Providence* do not speak of theurgy. This lacuna is compensated by the last chapters (XXV, XXVI, and XXVII) of Hierocles' commentary on the *Carmen aureum,* which describe in detail the conditions that must be filled so that the rational human soul may return to its homeland. These conditions are the same as in Iamblichus: the acquisition of virtue; learning the mathematical sciences and philosophy, which together purify the rational soul; and theurgy, which purifies the pneumatic or luminous body. For Hierocles, however, theurgy has two parts, telestics and hieratical elevation, a bipartition that we will find clearly expressed again in Proclus, albeit probably not with the same meaning. For Hierocles, as we shall see, telestics includes the totality of local pagan rites, whereas for Proclus this term seems to signify in particular the art of animating statues.[178] I quote Hierocles:

> The purifications required for the rational soul are the mathematical sciences, and the elevating deliverance is the dialectical vision of beings (ἡ διαλεκτικὴ τῶν ὄντων ἐποπτεία). This is why "deliverance" has been stated [sc. in the *Carmen aureum*] in the singular: "in the soul's deliverance," because deliverance is completed in a single science, whereas mathematics contains a plurality of sciences. It is also necessary to ordain for the luminous body prescriptions analogous to those that are appropriately transmitted for the soul's purifications and deliverance. Telestic purifications must therefore come together with those of mathematics, and hieratic elevation must accompany dialectical deliverance. For these things are particularly apt to purify the pneumatic vehicle of the rational soul and render it perfect, to separate it from matter's lack of life, and to prepare it to be apt to have converse with the pure pneumas [*scil.* pneumatic bodies]. . . . Just as it is fitting for the soul to be adorned with science and with

---

[177] Cf. above, chap. II, sec. 1, p. 9 with n. 29.
[178] On Proclus, cf. C. van Liefferinge, 1999, pp. 93ff.

virtue, so that it may keep company with those who are permanently in possession thereof, so the luminous vehicle must be rendered pure and immaterial, so that it may endure community with the ethereal bodies.[179]

After saying that we must neglect neither the purification of the rational soul nor that of the luminous vehicle, Hierocles continues a bit further on:

This is why philosophy is united with the art of sacred things (τῇ τῶν ἱερῶν τέχνῃ), since it is concerned with the purification of the luminous vehicle, and if you separate the philosophical intellect from this art, you will find that it no longer has the same power (δύναμις).[180] Indeed, of the factors that work together to complete our perfection, some were first discovered by the philosophical intellect, and others were introduced by telestic activity, following the philosophical intellect. I call "telestic activity" the power that purifies the luminous vehicle, so that, of the whole of philosophy, the theoretical part may come first as intellect, and the practical part may follow, as a power. Yet let us postulate two species of practice: one is civic morality, and the other telestics. One purifies us from irrationality through the virtues, and the other by excising material imaginations through the sacred methods. A not inconsiderable manifestation of political philosophy are the laws that regulate a collectivity, and of telestic philosophy, the sacred rites (τὰ τῶν πόλεων ἱερά) practiced in the cities. But the summit of all philosophy is the theoretical intellect; in the middle is the political intellect, and third is the telestic intellect . . . this is why we must join together into one single totality the science that finds the truth, the power that projects virtues, and that which produces purity, so that political activity may be accomplished in conformity with the dominant intellect, and that the sacred act may be shown to be in accord with both.[181]

The contents of these texts may be schematized by the two following figures:

[179] Hierocles, *In Carmen aureum*, XXVI, 21f., p. 116, 20–117, 10. On the soul's vehicle, cf. above, pp. 36–42. On the role of mathematics in Neoplatonic education, see I. Hadot, 1998; D. J. O'Meara, 1989.

[180] Cf. Hierocles, *In Carmen aureum*, XXVI, 8–9, p. 113, 6ff. Köhler: The pneumatic body must be purified "by following the sacred laws and the techniques of the sacred rites. This purification is, as it were, more corporeal. This is why it has recourse to various matters . . . but this entire practice, if it is done in a way fitting to the gods and not in the manner of a charlatan, is in conformity with the canons of the truth and of virtue."

[181] Hierocles, *In Carmen aureum*, XXVI, 24–28, p. 117, 20–118, 21 Köhler.

```
                    purifications and deliverances

         of the                          of the pneumatic or
       rational soul                     luminous vehicle

        purification:                  purification: telestic art
     mathematical sciences            (sacred rites of the cities)

   deliverance: the dialectical            deliverance:
      vision of beings                    hieratic elevation
```

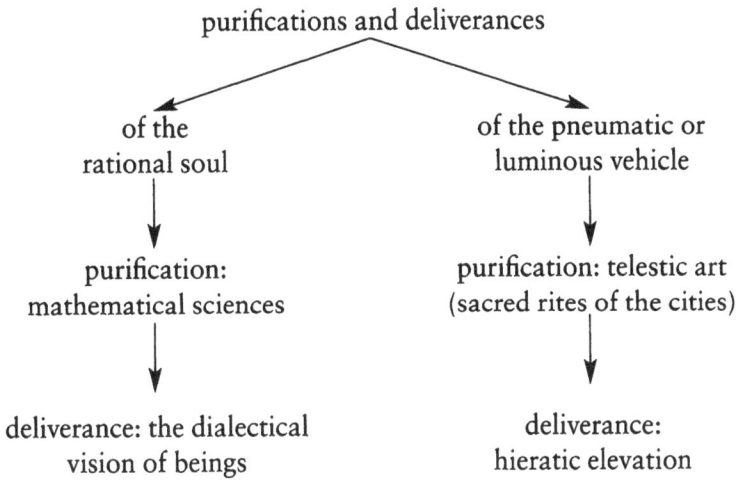

division of philosophy in hierarchical order:
theoretical (or contemplative) intellect
political intellect: civic morality
telestic intellect

In the last division, we no longer hear of "hieratic elevation," which certainly corresponds to the highest level of theurgy, whereas the telestic art probably includes the two lower levels of theurgy according to Iamblichus. What is interesting is that theurgy is by no means opposed to philosophy, but is integrated within it.

Chapter XXVII deals briefly with the fate of the rational human soul after its purification, and that of its vehicle. In accordance with the *Golden Verses* on which he is commenting:

> And if, having abandoned your body, you reach the free ether, you will be an immortal god. . .

Hierocles has both soul and vehicle arrive together in the ethereal region, which is situated below the moon. It is not, however, certain that what is at issue is anything other than a provisional affirmation, required both by the text to be commented upon and the elementary nature of this commentary; he may have refined this affirmation in another, more technical context. In any case, like Porphyry and Iamblichus, Hierocles is of the opinion that only a small number of human beings can arrive at this supreme goal.[182]

---

[182] Cf. Hierocles, *In Carmen aureum*, XXIV, 12, p. 100, 24ff.; XXV, 6–9, p. 106, 24–107, 23; XXV, 12, p. 108, 12–19 Köhler. For Iamblichus, cf. C. van Liefferinge, 1999, pp. 23–123. Cf. Porphyry *apud* Augustine, frag. 297 Smith.

9. The Essence of the Human Soul Is Subject to a Kind of Alteration

In his book *The Changing Self*, Carlos Steel (1978) was able to show the influence of the philosophy of Iamblichus on all the later Neoplatonists, and in particular on Damascius and Priscian, to whom he attributes the commentary on the *De anima* edited under the name of Simplicius. I have already expressed my reservations on this point.[183] Steel's readers are led to conclude that the doctrine that the very essence of the rational human soul can be subject to a certain alteration was admitted only by three Neoplatonists: Iamblichus, Damascius, and Priscian. Yet this way of presenting things risks falsifying our historical perspective. I therefore propose to contribute some supplementary elements to the history of this doctrine.

I have demonstrated elsewhere[184] that Simplicius, as a student of Damascius, also adopted this point of view. We shall see that Hierocles also adhered to this doctrine. I begin by quoting a text that speaks of the possibility of a certain corruption of the essence of the rational human soul:

> Since our nature is rational, and consequently apt to deliberate, and as it can, through its own choice, be led to deliberate well or badly, the form of life according to nature preserves and saves its essence, but the choice of what we ought not to have chosen corrupts, in so far as this is possible (ἡ μέν κατὰ φύσιν ζωὴ σῷζει τὴν οὐσίαν αὐτῆς, ἡ δὲ παρὰ τὸ δέον αἵρεσις διαφθείρει ἐφ' ὅσον οἷόν τε). For the corruption of an immortal reality is wickedness (κακία).[185]

This last sentence is explained a bit further on:

> Indeed, human nature risks slipping towards not-being as a result of its deviation towards what is contrary to nature, but thanks to its return towards what is in conformity with nature, it is brought back to its own essence, and it recovers its pure being, which had been blemished by mixture with the passions.[186]

Finally, I quote a third text in which Hierocles contrasts the ἀθάνατοι θεοί of the Pythagorean *Carmen aureum*, verse 1, with the θνητοὶ θεοί, the mortal gods, which are the rational human souls:[187]

---

[183] Most recently in "Simplicius or Priscianus? On the author of the commentary on Aristotle's *De anima* (CAG XI): A methodological study," *Mnemosyne* 55.2 (2002): pp. 159–199.

[184] Cf. I. Hadot, 1996, 70–100.

[185] Hierocles, *In Carmen aureum*, XIV, 4, p. 64, 10–15 Köhler.

[186] Hierocles, *In Carmen aureum*, XIV, 9, p. 65, 25–66, 1 Köhler.

[187] Hierocles, *In Carmen aureum*, I, 3–6, pp. 8, 19–9, 14 Köhler.

The *Golden Verses* call "immortal gods" those who always and identically intelligize the demiurgic god, who are arranged around the good of this demiurgic god, and who receive from him, indivisibly and immutably (ἀμερίστως τε καὶ ἀτρέπτως), being and well-being, since they are the impassible and unperverted images (ἀπαθεῖς καὶ ἀκακύντους) of the demiurgic cause. For it is fitting for the god to produce such images of himself as well, and not [only] images which are all changeable and subject to the passions (τρεπτὰς καὶ ἐμπαθεῖς), by their downward motion towards evil, as are human souls, which constitute the last kind of rational natures, just as, in contrast, the kind of the immortal gods, of which we are now speaking, is that which is highest. And perhaps it is by opposition to human souls that these gods have been called "immortal gods"[188] in so far as they do not die to the divine happy life (εὐζωία), and they are never in forgetfulness, either of their own essence, or of the goodness of the Father. But the human soul is subject to these passions, sometimes thinking the god, and recovering its own value (ἀξία); sometimes falling far away from all that. That is why human souls could reasonably be called "mortal gods," in so far as they sometimes die to the divine happy life, as a result of their flight from the god, and that they live that life once again when they turn towards the god; and in this way they live the divine life; but in that other way they die, and participate in the fate of death, so far as this is possible for an immortal essence (ὡς οἷόν τε ἀθανάτῳ οὐσίᾳ θανάτου μοίρας μεταλαχεῖν), not by deviation towards not-being, but by the negation of well-being. For death for a rational essence is the privation of divinity (ἀθεΐα) and of intelligence (ἄνοια).

In this text, we again encounter the opposition between souls that always adhere to the Good, and human souls, which can deviate toward evil. We also find in it the theme of the soul's death, which is not unusual in Neoplatonic texts. Our first quotation from Hierocles leaves no doubt that, in the third quotation, the death of the rational essence, and therefore of the rational soul, corresponds to an alteration of essence that is manifested in the loss of "well-being" or of virtue. Did this doctrine of the mutability of the human soul's essence reach Hierocles directly from a work by Iamblichus or through the intermediary of his teacher Plutarch of Athens? The fragments and testimonies concerning Plutarch, which D. Taormina[189] has collected and interpreted, do not allow us to answer this question.[190]

---

[188] Cf. Cicero, *De fin.*, II, 13, 40: mortalem deum (= Aristotle, *Protr.*, fr. 10c Ross); *Corpus Hermeticum*, X, 25; XII, 1.

[189] Catania, 1989.

[190] Elsewhere, however, it is clear (cf. above, p. 39) that Hierocles' commentary on the *Carmen aureum* does not reflect either Iamblichus' doctrine or that of Plutarch of Athens

Now that we have recognized the role of Iamblichus in the development of the doctrine of the mutability of the human soul's essence, we must not imagine that he had created this doctrine *ex nihilo;* that is, without basing himself on any previous elements. On the contrary, we must be well aware that the problematic in which the discussion of the mutability of the human soul's essence is situated goes back to the origins of Neoplatonism. How can a soul remain a soul, if, while its essence is rational, it falls into irrationality? How can a soul remain a soul, if, when its essence is to be life, it sinks into that kind of death that is vice? A Neoplatonist had to ask himself these types of questions. They are of the type raised, for instance, by Augustine during the Cassiciacum period, under the influence of Neoplatonism, and more particularly of the *Platonici libri,* which contained writings by Plotinus and Porphyry. Let us read a few texts by Augustine in which the human soul's relation to evil is discussed:

> For indeed, the soul is at fault when it consents to evil; it then begins to have less being, and, for this reason, to be worth less that it was worth when it did not consent to any evil, and remained in virtue. It is all the more evil in that it turns away from that which *is* in the highest degree, in order to tend towards that which *is* less, so that it itself is less. Now, the less it *is,* the closer it is to nothingness, for all things whose being diminishes tend towards absolute nothingness. And although the soul does not reach the point of being nothing, by dying altogether, it is nevertheless evident that any one of its lapses is the beginning of death. (*Contra Secundinum,* 15)

In this text, we encounter the Neoplatonic identification between being and "well-being," and between not-being and evil. When the soul ceases to be good, it loses its real being, and becomes more and more nullified as it becomes worse, without, however, ever managing to cross

---

faithfully and in all its details. As has been shown by J. M. Dillon (1973) and J. F. Finamore (1985, pp. 16ff.), Iamblichus held the view that the soul's vehicle—for him, there is only one vehicle, not the two that were distinguished by the late Neoplatonists— is immortal, as is the irrational soul or life. Hierocles also accepts the immortality of the soul's vehicle, but for him, as for all the later Neoplatonists, the irrational soul is mortal. This is very clearly explained at *In Carmen aureum,* XXVI, 4–6, p. 112, 5–17 Köhler (cf. above, p. 37 n. 133). On the question of the immortality of the irrational soul, Hierocles also takes his distance from Plutarch, who, according to Damascius (*In Phaed.,* I, 177, p. 107f. Westerink), also accepted the immortality of the irrational soul (cf. D. Taormina, 1989, pp. 79–80). Hierocles has thus adopted Iamblichus' thesis, according to which the essence of the rational human soul can undergo an alteration, but he did not want to follow Iamblichus in all the details of his doctrine of the soul. Damascius proceeds in the same way.

the limit that separates it from nothingness. It will never die completely, but it will undergo a beginning of death.

Let us translate a second text of Augustine, taken from the *De immortalitate animae*. In this treatise, the terms "anima" and "animus" are used indifferently.

> But, it will be said, the very remoteness of reason because of which the soul falls into folly cannot occur without a loss of its being. Indeed, if the soul *is* more intensely when it is turned towards reason and attached to it, because it is attached to an immutable thing which is the truth, which *is* in an eminent and primordial way, on the contrary, when the soul turns away from reason, it possesses being itself to a lesser degree, which is the same as a loss of being. Now, all that is loss of being tends towards nothingness; and inevitably nothing is more able to make us understand death than the fact that a thing that *was* is now nothing. This is why to tend towards nothingness is to tend towards death. Why should death not reach the soul in which there takes place a loss of being (*defectum ab essentia*): this is what is difficult to say. Here, we admit all the rest, and yet we deny the consequent; that is, that that which tends towards nothingness dies, or in other words reaches nothingness. (*De imm. an.,* VII, 12)

> But if the soul suspends itself from spiritual things and fixes itself in them and resides in them, the pressure of this habit [that is, of the habit of taking pleasure in sensible things] is broken, and being gradually repressed, it is extinguished. For this habit was more powerful when we yielded to it; when we restrain it, it is not reduced to nothing, but it is in any case less. Thus, by these stages which move resolutely away from all dissolute motions in which the soul suffers a loss of its essence, after recovering the enjoyment of the rational harmonies, our whole life turns back towards God . . . (*De musica,* VI, 11, 33)

These last two texts attest explicitly that, for Augustine, the soul's *minus esse* is an alteration of its essence. Moral degradation corresponds to ontological degradation. A fourth text sets forth this Augustinian conception once again:

> For the soul is nothing by itself; otherwise it would not be subject to change or exposed to the loss of its essence (*pateretur defectum ab essentia*). Since it is nothing by itself, all the being it possesses must come from God; when it remains faithful to its rank (*in ordine suo* = τάξις), it lives by the very presence of God in mind and con-

sciousness. The soul thus possesses this good inside itself. Thus, for it, to be filled with pride is to go towards external things and, so to speak, to nullify itself (*inanescere*), which consists in being less and less. (*De musica,* VI, 13, 40)

Did Augustine find this doctrine, according to which the rational human soul can undergo an alteration of its essence, but not its complete destruction, in the *Platonici libri,* or did he himself draw this final consequence from a few preparatory texts by Plotinus and Porphyry? Generally speaking, but with particular regard to the last text from Augustine I have quoted, W. Theiler thought that Augustine's source was found in the *Platonici libri,* made up above all of texts by Porphyry.[191] E. zum Brunn, who dealt with all the texts from Augustine I have just cited,[192] did not attempt an investigation of sources. Theiler's hypothesis can claim for itself a certain probability from the very fact that, elsewhere, for other texts and according to other historians, it has been supposed with probability bordering on certitude, that Porphyry was Augustine's source.

In what follows, we shall give a few examples of what we can find in Plotinus. The theme of *magis* and *minus esse* is stated clearly in the following text:

[W]e are more, when we tend towards the One, and well-being[193] is there; but being far from him is nothing other than being less (*Enn.,* VI, 9, 9, 11–13).

Did Plotinus, from a certain point of view or at a determinate moment of his life, go so far as to accept the mutability of the soul, as did Augustine? The following text suggests as much:

For if the soul goes completely as far as complete wickedness, then it no longer has wickedness [as an accident], but it exchanges its nature for "the nature that is other" [than form], which is inferior, for wickedness that is still mingled with some contrary is still human. It dies, then, as a soul might die, and death for it, since it is still plunged within the body, is to sink into matter, to be surfeited with it, and even when it has left the body, to lie there until it rises back up and somehow turns its gaze away from the slough. This is the

[191] W. Theiler, 1933, p. 27, where the text by Augustine is cited; cf. also pp. 22ff. But Theiler does not discuss the doctrine we are currently studying.

[192] E. zum Brunn, 1969.

[193] τὸ εὖ ἐνταῦθα: εὖ in the sense of εὖ εἶναι. For εὖ εἶναι, cf. Plotinus, *Enn.,* II, 1, 5, 20–25.

meaning of the expression "to go down into Hades, there to fall deeply asleep" [Plato, *Republic* 534c]. (*Enn.*, I, 8, 13, 18–26)

In the phrase ἀλλ' ἑτέραν φύσιν τὴν χείρω ἠλλάξατο, the expression "ἑτέρα φύσις" is taken from Plato's *Parmenides* (158b6), and has a particularly strong meaning. The "other nature" is the "alien nature," or the nature that is contrary (cf. Plotinus, *Enneads*, I, 6, 5, 57; I, 6, 6, 22). This text cannot be understood otherwise than in the sense that the soul changes in its essence.

From Porphyry, we may cite the following texts:

> For the essence whose being consists in life, and whose very affections are lives, death consists in a certain form of life, and not in absolute privation of life, because, for it, even affections (τὸ πάθος) do not lead to the complete absence of life. (*Sent.*, XXIII, p. 14, 1–4 Lamberz)

> For those who are capable of advancing by intelligence to their essence, and to know their essence, and to recover themselves in this very knowledge and in the consciousness of this knowledge according to the union of the knower and the known, for them, since they are present to themselves, being is also present. But for those who stray from their being towards other things, since they are absent from themselves, being is also absent. (*Sent.*, XL, p. 50, 16–51, 2 Lamberz)

These texts from Augustine, Plotinus, Porphyry, and Hierocles have a common denominator: when the rational human soul turns toward entities that are ontologically superior to it, and participates in them, it is completely what it *is*, and what it *must be* by its nature. When, however, it turns away from the beings superior to it, and away from itself, as it advances towards matter and sinks within it, it is *less;* its life is lessened, it becomes evil, and it dies, not completely, but in a sense. The object of its participation determines its moral quality and the degree of purity of its being, as well as the integrity of its essence.

I do not know any of the small number of texts by Porphyry that have been preserved, that declare *expressis verbis* that the rational human soul can change in its essence; yet the presence of this doctrine in Augustine makes it probable that some such texts existed. In any case, in a fragment of his treatise *On the soul against Boethos*,[194] we find the

---

[194] Porphyry, in Eusebius, *Praeparatio evangelica*, XI, 28, 4–5, vol. II, p. 63 Mras = fr. 242, p. 260, 23–37 Smith: "Since it (the soul) does not at all resemble what is mor-

idea that leads to the doctrine of the mutability of the essence of the human soul; that is, that the soul's activities follow from its essence, that the essence changes when the activities change, and *vice versa*.

I believe I have shown the continuity of this problem, which is linked to the fact that the rational human soul can pass from virtue to vice, approach the divine and move away from it, and *vice versa*. It is undeniable that, in the course of the history of Neoplatonic philosophy, the questions regarding this problem were raised with more and more precision, and that the answers also became more and more precise, detailed, and systematic, without, I believe, gaining in clarity and persuasion. In this development, Iamblichus is an important link; yet as far as the doctrine of the mutability of the essence of the soul is concerned, he does not appear to be an innovator without any precursors.

10. *The Attributes of the Demiurge: King, Father, Zeus, and Tetrad in Hierocles and Their Neoplatonic Background*

Let us now return to the demiurge of the universe. We have already learned that, according to Hierocles, the demiurge creates in an immobile way by his very being, by his thought, and by his will alone, and that he includes within him three different levels of demiurgic causes.[195] We also know that the demiurge, for Hierocles, is situated on the level

---

tal, soluble, and unintelligent, or what does not participate in life and can, for this reason, be touched and perceived by the senses, and is born and perishes; but on the contrary it resembles what is divine, immortal, and invisible; the intelligible living being, which is akin to the truth—and all the other notions Plato recapitulates with regard to it—Plato did not think it well to agree that all other similarities to the deity are present in it, and yet to wish to eliminate its resemblance to essence, thanks to which it was able to obtain the others. For just as those things that are unlike the deity in their activities, are immediately also utterly changed in the constitution of their essence, in the same way it follows that things that somehow (πως) participate in the same activities first possess similarity of essence. For it is through the fact that an essence is of a given quality, that its activities are also of a given quality, since they flow forth from it, and are its offspring." This text is situated in the context of the discussion of the proofs given by Plato for the immortality of the human soul. In this context, resemblance with the god concerns such aspects as being alive and vivifying, being immaterial, possessing reason, etc.; in short, aspects that Damascius was to resume by the phrase "the form of its original being" (I. Hadot, 1996, p. 71–77). From this viewpoint, Porphyry says further on (28, 12, p. 64 Mras) that the human soul always maintains its resemblance to the deity in its activities, even when it sinks down into the deepest parts of the world of becoming. However, as soon as he envisaged the possibility of dissimilarity between the activities of the human soul and the divine activities, which results from its possibly vicious state, should he not, according to the premises he has just stated, conclude to the possible alteration of its essence?

[195] Cf. above, chap. III, sec. 4–5, pp. 24–36.

of the *Noûs*.[196] We have seen that all these features that Hierocles attributes to the demiurge are found in all the Neoplatonists. Yet we have not yet interpreted the last phrase of the passage cited on page 30: "But the god who is their father and demiurge reigns as king over them all," and of the parallel passage from codex 251: "But the god who is their creator (ποιητής) and father reigns as king over them all."[197] The phrase "creator and father," which Hierocles applies to the demiurge, indicates that Hierocles does have in mind the demiurge of Plato's *Timaeus,* for the demiurge of the *Timaeus* is also called "creator and father."[198] In addition, nothing is more usual in a text of Platonic inspiration than to call the demiurge "king," since this appellation is the result of a learned combination of several texts of Plato[199] and of various attempts to harmonize them with the *Orphica*.[200] In Neoplatonic texts, we find a multitude of phrases, always similar, of which I will cite only one, used by Iamblichus, as an example: "the intellect, leader and king of beings and demiurgic art of the universe . . ."[201]

Besides these reflections of an exegetical nature, the title of "king" given to the demiurge is, for a Neoplatonist, laden with the meaning of Hellenistic research on the ideal government. In Hellenistic thought, royalty implied a government that respects the laws of the city, by opposition to tyranny, which knows only arbitrary procedures. Xenophon's Socrates (*Memor.* IV, 6, 12) already distinguished the king from the tyrant in this way. The ideal king is thus essentially loyal (νόμιμος); but he does not act like a blind, impersonal law, incapable of discerning what is best and most just in each individual case. On the contrary, he is a kind of living law (νόμος ἔμψυχος), a law in conformity with nature, that emanates from his own eminent wisdom. The king is not only just, but is in addition benevolent. His philanthropy makes him take care of his subjects like a father cares for his children.[202] It is

---

[196] This is already evident from the fact that Hierocles situates the demiurge above the hypostasis of the soul, but is, in addition, designated by formulas like νοῦ τῶν πάντων ἡγουμένου καὶ θεοῦ τῶν ὅλων ὄντος αἰτίου [in Photius, *Library,* cod. 251, 462b18 Bekker, vol. VII, p. 195 Henry—an allusion to Plato, *Tim.,* 48a1–2], and like πᾶς γὰρ εἰκὼν τοῦ νοητοῦ θεοῦ τὸ ἄλογον καὶ ἀνόητον [in Photius, *Library,* cod. 251, 462a26 Bekker, vol. VII, p. 194 Henry]. Cf. also *In Carmen aureum,* XX, p. 89, 12ff. Köhler: ἔστι γάρ, ὡς ἔφαμεν, δημιουργός, τῶν ὅλων αἰτία ἡ τετράς, θεὸς νοητός, αἴτιος τοῦ οὐρανίου καὶ αἰσθητοῦ θεοῦ. Cf. the end of the translation below, p. 66.

[197] Photius, *Library,* cod. 214, 172a41–42 Bekker, vol. III, p. 127 Henry; *ibid.,* cod. 251, 461b19 Bekker, vol. VII, p. 192 Henry.

[198] Plato, *Tim.,* 28c3: τὸν . . . ποιητὴν καὶ πατέρα τοῦδε τοῦ παντός. . . .

[199] Plato, *Tim.,* 28c3; 41a7; *Statesman,* 273b1; *Letter* II.

[200] Cf. for instance Proclus, *In Tim.,* vol. III, p. 168, 17 Diehl.

[201] Iamblichus, *De myst.,* I, 7 (22, 1), p. 50 des Places: νοῦς τοίνυν ἡγεμὼν καὶ βασιλεὺς τῶν ὄντων τέχνη τε δημιουργικὴ τοῦ παντός . . .

[202] Cf. P. Hadot, 1970, col. 572–607.

this Hellenistic image of the ideal king that Philo applies to God and Hierocles to the demiurge, when he speaks of his providence, an image that enables us to understand the expression "paternal royalty" that Hierocles attributes to the providence of the demiurge-king.[203]

In his commentary on the *Carmen aureum,* Hierocles, commenting on verse 61, identifies the demiurge of the *Timaeus*—"creator and father of this universe," with Zeus and Zen of the *Pythagoreans.*[204] Proclus, for his part, assimilates him to the Zeus of Homer and of Orpheus, to the decade of the Pythagoreans[205] and to the "Father of men and gods" of the *Chaldaean Oracles:*

> And this demiurge is celebrated, he says, by Plato, and by Orpheus and by the Oracles, as the unique Creator and Father of the Universe, "Father of men and gods," who engenders the multitude of the Gods, but also sends the souls, so that there may be generation of men, as the *Timaeus* also says.[206]

This identification of the demiurge with Zeus in "all of Hellenic theology," as Proclus says,[207] seems already to have been sketched by Iamblichus. Proclus tells us that Iamblichus had written a treatise entitled "On the Discourse of Zeus in the *Timaeus,*" where he drew a parallel between Plato's demiurge and the Third Intellect of the Pythagoreans.[208] We also have the testimony of Hermias,[209] who criti-

---

[203] Cf. the text from Hierocles, quoted p. 101 with n. 350. Compare this with Philo, *De provid.,* II, § 15 (after the trans. by M. Hadas-Lebel, *Philon, De providentia,* p. 227): "God is not a tyrant who indulges in cruelty, violence, and all the practices of a brutal despot in his domination, but a king who holds a temperate power in conformity with the law, who governs all the heaven and the universe in justice. For a king, there is no appellation more appropriate than that of father. For what parents are to children in the family, the king is to the city and God to the universe [this is why in Homer, the most appreciated and praised of the poets, Jupiter has been called "father of gods and of men" = Armenian version], he who, by the immutable laws of nature, has joined together in indissoluble union two very beautiful attributes: authority and solicitude (τὸ ἡγεμονικὸν μετὰ τοῦ κηδεμονικοῦ)." Cf. also the Introduction by M. Hadas-Lebel, p. 98.

[204] Hierocles, *In Carmen aureum,* XXV, p. 105, 4ff. Köhler: "The Pythagoreans had the custom of honoring the creator and father of this universe with the names of Zeus or Zen; for it is just to call him by whom all things have their being and their life after his activity." For the etymology, cf. Plato, *Cratylus,* 396a–b; cf. Proclus, *In Tim.,* vol. I, p. 315, 4–8 Diehl.

[205] Proclus, *In Tim.,* vol. I, p. 316, 4–317, 2 Diehl; 313, 2 Diehl. On Hierocles, who identifies the demiurge and the tetrad, see below, chapter III, sec. 12A, pp. 63–82.

[206] Proclus, *In Tim.,* vol. I, p. 318, 25–319, 1 Diehl (trans. based on Festugière, 1966–1968, 2:176).

[207] Proclus, *In Tim.,* vol. I, p. 316, 12–13 Diehl.

[208] Proclus, *In Tim.,* vol. I, p. 308, 19ff. Diehl.

[209] Hermias, *In Phaedr.,* p. 136, 17 Couvreur. On the different Zeus, cf. also Proclus, *In Tim.,* vol. III, p. 190, 20 Diehl; Hermias, *In Phaedr.,* p. 142, 10.

cizes Iamblichus for not having distinguished this Zeus, that is, the demiurge of the *Timaeus*, from the Zeus mentioned in Plato's *Phaedrus*. Hermias himself, in agreement with the *Chaldaean Oracles,* gives to the Zeus of the *Phaedrus* a place lower than that of Zeus the demiurge.[210]

In the metaphysical system of the Neoplatonists, however, this Zeus of Hellenic theology, identified with the demiurge of Plato's *Timaeus* and called "king" and "creator and father," was far from occupying the first place in the hierarchy. In general, we can say that neither Plotinus, nor Porphyry, nor Iamblichus, Syrianus, Hermias, nor Proclus made the demiurge the supreme god of their theological system; instead, the precise place occupied by the demiurge varied over time. Moreover, it was precisely because of the effort to assimilate various foreign systems to Platonism, such as the *Orphica,* Pythagoreanism, and the *Chaldaean Oracles,* that the Neoplatonists after Plotinus found themselves obliged, on the one hand, to multiply and subdivide continually the hypostases after the One and above all the hypostasis of the *Noûs;* and, on the other hand, to situate the demiurge ever lower on the hierarchical scale of Intellects.[211] The attributions of "king" and "father" do not imply the contrary; that is, they do not designate in and of themselves the summit of a hierarchy, as might be implied by the analogy with social and family status, for the late Neoplatonic system was familiar with several "fathers," and several "kings." For Syrianus and Proclus, the demiurge of the *Timaeus* is the fifth in the series of kings,[212] and the third of the fathers.[213] For Iamblichus, this demiurge seems to have been identical to the third king of Plato's *Second Letter.*[214]

We have seen that Proclus identified the demiurge with the Pythagorean decade. Hierocles, for his part, identifies him with the tetrad of these same Pythagoreans:

---

[210] Hermias, *In Phaedr.,* p. 136, 25ff. Couvreur: "We, following Plato and the Theologians, say the following: After the demiurgic monad, the unique and transcendent Zeus, there are three Zeus: Zeus, Poseidon, Pluto." This triad is subdivided into twelve gods, of whom the first is the Zeus of the *Phaedrus.*

[211] This did not, however, prevent the Neoplatonists—even the later ones—from speaking of the demiurge simply as the *Noûs* in works intended for a wide public.

[212] This classification was carried out in Syrianus' work entitled "Orphic Discourses"; cf. Proclus, *In Tim.,* vol. I, p. 314, 27ff. Diehl.

[213] Proclus distinguished between the "Father," the "Father and Creator," the "Creator and Father," and the "Creator," in an order of decreasing dignity. Cf. *In Tim.,* vol. I, p. 311, 25ff. Diehl; vol. III, p. 208, 5ff. Diehl.

[214] Cf. the testimony of Proclus (above, p. 58f.), where he affirms that Iamblichus identified Plato's demiurge with the Third Intellect of the Pythagoreans; and the exposition by H. D. Saffrey and L. G. Westerink on "The history of exegeses of Plato's *Second Letter* in the Platonic tradition," in Proclus, *Théologie platonicienne,* vol. II, pp. xx ff., especially pages LIII and following.

"The author of the *Golden Verses*," he writes, ". . . declares that the tetrad,[215] which is the source of the sempiternal cosmic arrangement, is identical with the demiurgical god."[216]

Immediately afterwards, he wonders how this is possible. To answer this question, he gives a brief summary of Pythagorean arithmology,[217] whence it results that the tetrad is the power of the decade. The decade represents "detailed" perfection, while the tetrad represents "unified" perfection. The tetrad is the arithmetical mean between the monad and the hebdomad (1 + 3 = 4); (4 + 3 = 7). The monad and the hebdomad have the most beautiful and excellent properties of all numbers, for the monad, being the principle of all numbers, unites within itself all the powers of all numbers, whereas the hebdomad, which is "motherless" and "virgin," has the dignity of the monad in secondary rank:[218]

> Since the tetrad lies between the unengendered monad and the motherless hebdomad, it has gathered together the powers of those that generate and those that are generated, and it is the only one of the numbers within the decad that both is generated by some number and generates one. For the dyad, by doubling itself, generates the tetrad, and the tetrad, coming about twice, completes [the number] eight. The first reflection of the solid is also found in the tetrad; for the point is analogous to the monad, and the line to the dyad, for it departs from something and goes towards something; and the surface is appropriate to the triad, for the most elementary of rectilinear figures is the triangle . . . the tetrad is the demiurge, cause of all things, intelligible god, cause of the heavenly and sensible god.

An initial result leaps to the eyes after reading these texts. If Hierocles identifies the tetrad and the demiurge with such arguments, he cannot conceive of the demiurge as the supreme god. In the argument we have just summarized, the tetrad occupies an intermediate position. In particular, Hierocles alludes to the Pythagorean classification of numbers within the decade into four categories: those that engender without being engendered (= 1), those that engender and are engendered (= 4), those that are engendered and do not engender (= 8), and those that do not engender and are not engendered (= 7).[219] Obviously, in this

---

[215] Or rather, the number four. See below, pp. 67f.

[216] Hierocles, *In Carmen aureum*, XX, p. 87, 17ff. Köhler.

[217] Hierocles, *In Carmen aureum*, XX, pp. 87, 19–89, 14 Köhler.

[218] Hierocles, *In Carmen aureum*, XX, 16–19, pp. 88, 20–89, 14.

[219] Cf. Philo, *De op. mundi*, §§ 99–100; Macrobius, *In Somn. Scip.*, I, 5, 16; Johannes Lydus, *De mens.*, II, 12, p. 33, 8 Wünsch.

classification the number four appears as inferior to the unengendered monad. If the demiurge is identified with the tetrad, it is, of course, because it is engendered by a superior hypostasis (that corresponds to the monad, but is not necessarily the One), and because it engenders inferior hypostases in its turn. The demiurge thus occupies a median position; that is, it represents a median hypostasis.

In the second place, we note here again that Hierocles indulges in the same kind of speculation as the late Neoplatonists. Proclus identified the demiurge or "Creator and Father" with the decade, but he identified the "Father and Creator," the second of the "Fathers," with the tetrad and the first of the "Fathers," who is "Father only," with the monad.[220] As we see, Proclus' demiurge is thus placed a bit lower in the hierarchy of beings than Hierocles' demiurge. This complication corresponds to the overall tendency of the evolution of Neoplatonism.

11. Hierocles' Demiurge Cannot Be the Supreme Principle

Nowhere does Hierocles tell us the exact place he reserves for his demiurge in the hierarchy of beings. Taken in isolation, all the demiurge's designations, such as *Noûs,* father, creator, king, Zeus, and tetrad, are open to multiple interpretations with regard to the demiurge's exact place within this hierarchy.

One thing is certain, however: this place cannot be the first. First of all, as we have seen, Hierocles' demiurge has a triadic structure, perhaps still further complicated by subdivisions. In order for the demiurge to be the supreme cause, he would have had to be simple, but because he is characterized by internal multiplicity—of a structure that is, moreover, typically Neoplatonic—the logic inherent to Platonic philosophy demands that he occupy an inferior place. Moreover, as we have seen, Hierocles does not hesitate to assimilate his demiurge to the tetrad, or the number four, and he describes this tetrad in terms that all imply a middle position, which therefore presuppose the existence of one or more entities prior to this demiurgic tetrad.[221]

Let us add that all the other features of Hierocles' philosophy, which Photius' summaries and the *Commentary on the Golden Verses* allow us to glimpse, reveal themselves as purely Neoplatonic. Better yet, they are close to Iamblichus, and we have not found any element that allows us to distinguish Hierocles from surrounding Neoplatonism. Matter as

---

[220] Proclus, *In Tim.,* vol. I, p. 316, 16–26 Diehl.

[221] The arithmological passage in which the designation of the demiurge as tetrad is found will be interpreted in chapter III, sec. 12A.

engendered; the demiurge as creating by his being, his thought, and his will; the demiurge counted among the immobile causes; the three classes of rational souls; their distinction without confusion; their vehicles; the means of purification of the rational human soul and its vehicle;[222] the inability of rational human souls to participate directly in the Intellect: this entire series is typically Neoplatonic and, to a large degree, characteristic of the development that Neoplatonism had reached between Iamblichus and Proclus. None of this reveals any compromise with Christianity, and it does not indicate a return to Middle Platonism.

Yet how can we explain the fact that Hierocles never names the One, or any hypostasis higher than the demiurge, other than implicitly, either in his treatise *On Providence,* or in his commentary on the *Carmen aureum?* Why does he not set forth all the details of his system once and for all? The explanation is easy to find. As far as the seven books of Hierocles' treatise *On Providence* are concerned, Photius gives us two summaries of them, which do not fill twenty pages in total. How can we know if this silence is due to the fact that Hierocles did not mention a hypostasis higher than the demiurge in these seven books or to the fact that Photius did not take the trouble to recount all the details of Hierocles' theological system?[223] Because we possess neither a systematic treatise on theology nor a commentary on Plato's *Timaeus* written by Hierocles, it is impossible for us to make any certain deductions. As far as the commentary on the *Carmen aureum* is concerned, I would say the following: because the *Carmen aureum* deals only with the gods of the cult and with Zeus, the highest of these gods, and therefore with gods who, according to the Neoplatonic system of his contemporaries, do not transcend the level of the *Noûs,* it is not surprising if, in his commentary, Hierocles did not go beyond this level. We must not forget, moreover, that the commentary on the *Carmen aureum* was intended only for auditors or readers who were at the very first stage of the study of philosophy.[224] It would have been pedagogically inappropriate to wish to set forth all the details of the Neoplatonic theological system in all its complexity. Hierocles tells us as much, moreover, at the end of his commentary,[225] as we shall see further on.

In conclusion, nothing in Hierocles' doctrine on matter, souls, and the demiurge allows us to distinguish him from surrounding Neoplatonism. On the contrary, in everything Hierocles has to say on these themes, we find precise, characteristic, and structured details, which

---

[222] Cf. above, the section on "Theurgy."
[223] On this point, cf. T. Hägg, 1975.
[224] Cf. I. Hadot, 2001, pp. XCII–XCVII; *eadem,* 1997, in particular 173–176.
[225] Hierocles, *In Carmen aureum,* XXVII, p. 121, 19ff. Köhler, cited at pp. 96–97. Cf. p. 100.

correspond precisely to the Neoplatonism of his time, and are very close to Iamblichus. In particular, his doctrine of the demiurge quite clearly implies the existence of higher hypostases, which extend from the One to the first subdivisions of the *Noûs*. In order to prove these claims, we shall give a detailed interpretation of Hierocles' arithmological passage, contained in his commentary on the *Carmen aureum*.

12. The Ontological Position of the Demiurge in Hierocles' Philosophical System

A. An Interpretation of Hierocles' Text on the Theology of Numbers

At the conclusion of the preceding chapter, we mentioned, in the context of our interpretation of the fragments from Hierocles' treatise *On Providence*, some reasons why Hierocles' demiurge cannot be the supreme principle of his ontological system. On that occasion, we alluded briefly to a text from the commentary on the *Carmen aureum*, where Hierocles identifies the demiurge with the tetrad, or rather with the number four.[226] We shall comment on this text in detail here, taking up the essential parts of two articles I wrote in 1990 and 1993 in response to N. Aujoulat, which have lost none of their currency.[227]

In a book published in 1986, entitled *Le Néoplatonisme alexandrin: Hiéroclès d'Alexandrie,* N. Aujoulat partially accepted my demonstration, admitting "that nothing allows Hierocles' doctrine on matter, souls, and the luminous body, to be distinguished from the Neoplatonism that surrounded him. Thus, Hierocles is naturally located between Iamblichus, on the one hand, and Syrianus and Proclus on the other" (p. 416). However, he refused to accept my thesis that the demiurge did not represent the first ontological principle for Hierocles, but a principle derived from a superior cause. For Aujoulat, Hierocles' supreme God is, on the contrary, the creative Intelligence, as it was for Origen the pagan, but also for the Christians. Hierocles' theology would thus somehow be simultaneously archaic, pre-Plotinian, and influenced by Christianity with regard to the highest principle; and yet somehow modern and post-Iamblichean as far as souls and their luminous bodies are concerned.

There was an inconsistency here that was, to say the least, surprising. Yet the fundamental problem remained that of the exact position of the demiurge within Hierocles' system. For if Hierocles assimilates him explicitly to the tetrad, he cannot be the first principle, as I showed in my German article "*Ist die Lehre des Hierokles vom Demiurgen*

---

[226] Cf. above, pp. 60f.
[227] I. Hadot, 1990; 1993.

christlich beeinflußt?"[228] Aujoulat hopes to elude my arguments by contenting himself with writing (p. 63):

> With regard to the Tetrad, which represents the demiurge in the *Commentary on the Golden Verses,* according to I. Hadot it occupies an "intermediate position," for it is "midway between the unengendered monad and the 'motherless' hebdomad." It is inferior to the unengendered monad. These remarks, while correct in themselves, nevertheless fail to take account of the fact that, for Hierocles, the tetrad is equivalent to the tetractys, the sacred number of the Pythagoreans, "source of all things," and that the Alexandrian, in addition, wishes to emphasize the tetrad or tetractys, as well as its generative property, with regard to the other numbers, in opposition to the negative qualities of the unengendered monad and the motherless septenary. The fact is that Hierocles says almost nothing about the monad in his *Commentary,* whereas he devotes a copious exposition to the tetrad. He does not seem to have placed the monad above the tetractys at all, and to claim the contrary is, it seems, to falsify the meaning of Hierocles' arithmology. Hadot admits, moreover, that "it must be admitted as likely that the monad did not once represent the highest principle for Hierocles" and that "The comparison with other Neoplatonists leads us to this conclusion."

Later, Aujoulat took up the same theme once again: "I. Hadot herself admits . . . that 'it must be admitted as probable that the monad is not once represented as the highest principle for Hierocles'" (p. 132). In fact, my German text does not "admit" anything of the kind, but the German phrase in question must be translated as follows: "It must be considered probable that it is *not even* the monad that represents the highest principle for Hierocles." I meant that it can be legitimately supposed that, for Hierocles, it is not even the monad, but the One that transcends the monad, which represents the first principle, as is, moreover, the case for other Neoplatonists. Aujoulat has confused the adverbial expression I had used, "*nicht einmal*" (= not even) with another German expression: "*nicht ein einziges Mal*" (= not even once). The context, in which it was said that Hierocles knew of principles higher than the tetrad identified with the demiurge, namely the triad, the dyad, and the monad, should, however, have set him on the right track, but Aujoulat probably did not understand the context, either.

I was thus obliged to take up my argumentation once again, developing it and specifying the relations between the tetrad and the tetrac-

[228] I. Hadot, 1979.

tys in Hierocles, on the one hand, and on the other between the monad and the first principle.

Let us therefore begin by rereading the text by Hierocles that deals with the tetrad, a passage from his commentary on the *Carmen aureum* devoted to the explanation of verses 47 and 48.[229] To allow the reader to form an exact notion of Hierocles' usage, I shall translate the Greek word *monas* by "monad," *hen* by "one," *duas* by "dyad," *duo* by "two," *tetras* by "tetrad," *tessares* by "four," *tetraktus* by "tetractys," *dekas* by "decad," *eikas* by "eikad," and so on, without carrying out an unjustifiable mixture:

> At the same time as he [*scil.* the author of the *Carmen aureum*] swears by the conjunction of the finest states (*hexeis*) of the soul [*scil.* the tetractys], he theologizes about the tetrad as well, which is the source of the sempiternal cosmic arrangement, and he declares that it is identical with the demiurgical god. In what sense this god is a tetrad,[230] you will clearly discover from the *Hieros Logos* attributed to Pythagoras, in which this god is celebrated as the number of numbers. For if all beings come into existence by means of his sempiternal will, it is clear that that number which is in each form of beings also depends on the cause within him [*scil.* in this god], and that the first number is there; for it comes here from there. Now, the interval accomplished by number is the decad, for in every case he who wishes to continue to count comes back to one, two, three; and he counts a second decad with a view to the fulfillment of the eikad (twenty), and likewise a third, that he might say "thirty," and so forth, until he counts the tenth decad and arrives at one hundred. Again, he counts "one hundred ten" in the same way, and thus, by the revolving of the interval of the decad, he may proceed to infinity. The power (δύναμις) of the decad is the tetrad, for prior to the detailed perfection (*kata diexodon teleiotês*) that is in the decad, a kind of unified perfection (*hênomenê tis teleiotês*) is observed in the tetrad; for the total sum of the decad comes about from the addition of the numbers from the monad to the tetrad. For one plus two plus three plus four fulfill the decad. And the tetrad is the arithmetical mean between the monad and the hebdomad, for in a way[231] it exceeds and is exceeded by the same number, since it falls short of the hebdomad by a triad, but surpasses the monad by a triad. Now, the

---

[229] These two verses are as follows: "By him (*scil.* Pythagoras), who gave to our soul the tetractys, source of inexhaustible nature." Hierocles' commentary is found on pp. 87, 16–89, 18 of Köhler's edition.

[230] Aujoulat's version follows an outdated text here; cf. below, p. 69 with n. 238.

[231] πως (XX, 15) is missing in Aujoulat; cf. below, p. 77.

characteristic features of the monad and the hebdomad are the best and the finest, for the monad, as principle of all number, contains within itself the powers of all, whereas the hebdomad, as motherless and virginal, has the value of the monad in a secondary [*scil.* derivative] way; for it is neither engendered from one of the numbers within the decad—as is 4 from twice 2, and 6 from twice 3, and 8 from twice 4, and 9 from thrice 3, and 10 from twice 5—nor does it generate any of the numbers within the decad, as 2 generates 4 and 3 generates 9 and 5 generates 10. Yet since the tetrad lies between the unengendered monad and the motherless hebdomad, it has gathered together the powers of those that generate and those that are generated, and it is the only one of the numbers within the decad that both is generated by some number and generates one. For the dyad, by doubling itself, generates the tetrad, and the tetrad, coming about twice, completes [the number] eight. The first reflection of the solid is also found in the tetrad; for the point is analogous to the monad, and the line to the dyad, for it departs from something and goes towards something; and the surface is appropriate to the triad, for the most elementary of rectilinear figures is the triangle. But solidity is proper to the tetrad, for the first pyramid is observed in the tetrad, for [the number] "three," as the base of the triangle, is its foundation, whereas the number "one" is added to it as its vertex. And there are four critical faculties in the field of beings: intellect (*noûs*), science, opinion, and sensation; for all beings are judged by intellect or science or opinion or sensation. In general, the tetrad, number of the elements, binds up all things: the seasons of the year, the ages of man; life in common;[232] and it is impossible to say what does not depend on the tetractys as its root and its principle. For, as we have said, the tetrad is the demiurge, cause of all things, intelligible god, cause of the heavenly and sensible god. The knowledge of him was handed down to the Pythagoreans by Pythagoras himself, by whom the author of this poem now swears that the perfection of virtue may lead us to the illumination of truth.

One more word on the subject of translation. Following international usage in the context of the Idea-Numbers of the Old Academy and the doctrinal tradition of "number mysticism" that derives therefrom, I have translated the terms *monas, duas, trias, tetras,* and so on,

---

[232] What is meant here becomes clear from a parallel passage in Theon of Smyrna, *Expositio rerum math.*, p. 97, 21–24 Hiller, where we find the following text in an enumeration of all the groups of four represented in nature: "The seventh tetractys is that of communal lives. The origin and, as it were, the monad is man, the dyad is the house, the triad the village and the tetrad the town, for a people is made up of all these."

by "monad," "dyad," "triad," "tetrad," and so on. Yet this is not without a certain ambiguity: the English term "tetrad," for instance, no longer means exactly the same thing as in ancient Greek. If we consult Liddel-Scott's Greek-English dictionary or Bailly's Greek-French dictionary, we find the following indications for the word "tetras":[233] "(1) the number 4; (2) the fourth day of the first part of the month (in a bipartite division), or of the decad or of the week; (3) a duration of 4 days." Liddel-Scott adds "the four quarters of the moon." Yet the *Grand Robert de la Langue Française* gives for the word "tetrad" the general explanation "group of four," before going on to speak of the special applications of this term in the sciences. "Group of four" does not necessarily mean that we have to do with the assemblage of four equal elements—four days, four quarters—as is the case for the Greek term, and the principal signification, that of "the number four," has completely disappeared. To be completely clear, I should therefore always have translated "tetrad" by "the number four," "triad" by "the number three," and so forth. For instance, the beginning of the text should be translated as follows: "At the same time as he (*scil.* the author of the *Carmen aureum*) swears by the conjunction of the finest states of the soul, he theologizes about the number four as well, which is the source of the sempiternal cosmic arrangement, and he declares that it is identical with the demiurgical god. In what sense this god is the number four, you will clearly discover," and so on. Analogously, the subtitles Περὶ δυάδος, Περὶ τριάδος, Περὶ τετράδος of the anonymous treatise *Theologoumena arithmeticae*, attributed to Iamblichus, are translated as precisely as possible by "On the number two," "On the number three," "On the number four," and so on, and the texts of the chapters show that this translation is adequate. In addition, the term "tetractys" among the ancient Pythagoreans and elsewhere has the general meaning of "group of four unequal or different elements"[234] and consequently also the special meaning of "group of the first four numbers," whose sum is ten. Since, in our text, Hierocles assimilates the tetractys of the *Carmen aureum* to the tetrad, the question may be raised of whether, for Hierocles, the meaning of the term "tetractys" takes precedence over that of "tetrad"—this is Mr. Aujoulat's opinion[235]—or whether, on the contrary, the tetractys takes over the meaning of "tetrad." In other words, we may wonder whether, for Hierocles, the tetractys of the *Carmen aureum* is simply the num-

---

[233] I reproduce Bailly's indications, which are not different from those of Liddel-Scott.

[234] But never the meaning of "supreme god or first principle." Cf. below, p. 82, with n. 288.

[235] Aujoulat, 1986, 123: ". . . [T]he tetrad is thus equivalent to the tetractys . . . the tetractys had the same value as the decad."

ber four. Let us look at what the text says: for instance, the tetrad is said to be "the arithmetical mean between the monad and the hebdomad"; but it could not be their arithmetical mean if it represented the sum of numbers from one to four. To take another example, among many others: "the dyad, by doubling itself, engenders the tetrad, and the tetrad, coming about twice, completes <the number> eight." How could all this be possible if the tetrad were not the number four, but the sum total of the first four numbers, and therefore in fact the number ten? The whole of the text just quoted and translated demonstrates without any ambiguity that for Hierocles, the "tetrad," as the "tetractys" is the number four.[236]

This entire text is intended to comment on the following passage from the *Golden Verses* (verses 47–48; cf. above, p. 65): "by him [*scil.* Pythagoras] who has given to our soul the tetractys, source of inexhaustible nature." In his commentary, Hierocles assimilates the "tetractys" to the tetrad [= the number four] and to the demiurge, and "nature" to the sempiternal ordering of the world. We may note that at the beginning of his exposition, Hierocles immediately assimilates the tetractys to the tetrad, without himself adopting the term "tetractys" again. It is only near the end of his praise of the tetrad that Hierocles—only once—uses the word "tetractys," in order to stay close, as it were, to the text on which he is commenting. This may be an instance of *Ring-komposition,* or circular composition.

The exposition itself goes through the following stages. First, basing himself on a Pythagorean *Hieros Logos,* Hierocles proves that the tetrad is identical with the demiurge insofar as it is the number of numbers. Hierocles then situates the tetrad with respect to the other numbers, first to the decad (the tetrad is the power of the decad), then to the monad and the hebdomad (the tetrad is the arithmetical mean between these two numbers, as both engendering and engendered); and, finally, with regard to the monad, the dyad and the triad (whereas the monad corresponds to the point, the dyad to the line, and the triad to the surface, the tetrad corresponds to the solid, or the first pyramid). We then find a brief exposition on the importance of groups of "four" within reality. We are thus brought back to our starting point: the tetrad appears as the cause of all things, an intelligible god who produces that visible god known as the world.

---

[236] This was also the case later for Damascius. Cf. Damascius, *In Parm.,* (201), vol. II, p. 27, 18–20 Combès-Westerink: "Let there be a tetrad up above as well, and let it be as the principle of number, 'the source of inexhaustible nature' according to the poem." Damascius can certainly not be suspected of having made the tetrad his supreme ontological entity.

Let us therefore examine the various points of this exposition. First of all, Hierocles alludes to the *Sacred Discourse* attributed to Pythagoras: "In what sense," he says,[237] "this god is a tetrad, you will clearly discover from the *Hieros Logos* attributed to Pythagoras, in which this god is celebrated as the number of numbers." Mr. Aujoulat (p. 124), who follows the text of Mullach's 1853 edition, instead of utilizing the only worthwhile text—that is, Köhler's 1974 critical edition—cites the beginning of the phrase as follows: "But how is the Tetrad God?" Aujoulat remarks in a note[238] that "Köhler has retained the reading Πῶς δὲ τετρὰς ὁ θεὸς οὗτος;" this, like the punctuation,[239] is entirely false: here, Köhler has not retained one reading among other valid readings, but he has edited the only text that the independent witnesses allow to be established. I refer to the critical apparatus of Köhler's edition, as well as to his excellent *Textgeschichte von Hierokles' Kommentar zum "Carmen aureum" der Pythagoreer,*[240] which also contains an entire chapter dealing with the deficiencies and sloppiness of Mullach's edition. Obviously, this choice of a bad reading has the result of turning all the data upside down; the quite determinate god (*this* god) to whom Hierocles' tetrad corresponds in the pantheon of Neoplatonic gods has thus, for Aujoulat, become simply God. By working on an outdated text, Mr. Aujoulat has invalidated the bases of his interpretation right from the start.

The *Sacred Discourse,* or *Discourse on the Gods,* as it is also entitled,[241] is a pseudepigraphic work, as we know today. This *Sacred Discourse,* in Doric prose, must not be confused with another *Sacred Discourse* in hexameters, also attributed to Pythagoras. According to H. Thesleff's collection of the testimonies and fragments concerning this text, the *Sacred Discourse* is mentioned rather late, and exclusively by Neoplatonists. The first person to quote it is Iamblichus (from the end of the third century to the first half of the fourth century). In the fifth century, Syrianus and Hierocles, who were contemporaries and probably classmates—both were students of Plutarch of Athens—refer to this work, as does Syrianus' student Proclus. I first quote a text by Iamblichus, where the subject is the presumed sources of the *Sacred Discourse:*[242]

---

[237] *In Carmen aureum,* xx, p. 87, 19ff. Köhler.

[238] Page 124, n. 159. Aujoulat and Mullach: πῶς δὲ τετρὰς ὁ θεός; οὗτως . . .

[239] Köhler's text does not have a question mark after *houtos,* but a comma, after which the text continues.

[240] Dissertation (Münster/Westfalen, 1966).

[241] Cf. the text by Iamblichus, cited in the following note.

[242] Iamblichus, *Pythagorean life,* XXVIII, 145–147. I follow the text edited and translated by Michael von Albrecht, *Iamblichos, Pythagoras* (Zürich, 1985²).

If someone wishes to know from what source those men [*scil.* the Pythagoreans] derived such piety, it must be said that in Orpheus there existed a clear model for the Pythagorean theology of numbers. There is no doubt but that Pythagoras took his point of departure from Orpheus when he wrote the *Discourse on the gods,* which he also entitled *Sacred discourse* because it was derived from the most mystical place in Orpheus, whether this work is really by Pythagoras, as most people say, or whether it is by Telauges [*scil.* Pythagoras' son]—as is firmly asserted by several members of the school, who are held in high esteem and who are trustworthy ...— on the basis of writings which Pythagoras himself had left to his daughter Damo ... *The Sacred discourse* or the *Discourse on the gods*—for both titles exist—also reveals who it was that transmitted the *Discourse on the gods* to Pythagoras. For it says: "This is the discourse on the gods which I, Pythagoras, the son of Mnemarchos, initiated into the mysteries in Thracian Libethra, learned from Aglaophamos, the priest in charge of initiations into the mysteries, who communicated to me (what follows): Orpheus, son of Calliope ... has proclaimed: "The sempiternal essence of number is the highest providential principle in all the heavens, the earth, and intermediate nature. It is also the root of the permanence of divine <men>, gods, and demons." From this, it is obvious that he received from the Orphics the teaching that affirms that the essence of the gods is defined by number.

Proclus alludes to this passage in his commentary on the *Timaeus,*[243] where he says:

These are the doctrines that could be derived from the present text [*scil.* by Plato]. But it is also Pythagorean to follow the *Orphic Genealogies,* for it is from the Orphic teachings that the science of the gods has come down, through Pythagoras, to the Greeks, as Pythagoras says himself in his *Sacred discourse.*

In his *Platonic Theology,*[244] Proclus insists once again on the fact that the whole of Greek theology has come down to the Greeks through the intermediary of Orpheus, Pythagoras via Aglaophamus, and Plato, in that order. In his commentary on the first book of Euclid's *Elements,*[245]

---

[243] Proclus, *In Tim.,* III, p. 161, 2–6 Diehl; trans. based on that of Festugière, 1966–1968, 4:204.
[244] Proclus, *Theol. Plat.,* I, 5, 26ff.; vol. I, p. 25, 25ff. Saffrey-Westerink.
[245] Proclus, *In Primum Euclid.,* p. 22, 9–16 Friedlein.

Proclus makes the Platonic doctrine of Idea-Numbers depend explicitly on the teaching concerning the gods given by Pythagoras in his *Sacred Discourse.*

The testimonies cited so far have enabled us to understand that the *Sacred Discourse* contained a theology that placed the hierarchy of the gods in relation with certain numbers. Five testimonies and fragments from Syrianus' commentary on Aristotle's *Metaphysics* tend in the same direction. I shall limit myself to translating two of them:

> "If one were able to follow Pythagoras' *Sacred discourse,* he would find all the ranks of monads and of numbers in it, celebrated uninterruptedly. . . ."[246] and "Pythagoras himself, when he explains all the numbers from the monad to the decad, expands upon this subject in a way that is simultaneously theological and physical, without indulging in a paltry or cold presentation."[247]

In two other passages of his commentary, Syrianus gives precise examples of the equations between gods and numbers contained in the *Sacred Discourse:* here, the monad is identified with Proteus, and the dyad with Chaos.[248] I add one more testimony from Iamblichus,[249] which emphasizes as much as one could wish the progressive abasement in the ontological rank of the ideal numbers from one to four, and of the four mathematical sciences that correspond to them:

> [M]oreover, if number is the ideal type [εἶδος: form] of beings, and if the roots and as it were the elements of number are the first terms as far as the tetrad, the above-mentioned characteristic features would be in them, as well as the reflections of the four sciences: that of arithmetic in the monad, of music in the dyad, of geometry in the triad, of the science of spheres in the tetrad, according to what Pythagoras defines in the treatise denoted as *On the gods:* "Four are also the foundations of wisdom: arithmetic, music, geometry, the science of spheres, which have the rank of one, two, three, and four."

All these testimonies, as well as those of the texts collected by Thesleff that I have not cited, make it clear that the *Sacred Discourse* dealt with

---

[246] Syrianus, *In Metaph.,* p. 140, 16 Kroll.

[247] Syrianus, *In Metaph.,* p. 192, 10ff. Kroll.

[248] Syrianus, *In Metaph.,* pp. 10, 5; 175, 4ff. Kroll.

[249] [Iamblichus]—Scholars today agree that this work consists of extracts put together by Iamblichus—*Theol. arithm.,* p. 21, 2ff. de Falco (excerpt from Nicomachus' *Theol. arithm.*), cited after the trans. by A.-J. Festugière, 1949, 213. This very important article on the tetrad-pyramid is unknown to N. Aujoulat.

a hierarchy of gods, situated in parallel with a hierarchy of numbers proceeding from the monad to the decad. Yet the *Sacred Discourse* was not the only pseudo-Pythagorean text studied by the Neoplatonists of the fifth century. There was also the *Hymn to Numbers,* four verses of which are cited once by Syrianus in his commentary on the *Metaphysics*[250] and three times by Proclus in his commentary on the *Timaeus:*[251]

> [U]ntil it [*scil.* the divine number in its progression] reaches, from the inviolate hollows of the Monad, as far as the sacred Tetrad; lo it [*scil.* the Tetrad] has born the universal Mother, the all-receiving, the Venerable one, she who imposes a limit on all things, the Inflexible, the Indefatigable one; they call her the pure Decad.

This hymn, which, like the *Sacred Discourse,* the Neoplatonists attributed to Pythagoras, also sings of the hierarchy of divine numbers from the monad to the decad. In general, we can even say that from the time of Moderatus (second half of the first century of our era), all Neopythagorean texts concerning theological number speculations agree with one another—as is, moreover, logical—in making the progression of numbers begin either with the monad or with the One, conceived as the supreme principles.[252] In these circumstances, and given the fact that the *Sacred Discourse* or *Discourse on the Gods* was obviously very widely read, at least in the Neoplatonic milieu of his time, how could Hierocles, who refers *expressis verbis* to this same *Sacred Discourse* as a text that clearly defines the exact position of the god who corresponds to the tetrad-tetractys, possibly dare to maintain that this *Discourse* made this god the supreme God? And yet, this is Aujoulat's hypothesis.

What, then, does Hierocles' reasoning consist in? In affirming, first of all, that the *Golden Verses* identify the tetrad with the demiurge, and secondly, that the *Sacred Discourse* attributed to Pythagoras explains how the tetrad is identical with the demiurge. The first point is implied, in his view, in the formula used by the *Golden Verses:* "the tetractys, source of inexhaustible nature." The second point presupposes the following reasoning: the demiurgic god is celebrated by Pythagoras' *Sacred Discourse* as "number of numbers." This is because in each form of beings, there is a number, and this number is produced by the first number found within the demiurge. Number flows from up above to

---

[250] Syrianus, *In Metaph.*, p. 106, 16ff. Kroll.

[251] Proclus, *In Tim.,* I, p. 316, 20ff. Diehl; trans. based on Festugière, 1966–1968, 2:173. Cf. also Proclus, *In Tim.,* III, p. 107, 13, and II, 53, 2–7 Diehl.

[252] Cf. A.-J. Festugière, 1944–1954, 4:18.

this world. We note that the first number is not the monad, for according to Hierocles the monad is the "principle of numbers" (in this regard, it is impossible to say, with Mr. Aujoulat [p. 127], that the monad is the number of numbers, especially since Hierocles clearly identifies the tetrad with the "number of numbers").[253] As Syrianus says, "It is from the intelligible monad that the first number (ὁ πρώτιστος ἀριθμός) proceeds 'from the inviolable hollows of the monad.'"[254]

If we were to judge by the rest of the text of the *Hymn to Numbers* cited by Syrianus, the first number Hierocles mentions—that first number that comes forth from the monad—should be the tetrad, which could be considered as the first number insofar as the procession that begins from the monad stops at the tetrad. Proclus' citation of the *Hymn to Numbers*[255] has the same meaning; and this interpretation might find additional support in the following text by Hermias:[256]

> According to other viewpoints, they attribute the tetrad to Dionysos, for it is the first to have all the harmonies within it . . . and because all numbers are also contained within it. The tetrad is the root of all the numbers, for, if one adds up (the numbers) as far as it, the decad is accomplished, and the decad is the total number; and, in general, theology calls Dionysos "the four-eyed," and "the four-faced."

Yet it is possible that by the expression "the first number" Hierocles means to designate intelligible number in general, from which the numbers within being come forth. This is the sense of "first number" in Iamblichus' treatise *On Pythagoreanism, V: On Physical Number.*[257]

Let us return to Hierocles' text. This arithmological exposition takes its place within a rich and lengthy tradition of Pythagorean speculation on numbers, which begins with the Old Academy and remains alive down to the end of Neoplatonism. The decisive point in this text is the identification of the demiurge with the tetrad. As we shall see, this identification is characteristic of Hierocles' median position between Iamblichus and Proclus, which I have described in detail above.[258] First, however, let us pause for a moment over the traditional elements of Pythagorean number speculation that we encounter outside the *Sacred*

---

[253] Hierocles, *In Carmen aureum*, xx, p. 87, 19–21 Köhler. Cf. above, the trans. on p. 65.

[254] Syrianus, *In Metaph.*, p. 140, 11 Kroll.

[255] Cf. the citation from this hymn by Proclus, above, p. 72 and n. 251, as well as the quotation from Iamblichus, p. 71.

[256] Hermias, *In Phaedr.*, p. 90, 30–91, 6 Couvreur.

[257] Cf. D. O'Meara, 1989, Appendix I: "The excerpts from Iamblichus' *On Pythagoreanism* V–VII in Psellus," p. 219, 6; 24.

[258] Cf. Chap. III, secs. 6 and 11, pp. 36–42; 61–63.

Discourse and the *Hymn to Numbers* in numerous texts, both prior to and later than Hierocles. We begin with the role played by the decad as "interval accomplished by number." "The decad," writes Philo of Alexandria, "is the limit of the infinity of numbers, around which they swing and return, as around a turning-point."[259] We find parallel texts in the pseudo-Aristotelian *Problemata*,[260] in the *Placita* of Aetius (written around A.D. 100),[261] in Anatolius,[262] in Theon of Smyrna,[263] in Calcidius,[264] in the *Theologoumena arithmeticae*,[265] and in Johannes Lydus.[266] The most ancient testimony is that of Speusippus.[267]

Another traditional element is the perfection of the decad and the definition of the decad as a perfect number. For instance, we encounter this idea in Porphyry, Hippolytus, and Macrobius,[268] Sextus Empiricus,[269]

---

[259] Philo, *De opif. mundi*, § 47.

[260] *Problemata*, 15, 3, 910b23ff.: "Why do all men, both Barbarians and Greeks, count as far as ten . . . and then repeat the process?"

[261] Aetius, *Placita*, 1, 3, 8 = *Doxographi Graeci*, p. 281, 13ff. Diels: "All the Barbarians, and all the Greeks count as far as ten, and, once they have reached it, return to the monad."

[262] Anatolius in [Iamblichus], *Theol. arith.*, p. 86, 2–5 de Falco (= Anatolius, *On the First Ten Numbers*, p. 39 Heiberg in *Annales internationales d'histoire, Congrès de Paris, 1900*, 5ᵉ section, Histoire des Sciences, Paris 1901): "The decad is the cycle and the limit of every number, for turning around it as around a turning-point and going back in the other direction, they run a long race. Again, it is the limit of the infinity of numbers."

[263] Theon of Smyrna, *Expositio rerum math.*, p. 99, 17–20 Hiller: ". . . [T]here is no number above the decad, for we always return, in increase, to the monad and the dyad." Cf. Iamblichus, *In Nicom. Arithm.*, p. 88, 17–21 Pistelli.

[264] Calcidius, *In Tim.*, cap. 35, p. 84, 5–11 Waszink: "Nam perfectus quidem numerus est decem ideo, quod a singularitate orsi usque ad decem numerum numeramus, residua vero numeratio non tamen numeratio est quam eorundem numerorum, quibus ante usi sumus in numerando, replicatio; undecim enim et duodecim et ceteri tales nascuntur ex praecedentium replicatione."

[265] [Iamblichus], *Theol. arithm.*, p. 27, 12ff. de Falco (excerpt from Nicomachus): "The decad is the measure and the perfect limit of all number, and after it there is not a single natural number, but all are secondary, and they recur to infinity, according to participation in the decad."

[266] Johannes Lydus, *De mens.*, 3, 4, p. 38, 17–22 Wünsch: "The decad is the circle and the limit of every number. Around it, as around a turning-point, the numbers swing and run a long race, going back where they came from . . . from the monad, we count as far as it and only as far as it; and when we stand upon it, we turn back to the monad."

[267] Speusippus, *De numeris Pythag.*, in [Iamblichus], *Theol. arithm.*, p. 83, 6–9 de Falco: "For the decad is a perfect <number>, and it is right and in conformity with nature that the Greeks and all people, when they count, reach it in all kinds of ways, without doing so deliberately."

[268] Porphyry, *Vita Pyth.*, 52, p. 61 des Places; Hippolytus, *Refutatio omnium haeresium*, I, 2, 8 = *Doxographi Graeci*, p. 556 Diels; Macrobius, *In somnium Scip.*, I, 6, 77, p. 32, 24 Willis: ". . . decas, qui et ipse perfectissimus numerus est. . . ."

[269] Sextus Empiricus, *Adv. math.*, 4, 3, vol. 3, p. 133, 18ff. Mau: "The 'fourth number' which is made up of the first four numbers, is called by them [*scil.* by the Pythagoreans] tetractys,' for 1 plus 2 plus 3 plus 4 make 10, which is the most perfect number, for once we have reached it, we return to the monad and begin to count all over again."

Calcidius,[270] Iamblichus,[271] in the *Theologoumena arithmeticae*,[272] and in Speusippus.[273] Hierocles (pp. 88, 5ff.) specifies what distinguishes the perfection of the decad from that of the tetrad: the tetrad possesses a perfection ontologically superior to that of the decad; it is "somehow" unified, by contrast with the more diversified perfection of the decad. Hierocles takes care to add "somehow" (πως) when describing the unified perfection of the tetrad; this is because he wants to avoid any confusion with an even higher principle that would be unified in the true sense of the word, for the tetrad is not truly unified, like the monad is, but only compared to the decad, which is perfect in accordance with a "detailed development." This means that the decad, by specifying and diversifying the seminal reasons contained in the tetrad, has already moved away, to a greater extent than the tetrad, from the first principle. The same clarification is found in Proclus:[274] "For the tetrad contains all things, and so does the decad, but one contains them unitively, and the other in a separated way; and although the decad contains all that the tetrad contains, yet because it contains them in a separated way, it is less perfect than the tetrad. For that which is closer to the monad is more perfect, and the smaller the quantity, the greater the power (*dunamis*)." Here, Proclus identifies the tetrad with the Intelligible Living Being, and the decad with the demiurge.

The idea that the tetrad is the power (*dunamis*) of the decad is also mentioned and commented often in this tradition. Hierocles speaks of it in the same phrase as that in which he distinguishes the perfection of the tetrad from that of the decad (p. 88ff.). Aujoulat (p. 128), citing J. Souilhé, thinks that the word *dunamis* applied to the tetrad means that it is "the fundamental or distinctive property" of the decad; that is, that the tetrad "realizes and expresses" the decad. This explanation is rather obscure; it seems much simpler to consider the use of *dunamis* in the arithmetical expositions of Philo, for instance, or of Iamblichus, where we observe that *dunamis* is opposed to *entelecheia*,[275] and, most often, to *energeia*.[276] We are thus in the presence of a pair of opposites of

---

[270] Cf. the citation at n. 264.

[271] Iamblichus, *In Nicom. arith.*, p. 43, 15–16 Pistelli.

[272] [Iamblichus], *Theol. arithm.*: cf. the citation n. 265.

[273] Speusippus: cf. the citation n. 267.

[274] Proclus, *In Tim.*, I, p. 432, 19–23 Diehl; trans. based on Festugière, 1966–1968, 2:311.

[275] Philo, *De opif. mundi*, § 47: "For what the decad is in act (ἐντελεχείᾳ), the tetrad, it seems, is in potentiality."

[276] [Iamblichus], *Theol. arithm.*, p. 58, 15 de Falco (excerpt from Nicomachus): ". . . [T]he numbers from the monad to the tetrad are potentially the decad, but in act (ἐνεργείᾳ) it is the decad itself; seven is the arithmetic mean between the tetrad and the decad, and therefore, in a way, between two decads: the potential one and the actual

Aristotelian origin: power or potentiality and act, but with the difference that for the Neoplatonists, power, compared to act, has a superior ontological reality. Hierocles thus meant that "What the tetrad is in power/potentiality, the decad is in act." We therefore need not wonder, with Mr. Aujoulat (p. 128): "In what sense, then, does the tetrad realize the decad?" It is not the tetrad that realizes or concretizes the decad, but the other way around: the decad realizes the tetrad; that is, the decad is an emanation from the tetrad, and is the unfolding of the forces contained within the tetrad. Hierocles himself has said so, moreover, in language which is perfectly clear for a Neoplatonist or someone knowledgeable in their philosophy: "The power of the decad is the tetrad, for prior to the detailed perfection that is in the decad, a kind of unified perfection is observed in the tetrad."

To prove that the tetrad is the power of the decad, Hierocles instances the fact that the decad results from the addition of the numbers from one to four (1 + 2 + 3 + 4). This detail, alone or linked with the qualification of the tetrad as a potential decad, is also mentioned very often in parallel texts.[277] For three of the parallel texts we have reproduced in

---

one." Cf. p. 1, 1–12 de Falco: "The monad is the principle of number. . . . For everything is set in order by the monad, which contains everything potentially; for the monad contains, even if not yet in actuality (ἐνεργείᾳ), but seminally, all the formative principles contained in all the numbers, and naturally also those contained in the dyad, since it is even and odd. . . ." Cf. Iamblichus, *In Nicom. Arithm.,* p. 72, 6ff. Pistelli: "Since these most wise people [*scil.* the Pythagoreans] noticed that all the formative principles contained in number were highly various and infinite in multitude, all of them sprouting from the monad as from a common root, and changing from potentiality to actuality (εἰς τὸ ἐνεργείᾳ ἀπὸ δυνάμεως). . . ."

[277] Sextus Empiricus: text cited n. 269. Philo, *De opif. mundi,* § 47, p. 170 Arnaldez (the continuation of the text cited n. 275: ". . . to be sure, if the numbers from the monad to the tetrad are added in succession, they will engender the decad. . . ." Anon., *Vita Pythag.,* in Photius, *Library,* cod. 249, 439a2–8, Bekker, vol. VII, p. 127 Henry: "And since they [*scil.* the Pythagoreans] referred all things to numbers, deriving them from the monad and the dyad, they also called all beings 'numbers,' and number is completely fulfilled by ten, and ten is the addition of the <first> four <numbers> as we count successively, for this reason also they call the total number 'tetractys.'" Hermias, *In Phaedr.,* p. 90, 30–91, 6 Couvreur, cited p. 73. Simplicius, *In Cat.,* p. 44, 9–10 Kalbfleisch: "and the decad is contained within the tetrad, for as we add up one, two, three, and four, we obtain the number ten." [Iamblichus], *Theol. arithm.,* p. 20, 1–9 de Falco (excerpt from Nicomachus): "In the natural increase as far as the tetrad (*scil.* the number four), the things in the world appear accomplished together, universally and particularly, as well as the things that are in number; in short, in all the natures. In particular, what contributes especially, and in an extraordinary way, to the harmonious union of the finished product is the fact that the decad [the number ten] is completed at the same time by it [*scil.* the tetrad] and by the numbers that come just before it [*scil.* 4 + 1 + 2 + 3 = 10], since it [*scil.* the decad] is a gnomon and a meeting-point [*scil.* of the entire decimal system], but also the fact that it [*scil.* the decad] is the limit of corporification and of three-dimensional extension." Johannes Lydus, *De mens.,* 2, 9, p. 30, 45f. Wünsch: "For if they add the numbers from the monad to the tetrad in order, they obtain ten." Cf. Aetius, *Placita,* 1, 3, 8 = *Doxographi Graeci,* p. 281–82 Diels; Hippolytus, *Refutatio omnium haeresium,* 1, 2, 8–9 = *Doxographi Graeci,* p. 556 Diels.

n. 277—that of Sextus Empiricus, that of Hippolytus, and that of the Anonymous of Photius—the decad is the tetractys. For Hierocles, by contrast, the terms "tetrad" and "tetractys" signify one and the same thing: this is proved by the beginning and the end of the passage from the commentary on the *Carmen aureum*, which I have translated above. Proclus, too, in his commentary on the *Timaeus*,[278] identifies the tetrad of the *Hymn to Numbers* with the tetractys of the *Carmen aureum*. Aetius[279] and Macrobius[280] also assimilate the tetractys of the same Pythagorean oath to the tetrad.

In the following sentence (p. 88, 10ff.), Hierocles affirms that the tetrad constitutes the arithmetical mean between the monad and the hebdomad. The reason for this is, he says, that the tetrad "somehow" (πως) surpasses the monad by the same number by which it is surpassed by the hebdomad. Here again, Hierocles takes care, by the addition of the adverb πως, to specify that the tetrad does not *really* surpass the monad, that is, in an ontological sense, but only "somehow," that is, in quantity, and for a Neoplatonist greater quantity is a clear sign of ontological inferiority. Mr. Aujoulat, who simply reproduces Meunier's old translation, omits the specification, as Meunier does, although it is found even in Mullach's text. In any case, the designation of the tetrad as the arithmetical mean between the monad and the hebdomad should already suffice to show that the tetrad, because of its medial position, cannot be the supreme god.

The mention of the monad and the hebdomad, between which the tetrad is the arithmetical mean, gives Hierocles the opportunity briefly to describe the qualities of both: "The monad," he says, "as the principle of all number, contains within itself the powers of all the numbers." If the monad is the principle of every number, that means beyond all possible doubt that it is the cause that precedes and engenders all other numbers, and that all other numbers depend on it and derive their origin from it. In addition, if the monad contains the powers of all the numbers within itself,[281] we cannot doubt that it also contains within it the power of the tetrad. The monad is potentially the tetrad, as it is potentially every number; analogously, Hierocles had stated above that the tetrad is the power of the decad. Since this implies that the tetrad is

---

[278] Proclus, *In Tim.*, II, p. 53, 1–7 Diehl.

[279] Aetius, *Placita*, 1, 3, 8 = *Doxographi Graeci*, p. 282 Diels. He too identifies the tetrad with the tetractys of the Pythagorean oath.

[280] Macrobius, *In somnium Scip.*, 1, 6, 41, p. 25, 24–31 Willis: ". . . quaternarium quidem Pythagorei, quem τετρακτύν vocant, adeo ad perfectionem animae pertinentem inter arcana venerantur, ut ex eo et iuris iurandi religionem sibi fecerint: οὐ μὰ τὸν ἀμετέρᾳ ψυχᾷ παραδόντα τετρακτύν per qui nostrae animae numerum dedit ipse quaternum." *Quaternarius, ternarius, septenarius*, etc., translate in this context the Greek terms *tetras, trias, heptas* (or *hebdomas*), etc.

[281] Cf. the texts cited n. 276.

ontologically superior to the decad—which Aujoulat admits—the monad is necessarily superior ontologically to all other numbers, including the tetrad. This sentence from Hierocles' commentary should thus be enough by itself to demonstrate the demiurge-tetrad's dependency on the monad, as on a god far superior to it. No ancient reader, pagan or Christian, could have been mistaken on this point, for all ancient authors who mention or use the Pythagorean theory of numbers, like Hierocles, make the monad (or the One) the supreme principle of all numbers.[282] This is required by the logic inherent in the theology of numbers.

Everything that follows in Hierocles' text from page 88, 21 on merely confirms our interpretation. Before we come to that, however, let us say a few more words on the hebdomad. Hierocles describes it as being virginal and motherless. In parallel texts,[283] moreover, it is very often iden-

---

[282] Cf. [Iamblichus], *Theol. arithm.*, p. 1, 1–12 de Falco, cited n. 277; cf. also *ibid.*, p. 26, 20ff. Cf. Iamblichus, *In Nicom. Arithm.*, p. 15, 18–25 Pistelli: "And the most astonishing fact, which is peculiar to the monad and proves that it is not yet a number, is that it is surrounded (by numbers) only on one side, and not on both; it is half of the dyad only, and is content with one neighbor alone. Thus, potentially all the species of the odd and the even are observed within it in common, as in a spring and a root, undetermined with regard to both, and necessarily indivisible with regard to all the others." Cf. also *ibid.*, p. 11, 11–17; p. 81, 23–24. Cf. Syrianus, *In Metaph.*, p. 140, 7–9 Kroll: "When they [*scil.* the Pythagoreans] say that the monad is the form of forms, they thereby allude to their originary cause, which has taken up in itself the species of all numbers in advance." Cf. Macrobius, *In somnium Scip.*, 1, 6, 7, p. 19, 24–27 Willis: "unum autem quod μονάς id est unitas dicitur et mas idem et femina est, par idem atque impar, ipse non numerus sed fons et origo numerorum." Cf. the quotation from the Anonymous of Photius at n. 277. Cf. Aetius, *Placita*, 1, 3, 8, p. 201 Diels; Hippolytus, *Refutatio omnium haeresium*, 1, 2, 6–7 = *Doxographi Graeci*, p. 556 Diels.

[283] Cf. [Iamblichus], *Theolog. arithm.*, p. 71, 3–10 de Falco (excerpt of Nicomachus): "They gave the heptad the names 'Athena,' 'opportune moment,' and 'fortune'; Athena because it is a virgin, like the one whose story is told in myth, and because it is not subject to the yoke of marriage, and it was not engendered by a mother—that is, by even number—nor by a father, which is odd number, except that it has come forth from the head of the father of all things; that is, from the monad, which is the head of number; and, like Athena it is somehow non-feminine; for number that is easily divisible is feminine." Cf. Macrobius, *In somn. Scip.*, 1, 6, 11, p. 20, 14ff. Willis: "nulli enim aptius iungitur monas incorrupta quam virgini. huic autem numero id est septenario adeo opinio virginitatis inolevit ut Pallas quoque vocitetur. nam virgo creditur, quia nullum ex se parit numerum duplicatus qui intra denarium coartetur, quem primum limitem constat esse numerorum: Pallas ideo quia ex solius monadis fetu et multiplicatione processit, sicut Minerva sola ex uno parente nata perhibetur." Cf. Philo, *De opif. mundi,* § 99–100, p. 206f. Arnaldez: "So great is the sacred character that naturally resides within the number seven, that it has a special account (*logos*) among all the numbers in the decade. For of those numbers, some engender without being engendered, the others are engendered and do not engender, and others both engender and are engendered. Only the number seven is not observed in any part. This statement of principle must be confirmed by demonstration. The one (*hen*) engenders all the numbers in succession, without being engendered by any other whatsoever. Eight is engendered by two times four, but it does not engender any number of the decad; with regard to four, it has the rank

tified with Athena, who burst forth from the head of her father, Zeus, without being engendered by a mother. The hebdomad "is not engendered by any of the numbers contained within the decad"; that is, it is not the result of the multiplication of two numbers, but derives its origin from the monad alone, which is generally conceived as not being a number itself.[284] It is virginal, because it does not give birth (through multiplication by another number of the decad) to any other number within the decad. Its position within the decad is therefore singular, and in some aspects it resembles that of the monad. This is why Hierocles can say that it "possesses the merit of the monad in a secondary way."

Hierocles continues (p. 88, 21ff.):

> Yet since the tetrad lies between the unengendered monad and the motherless hebdomad, it has gathered together the powers of those that generate and those that are generated, and it is the only one of the numbers within the decad that both is engendered by some number and engenders one.

In this phrase and the following one (p. 88, 25), Hierocles again assigns to the demiurge-tetrad a position ontologically intermediate between the monad and the hebdomad. The demiurge-tetrad is engendered by the dyad, and insofar as it is engendered by it, it can consequently not be the first principle, that from which all things, including the dyad, come forth. For a Neoplatonist, it goes without saying that an engendered god can be only a derived principle. Yet Mr. Aujoulat thinks Hierocles was influenced by Christianity. Is it conceivable that a Christian could have represented the demiurge or world-creator, God the Father, as having been engendered? *A fortiori,* could that Christian have seen in the demiurge the first signs of the materiality Hierocles attributes to him in the lines that follow? Instead of taking up Hierocles' text once again, I prefer to cite a parallel text from Philo of Alexandria, which reports the same details. I think it is useful to insist yet again on the fact that the ancient tradition on the theology of numbers is unanimous in making all numbers and all gods derive from the monad or the One. Here is the text in question:

---

of both the generators and the offspring, for it engenders eight as it comes about twice, and it is engendered by twice two. As I have said, only seven neither engenders by nature nor is it engendered. This is why, whereas the other philosophers assimilate this number to Nikê, the motherless virgin, who is said to have come out the head of Zeus ..." Cf. Calcidius, *In Tim.,* cap. 36, p. 85, 1–18 Waszink; cf. Proclus, *In Tim.,* I, p. 151, 11–18; II, p. 95, 5; p. 236, 17–20 Diehl.

[284] Cf. the quotations from Iamblichus, Macrobius, and Philo of Alexandria in the preceding note.

There is another power of the tetrad which is most amazing to state and to think upon; for it is the first to show the nature of the solid, whereas the numbers that precede it are referred to the incorporeals. For according to the one is ranged what is called the point in geometry; according to two is the line, for the dyad comes about by the flow of the one, while the line arises through the flow of the point. Now the line is a length without breadth, but when breadth is added to it, there comes about the surface, which is ranged according to the triad. The surface lacks one element with regard to the nature of the solid, and this is depth, which, when added to the triad, there comes about the tetrad. Hence it is that this number is such a great thing, which from the incorporeal and intelligible essence has brought us to have a conception of three-dimensional body, the first sensible by nature.[285]

In this text by Philo, as in that by Hierocles, and in the numerous parallel texts cited in the notes, the theology of numbers serves to indicate how, from a supreme principle that is one without qualification, the multitude of sensible phenomena of the sensible world can be realized, through several levels of intelligible hypostases. In this passage from the intelligible and the incorporeal to the sensible and the corporeal, the intelligible seeds of the sensible world are manifested for the first time in the tetrad, which proves yet again that it is already considerably far removed from the first cause.

If, as Mr. Aujoulat would have it, Hierocles had been influenced by Christianity, and if, for this reason, he had wished to make the creator of the world the supreme god, and if he had insisted on illustrating the position of this supreme god by the Pythagorean theory of numbers, which was very widespread in his time, only one solution remained to

---

[285] Philo, *De opif. mundi*, § 49, pp. 172–173 Arnaldez. Cf. Philo, *ibid.*, § 98, pp. 204–207 Arnaldez. Cf. [Iamblichus], *Theol. arithm.*, p. 20, 9–12 de Falco (continuation of the text quoted n. 277: "For the minimal body (σῶμα ἐλάχιστον) and the first to appear, the pyramid, is seen in a tetrad, either of angles or of planes, as the sensible body, made out of matter and form, which is a three-dimensional accomplishment, is contained within four delimitations." Cf. *ibid.*, p. 29, 10–12: "The tetrad shows the first nature of the solid, for there is the point, then the line, then the surface, then the solid, which is a body." Cf. Macrobius, *In somnium Scip.*, 1, 6, 36, p. 21f. Willis; Johannes Lydus, *De mens.*, 4, 64, p. 115, 14–17 Wünsch: "This number is the first quadrangular number and tetractys, but it is also the first to show the nature of the solid: for there is the point, then the line, then the surface, then the solid, which is a body." Cf. Syrianus, *In Metaph.*, p. 150, 29–31 Kroll; Proclus, *In Primum Euclidis*, p. 97, 18–22: "But let us recall the more Pythagorean accounts, which postulate the point as analogous to the monad, the line to the dyad, the surface to the triad, and the solid to the tetrad." Cf. Sextus Empiricus, *Adv. math.*, X (= *Adv. physicos* II), 281–282; and the texts cited by A.-J. Festugière, 1949.

him: to identify this god with the monad, or an even higher principle. This is what is done, for instance, by Philo the Jew in Alexandria, for whom God, the creator god of the Old Testament, is sometimes higher than and sometimes identical with the monad, according to the notion of the monad used by his sources.[286] To wish to assimilate the supreme God to a derivative principle like the tetrad would have been nonsense, not only for a Neoplatonist, but also for a Christian or for a Jew. A Christian or a Jew who affirmed that God the Father, the creator of the world, was engendered, would obviously have exposed himself to incurring every kind of anathema.

To be sure, Aujoulat attempts to explain his own interpretation by writing (p. 133): "Clearly, Hierocles here wishes to emphasize the generative properties of the Tetrad (that is, the Demiurge), even if strict logic should suffer therefrom. . . ." Further on, he continues:

> These last two numbers (that is, the Monad and the Septenary) are stated under a negative aspect, and the Tetrad under a positive one. One even ends up considering the fact of being unengendered as an inferiority of the Monad with regard to the Tetrad! whereas, in good Platonic philosophy, it constitutes a superiority . . . The Tetrad is movement and life; the Monad and the Septenary are immutable in their cold impassibility. How, then, could the Tetrad fail to be the active, creative God, who gives life to all beings, and orders them so as to form the cosmos . . . It is no small merit to have returned to the sources of authentic Pythagorean tradition, causing a breath of life to enter into a domain that was traditionally quite arid!

Such affirmations are highly questionable. First of all, the Neoplatonists did not refuse to recognize this "breath of life" in the tetrad, since they too saw in it the source of eternal nature. But they obviously considered that this situation of a number both "engendering and engendered" did not allow the tetrad to be at the summit of the hierarchy, any more than it did the demiurge. Aujoulat affirms, without any proof, that Hierocles somehow considers the "negative" qualities of the monad and the hebdomad as inferior. Yet Hierocles says absolutely nothing on this subject. In the whole of his text on the tetrad, the monad, and the hebdomad, which I have translated above in its entirety, there is not the slightest remark in the sense intended by Mr. Aujoulat. On the contrary, Hierocles there states that "the characteristic features of the monad

---

[286] Cf. Festugière, 1944–1954, 4, the chapter on "Philon et les spéculations pythagoriciennes de son temps," pp. 19ff., especially p. 21.

and the hebdomad are the best and the finest, for the monad, as principle of all number, contains within itself the powers of all. . . ." (p. 88, 17ff.). What more could he have said to affirm the superiority of the monad over all numbers? His language—completely conventional—is no different in content or in tone from the traditional pagan descriptions of the monad, the tetrad, and the hebdomad, as is proved by the numerous parallel texts I have cited in the notes. Moreover, it would have been unlikely at that time that the "fact of being unengendered" could have been considered "an inferiority." In a sense, being unengendered is, for the pagans, the definition of the first god, and for the Christians the definition of God the Father. In the Christian tradition, it is, as it were, the name of the Father, at least as early as Justin.[287]

Mr. Aujoulat (pp. 121–122) also seems to think that for the ancient Pythagoreans, the tetractys was God himself, and (p. 133) that Hierocles thus returns to the sources of authentic Pythagorean tradition. In fact, however, nothing allows us to suppose that the tetractys was considered identical to God in ancient Pythagoreanism. It is enough to consult W. Burkert's *Weisheit und Wissenschaft*,[288] authoritative as far as ancient Pythagoreanism is concerned, to see that this is by no means the case: the tetractys does not appear as a personalized power, but as a group of four different elements ("Vierheit von ungleichen Gliedern").

B. The Historical Background

From the entire passage from Hierocles that I have translated and commented upon, I thus draw the conclusion that the demiurge-tetrad could not represent, for this philosopher, the supreme principle of his theological system, and that no traces of Christian influence can be discerned in it. We must now determine the position of this demiurge more closely. Happily, Hierocles himself has clarified this point rather well, so that in his case, unlike that of many other Neoplatonic texts, there is no difficulty in knowing which one of the various demiurges of the Neoplatonic hierarchy is in question. As Hierocles himself says (p. 87, 17–18; 89, 12), the demiurge in question is "the source of the sempiternal ordering of the world," who, as an "intelligible god,"[289] is "the cause of the celestial and perceptible god" (and not, as Aujoulat writes

---

[287] *Apol.,* I, 14, 1–2; 23, 2; 49, 5; 53, 2; II, 6, 1; 12, 4; 13, 4.

[288] Nürnberg 1962, pp. 63ff.; 170ff. (where verses 47 and 48 of the *Golden Verses* are discussed); pp. 337; 442.

[289] The term νοητός (intelligible) designates in this context not the highest level within the hypostasis of *Noûs,* but, as occurs again in texts of the later Neoplatonists, the general fact of belonging to this hypostasis.

[p. 136] following Meunier, "cause of the God who reigns in the heavens and in the sensible world"). He is thus the cause of the world. This description designates, with all desirable precision, the demiurge of Plato's *Timaeus,* at the same time as it emphasizes the fact that he belongs to the hypostasis of the *Noûs.* This is the same demiurge whose structure was described above by Hierocles as triadic;[290] it is the same demiurge who, in the same context, is designated as the immediate cause of the triadic hypostasis of rational souls, and whom Hierocles identifies further on (p. 105, 1ff.) with the Zeus who is mentioned in the *Carmen aureum,* on which he is commenting. We find the same details—triadic structure of the demiurge as immediate cause of a triadic hypostasis of souls, and its identification with Zeus—in Iamblichus, Proclus, and other Neoplatonists.[291] It must be emphasized, however, that in these authors the Zeus in question is far from occupying the most eminent place in the Neoplatonic pantheon, as I have demonstrated above.[292] Moreover, the text by Hierocles we are interpreting shows that he is aware of other hypostases prior to the demiurge-tetrad, which should be placed in parallel to the monad, the dyad, and the triad. It is highly probable, however, that for Hierocles even the monad is not the supreme principle; the comparison with other Neoplatonists leads us to this conclusion. Calcidius, for instance, who is slightly earlier than Hierocles, but who, unlike Hierocles, is influenced not by Iamblichus but by Porphyry and Numenius, identifies the monad with the first intellect or the demiurge of the *Timaeus.*[293] However, other passages of his commentary on the *Timaeus* demonstrate that this intellect does not represent the first principle for him,[294] but occupies only the second place in the hierarchical order. Iamblichus also calls the second principle of his theological system "monad"; yet, for him, it is no longer identical with the Platonic demiurge,[295] but is "principle and god of gods, monad come forth from the One, prior to Essence and principle thereof."

In general, we can say that the idea of conceiving the demiurgic activity, or the process of the world's procession, on the Neopythagorean model of the relation of the tetrad to the decad, seems to be common

---

[290] Cf. *In Carm. aur.,* I, 8, p. 10, 2–7 Köhler. Cf. above pp. 30–36.

[291] On the triadic structure of the demiurge in Iamblichus, cf. the excellent article by W. Deuse, 1977. On the attributes of the demiurge in Hierocles, cf. above pp. 56–61.

[292] Pp. 30–36; 56–61.

[293] Calcidius, *In Tim.,* cap. 39, p. 88, 12ff. Waszink.

[294] Calcidius, *In Tim.,* cap. 176, p. 204, 3ff.; cap. 188, p. 212, 21ff. Waszink. Similarly, Macrobius also designates in particular the second ontological principle by the term "monad," but it can also happen that he uses it with regard to the first god; cf. Macrobius, *In somnium Scip.,* I, 6, 7–9, p. 19f. Willis.

[295] Cf. Iamblichus, *De myst.,* VIII, 2 (261, 9–262, 13), pp. 195–196 des Places.

in the Athenian school. This conception appears very clearly in Proclus. While explaining the text from the *Timaeus* (39e) in which Plato says that the demiurge sees the forms that are in the Intelligible Living Being, he identifies[296] the tetrad with the "Intelligible Living Being," and the decad with the "demiurge." In so doing, he bases himself on the *Hymn to Numbers,* which the Neoplatonists attributed to Pythagoras[297]:

> until it [*scil.* the divine number in its progression] reaches, from the inviolate hollows of the Monad, as far as the sacred Tetrad; lo it (*scil.* the Tetrad) has born the universal Mother, the all-receiving, the Venerable one, she who imposes a limit on all things, the Inflexible, the Indefatigable one; they call her the pure Decad.

We can easily understand, first, why Proclus identifies the tetrad with the Intelligible Living Being: it is because Plato (39e8–10) affirms that there are four forms in the Intelligible Living Being. Moreover, as we have seen above, for Proclus, as for the entire tradition, the decad is inferior to the tetrad.[298] This, he says,[299] is why the demiurge possesses a totality inferior to the totality proper to the Living Being in itself, although he contains everything the latter contains.

For Proclus, however, the Intelligible Living Being already has a demiurgic activity in a transcendent mode. Here, we can compare the formula Hierocles applies to the tetrad: τῶν ὅλων αἰτία ἡ τετράς with that of Proclus, *In Tim.,* III, p. 106, 18 Diehl: ἡ πρώτη ποιητικὴ τῶν ὅλων αἰτία τετράς ἐστι. Likewise, in the *Platonic Theology,*[300] speaking of the tetrad that is identical with the Intelligible Living Being and which is, for him, at the same time a monad plus a triad, he affirms: "It (the triad) is the very first cause of creation and of demiurgy."

These texts are interesting in that they show that the tetrad is related to demiurgic activity. More precisely, Proclus makes the monad, which is not a number but the source of numbers, correspond to the Father; the tetrad—that is, the Intelligible Living Being—to the Father and Creator; and the decad—that is, the demiurge—to the Creator and Father. The relations between the Intelligible Living Being and the demiurge for Proclus are, moreover, extremely complex, for he points out[301] that the Intelligible Living Being is simultaneously prior to the demiurge, in the

---

[296] Proclus, *In Tim.,* III, 107, 5–25.
[297] Cf. above, p. 72.
[298] Cf. above, pp. 75–77 and n. 274.
[299] Proclus, *In Tim.,* I, 432, 23–25 Diehl.
[300] III, 19, p. 67, 11–13 Saffrey-Westerink.
[301] Proclus, *In Tim.,* I, 431, 29ff. Diehl.

demiurge, and posterior to the demiurge, insofar as the demiurge thinks the Intelligible Living Being.

This Intelligible Living Being and this demiurge are both situated at a relatively low degree in the hierarchy of beings. In Proclus' system, the Intelligible Living Being is located at the level of the third intelligible triad. Before it, therefore, come the One, then the henads, then the first and the second intelligible triad. Between the Intelligible Living Being and the demiurge, five hierarchized levels are intercalated (the three intelligible and intellectual triads, and the first two degrees of the intellectual hebdomad).

It is also on the model of the relations of the tetrad to the decad that Proclus' master Syrianus pictures the relation of the Intelligible Living Being to the demiurge. Basing himself on the same Pythagorean *Hymn to Numbers* that Proclus, as we have just seen,[302] cited in this context, Syrianus affirms[303] that the forms are in the Intelligible Living Being in an intelligible and tetradic mode, and in a "decadic" and intellectual mode in the demiurgic intellect. We also find in Syrianus the idea that the first cause of the demiurgy is found in the tetrad:

[T]here are four principles of the overall demiurgy . . . for everywhere the form of the decad is produced by the tetractys.[304]

In conformity with the relation that exists between the tetrad and the decad,

the Model [that is, the Intelligible Living Being] is both above the Demiurge and in him, above him in an intelligible mode, in him in an intellective mode.[305]

As he reports his master's doctrine, Proclus notes that

Plato's very expressions [in the *Timaeus*] seem sometimes to postulate the Model as different from the Demiurge, and sometimes as identical to him.[306] And he continues: so that Plato too sometimes says they are the same, and sometimes different, and in both cases he is correct.[307]

---

[302] Above, p. 84.
[303] Syrianus, *In Metaph.*, p. 106, 15ff. Kroll.
[304] Syrianus, *In Metaph.*, p. 150, 35–151, 2 Kroll.
[305] Syrianus, in Proclus, *In Tim.*, I, p. 323, 20ff. Diehl.
[306] Syrianus, in Proclus, *In Tim.*, p. 323, 23ff. Diehl; trans. based on that by Festugière, 1966–1968, 2:182.
[307] Proclus, *In Tim.*, I, p. 324, 10 Diehl; trans. after Festugière, 1966–1968, 2:182.

The teacher of Syrianus and Hierocles had been Plutarch of Athens. Unfortunately, we do not know his conception of the demiurge; yet we do know, in general, that he had undergone the influence of Iamblichus. Now, it is interesting to observe that the hierarchy of the intelligible and of the intellectual world we found in Syrianus and in Proclus was already known, in its broad outlines, to Iamblichus, and that the problem of the relations between the Living Being in itself and the demiurge (therefore, as we have seen, of the relations between the tetrad and the decad) was already raised by this philosopher. According to the testimony of Proclus, Iamblichus distinguished three intelligible triads, three intelligible and intellectual triads, and one intellectual triad. For him, however, the Living Being in itself was identified with the three intelligible triads, and the demiurge with the intellectual triad. Or rather, according to Proclus, Iamblichus identified the Living Being in itself with the demiurge;[308] yet he attributed to the demiurge the third rank among the Fathers in the intellectual triad. We thus encounter here the problematic we have already met with in Proclus and Syrianus: the process of the demiurgy begins at the intelligible level and ends at the intellectual level. In a sense, the Living Being in itself and the demiurge are identical, insofar as the demiurge, as an intellect that knows the Living Being in itself, is identical with it; and also insofar as the demiurge reunifies within himself everything that has been deployed in the intelligible world. The Living Being in itself is the principle that contains within itself unitively (ἡνωμένως) everything that will henceforth be in a state of division. Thus, Iamblichus' insistence on the dynamic identity between the Living Being in itself and the demiurge would, if we take up once again the arithmological correspondences proposed by Syrianus and by Proclus, justify the identification between the tetrad and the demiurge, the Living Being in itself being considered as a tetrad, because of *Timaeus* 30c5–7. We must therefore suppose a system close to that of Iamblichus, if we wish to understand Hierocles' identification of the tetrad and the demiurge.

After commenting on pages 241–262 of Mr. Aujoulat's book *Le néoplatonisme alexandrin: Hiéroclès d'Alexandrie*, I here append a few remarks concerning his article "Le démiurge chez Hiéroclès d'Alexandrie: En réponse à l'article de Mme Hadot (R.E.G. 1990, pp. 241–262)."[309] These remarks are adapted from my second article of 1993.[310] First, on the subject of Origen the Pagan, whom Mr. Aujoulat supposes, with-

---

[308] Proclus, *In Tim.*, I, 307, 17ff. Diehl: "Iamblichus calls the entire intelligible world 'Demiurge.'"

[309] *R.E.G.* CVI (1993), pp. 400–429.

[310] *Ibid.*, pp. 430–459.

out supplying any proof, is Hierocles' source for his doctrine concerning the first god. On page 413, Mr. Aujoulat says:

> However, the former [*scil.* Plotinus] preaches the transcendence of the One, and the other [*scil.* Origen the Pagan] does not. We shall conclude that they did not interpret the elucubrations of the Pythagoreans and the Neopythagoreans on the world and the One in the same way. If the supreme god is a *noûs,* like the god of Aristotle, of Origen, and perhaps of Hierocles, the Pythagorean monad can no longer play its role of transcendental principle, just as the One of Plotinus no longer has a reason to exist. We must then make do with the tetractys as supreme god and creator.

I am afraid Mr. Aujoulat has not adequately grasped what separates Origen from Plotinus. Because of a different interpretation of the first hypothesis of Plato's *Parmenides*[311]—and not as a result of a divergent interpretation of the "elucubrations of the Pythagoreans"—Origen rejected Plotinus' One (*hen*), which transcends being, as non-existent; but that did not stop him from assimilating his own first cause—that is, absolute being identified with the demiurge—to another one (*hen*) that does not transcend being. The proof lies in a text from Proclus, which I cite after the translation by Saffrey and Westerink:[312]

> Indeed, he too [*scil.* Origen] stops at the intellect as the very first being, and he gets rid of the One, which is beyond all intellect and all being; and if this was because it is superior to all knowledge, all account, and all intellectual grasp, we would not say that he goes astray either from agreement with Plato or from the nature of things; but if it is because the One is completely non-existent and non-subsistent, that the intellect is what is best, and that primary being and the primary one are identical (ὡς ταὐτόν ἐστι τὸ πρώτως ὂν καὶ τὸ πρώτως ἕν), then we could not agree with him on this point. . . .

By identifying absolute being, the intellect-demiurge, and the absolute one, Origen was merely taking up once again the position of many Platonists prior to him; and, like them, he had no need to "make do with the tetractys as supreme god and creator," which, moreover, never occupied the place of the supreme god, even among the Py-

---

[311] On this subject, cf. H. D. Saffrey and L. G. Westerink, 1974, pp. xviiif., and H. R. Schwyzer, 1987, 52–53.

[312] *Theol. Plat.,* II, 4, t. II, p. 31, 9–18 Saffrey-Westerink.

thagoreans, as we have seen.[313] I could almost stop with this remark, for Mr. Aujoulat's argument is largely based upon the false hypothesis that Hierocles could not recognize the monad or the *hen* as first ontological entity, because his doctrine was based on that of Origen, and Origen did not accept the existence of the One. Yet I repeat: Origen refused the existence only of a One that transcends being; yet he did recognize as first cause or first principle an absolute "one," identical with absolute being and with the intellect-demiurge. If, therefore, Hierocles had wanted to follow Origen in his doctrine concerning the demiurge as first principle—which, once again, is a completely gratuitous supposition on the part of Mr. Aujoulat—he should, like Origen, have identified it with the one or the monad, and not with the tetrad. In all of ancient Greek literature, moreover—and the texts on number mysticism are quite numerous—there exists no example of an author having the idea, which could only be qualified as abstruse, of identifying his *first* principle with the number *four.*

Let us go through a few more objections from page 414 and following of Mr. Aujoulat's article.[314]

The first topic of discussion is the interpretation of the following passage:

> "The power of the decad (or the number ten) is the tetrad (or the number four), for prior to the detailed perfection (κατὰ διέξοδον τελειότης) that is in the decad, a kind of unified perfection (ἡνωμένη τις τελειότης), is observed in the tetrad."

Despite Mr. Aujoulat's objections, I remain convinced that the τις in ἡνωμένη τις τελειότης of the tetrad—I translated τις τελειότης as "a kind of unified perfection"—is a rapid allusion to the fact that the perfection in question is not the unified perfection *par excellence,* which is that of the monad, but a unified perfection that derives from the monad. I readily admit that a beginner would not have grasped all the meaning of this detail, but at least the teacher has expressed himself correctly, according to the good pedagogical principle that a simplification should not give rise to a falsification.[315] Let us first try to render the expressions *kata diexodon teleiotês* and *hênômenê tis teleiotês* more clear,

---

[313] Cf. above, p. 82.

[314] Cited above, p. 86, n. 309.

[315] For years, I have been working on the Neoplatonists' commentaries on the *Categories.* The *Categories* constitute the first philosophical work of the Neoplatonists' *cursus* of studies, and are therefore read by beginners and explained with beginners in mind. Although these commentaries avoid dealing with metaphysical questions, they contain terms and expositions that will be fully understandable to their students only at higher levels of their studies. And what shall we say of the term "trinity" in the Christian religion? Are most Christians ever aware of the complex problems involving this term, which is nevertheless used in the catechism?

with the help of another text from Hierocles, that I have already cited and interpreted above.[316] In his treatise *On providence,* Hierocles tries to explain the differences between the three classes of intelligent souls, all three of which are the work of the demiurge:[317]

> Since there are three encosmic intellective kinds, the first and highest of the demiurge's productions, which has received unchangeably and invariably its resemblance to him, is in all godlike good order, as we said of the kind of the heavenly beings. The second <kind>, which receives the divine order in a secondary (δευτέρως) and degraded way, does not share in the demiurgic resemblance unchangeably and indivisibly, but is unerringly and unafflictedly turned towards the paternal laws, which <characteristic> we attributed to the ethereal beings. The third, as the last of the divine kinds, is not only inferior to the excellence of the heavenly beings by the fact that it is to some extent subject to alteration, but because of the fact that it can sometimes be worsened it is situated below the worth of the ethereal beings. For the fact of always intelligizing the god, and of possessing knowledge of him in unified form (ἠνωμένως), pertains to the heavenly beings, whereas <intelligizing him> always, but discursively (διεξοδικῶς) belongs by essence to the ethereal beings. But the fact of not always intelligizing, and of intelligizing in a partial way in the very act of intelligizing, has been attributed as a proper characteristic to human souls, which by nature fall short of the undivided intellection of the heavenly beings and the knowledge, plurified in an orderly way, of the ethereal beings, since these souls do not intelligize either in a unified way (ἐνιαίως) or perpetually.

To think of the demiurge in a unitive or unified way—Hierocles uses the adverbs *hênomenôs* and *heniaiôs* indifferently—means that the heavenly souls have a total, intuitive vision of him, without distinction of the various Forms or Ideas that are in him in an intelligible mode, whereas the ethereal souls think of him *diexodikôs,* that is, passing from one Form or Idea to another, and introducing distinction into their mode of thinking. This text testifies to the fact that, for Hierocles as for all Platonists, from the beginning of Platonism to its end, that which is more or less unified, and thereby rendered more or less similar to the first principle, has a higher ontological rank than that which is more detailed. The perfection of the decad is therefore situated at an ontological level lower than that of the tetrad. We encounter the same ontological subordination of what exists in a detailed or differentiated

---

[316] Above, p. 43.
[317] Hierocles, in Photius, *Library,* cod. 251, 461b37 Bekker, vol. VII, p. 193 Henry.

way to what exists in a still undifferentiated mode in a text by Nico-machus of Gerasa.[318] We find it again in Syrianus,[319] Hierocles' con-temporary and, like him, a disciple of Plutarch of Athens, who defends the doctrine of the ancients against Aristotle: "the decad contains within itself the whole of number, no longer in a hidden way, like the monad, nor essentially, like the tetrad, but already with a great deal of alterity and division."

Yet let us see what Mr. Aujoulat has to say:[320]

> [T]he perfection of the decad is "detailed" (*kata diexodon*); that is, the decad analyses number, from one to ten, whereas that of the tetrad is *hênômenê tis,* because it proceeds by synthesis, by the ad-dition of the first four numbers. If we take the text *as it is,* and do not suppose *a priori* that the monad is a higher principle in Hier-ocles, we can understand that the tetrad presents a "veritable unity" with regard to the decad.

First of all, I cannot understand what is meant, in Mr. Aujoulat's text, by "the decad analyses number." For me, Hierocles' text means that the decad is in a detailed way what the tetrad is in a unified way; in other words, that all the forms-intelligible numbers included within the demiurge-tetrad in a more or less transcendent state where they re-main relatively indistinct[321] from each other, exist in the decad in a de-tailed way. Next, if we take the text "as it is," we find no trace in Hierocles' text that signifies that the tetrad "proceeds by synthesis." It is not the tetrad, or the number four, that proceeds to the addition of the monad, the dyad, the triad, and itself. Hierocles simply notes that by addition, or by placing together, "the numbers from the monad to the tetrad, their sum total gives the decad," and this, it seems to me, means that for the ontological or even purely numerical constitution of the decad, the monad, the dyad and the triad are just as indispensable as the tetrad itself. Hierocles is not saying anything different, for in-

---

[318] Nicomachus of Gerasa, *Arithmetical introduction,* I, VI, 1ff. Hoche: "Everything in the universe that is arranged by nature in accordance with a detailed technical devel-opment (κατὰ τεχνικὴν διέξοδον) appears, both individually and as a whole, to have been differentiated and adorned with order in accordance with number by providence and the intellect which created all things . . . from the fact that it maintains number, which was given previous existence in the mind of the god who made the universe; which num-ber is purely intelligible and entirely immaterial, yet also the veritable and perpetual essence, so that in relation to it as to a technical ratio, all these things might be accomplished: time, motion, the heavens, the stars, and all kinds of revolutions."

[319] *Commentary on the Metaphysics,* p. 147, 30 Kroll.

[320] p. 414 of the article cited above, n. 309.

[321] The degree of their transcendence and of their indistinctness depends on the on-tological level at which Hierocles has placed the demiurge.

stance, than Nicomachus of Gerasa in his *Theologoumena*, extracts or paraphrases of which are found in an anonymous treatise attributed to Iamblichus:[322]

> In the natural increase as far as the tetrad [*scil.* the number four], the things in the world appear as accomplished together, universally and particularly, as well as the things that are in number; in short, in all the natures. In particular, what contributes especially, and in an extraordinary way, to the harmonious union of the finished product is the fact that the decad [the number ten] is completed at the same time by it [*scil.* the tetrad] and by the numbers that come just before it [*scil.* 4 + 1 + 2 + 3 = 10], since it [*scil.* the decad] is a gnomon and a meeting-point [*scil.* of the entire decimal system], but also the fact that it [*scil.* the decad] is the limit of corporification and of three-dimensional extension.

Moreover, in the text "as it is" I cannot find anything to justify Mr. Aujoulat's affirmation that "the tetrad-tetractys is . . . an equilateral triangle formed by 4 + 3 + 2 + 1 points, which formed a total of 10 points."[323] That figure is compatible only with a tetractys, which would not be the number four,[324] as it is for Hierocles, but the assembly of the first four numbers. On the contrary, the geometrical figure corresponding to the tetrad is, as Hierocles himself says a bit further on (= p. 89, 5 Köhler), the pyramid, made up of four points.

What is truly unexpected is that Mr. Aujoulat affirms concerning this alleged figure of the tetrad, for which Hierocles' text does not offer the slightest support, that it gives an explanation of what the *dunamis* of the tetrad is

> which at least has the merit of confining itself to Hierocles' text, and not to appeal to an opposition between *dynamis* and *entelecheia*, through the intermediary of Philo and of Iamblichus. In fact, the Alexandrian does not use this last term. As far as the *dynamis/energeia* couple is concerned, it too appears to be absent from the *Commentary on the Golden Verses*.[325]

As is methodologically sound, I had indeed sought, with regard to the phrase "But the power of the decad is the tetrad," to explain the tech-

---

[322] [Iamblichus], *Theol. arithm.*, p. 20, 1–9 de Falco.
[323] p. 415.
[324] Cf. my demonstrations above, p. 67f.
[325] N. Aujoulat's article, p. 415.

nical term *dunamis* in Hierocles' text with the help of strictly parallel passages using the same term.[326] Among other texts, I had thus cited Philo, *De op. mundi*, § 47: "For what the decad is in act (*entelecheia*), the tetrad is, it seems, potentially." Needless to say, I maintain my interpretation of the *dunamis* of the tetrad. I merely add that the opposition δυνάμει—ἐνεργείᾳ is already found in the *Arithmetical introduction* by Nicomachus of Gerasa.[327]

At page 416 of his article, with regard to the phrase "And the tetrad is the arithmetical mean between the monad and the hebdomad, for in a way it surpasses [the monad] by the same number by which it is surpassed [by the hebdomad]," Mr. Aujoulat criticizes my way of translating πως by "somehow," which is nevertheless completely habitual and without artifice. I admit that πως here may well have the same meaning as τρόπῳ τινί, but this changes strictly nothing. One must really wish to force the text because of a preconceived idea to claim, as does Mr. Aujoulat, that one can here translate πως by "in a determinate way," which would give: "for it [the tetrad] surpasses [the monad] in a determinate way by the same number by which it is surpassed." Hierocles would then have rendered himself guilty of a tautology, for "in a determinate way" expresses the same thing as "by the same number," only slightly less precisely. Perhaps it was because he sensed this that Mr. Aujoulat finally translates πως by "precisely," which is not the same thing as "in a determinate way." This translation is certainly an amazing feat! In addition, whether Mr. Aujoulat translates πως by "in a determinate way" or by "precisely," πως still modifies "surpasses" (*huperekhei*), an interpretation which he sharply criticized with regard to my own translation at the beginning of the paragraph. In accordance with his own ideas, he should have translated "by the same, in a determinate way, number."

Then comes another highly revealing remark: "We must," says Mr. Aujoulat,[328] "note in passing how carefully the text on the tetrad is composed, and not forget that Hierocles is more of a 'littérateur' than a genuine scholar." The affirmation that Hierocles is more of a littérateur than a scholar is a judgment that comes out of thin air, and which Mr. Aujoulat does not even try to back up. The fact that it is stated in a peremptory tone does not make it any more true; yet Mr. Aujoulat uses it to treat Hierocles' text as he pleases. When he thinks it suits him, he recommends that the text be taken "as it is," but if the text "as it is" embarrasses him, he declares that it must not be taken literally, because

---

[326] Cf. I. Hadot, 1990, pp. 251ff.

[327] I, XVI, 8 Hoche. Cf. also the summary by Iamblichus of the *Theologoumena arithmeticae*, 1, 8ff., p. 1 de Falco, cited above, n. 276, second quotation.

[328] At p. 117 of his article.

Hierocles is a littérateur and likes literary effects, so that when, even in a passage that appears scientific, like our text on number mysticism, Hierocles uses current Platonist technical terms, he inserts into them a whole other meaning without any warning. Indeed, this is a very convenient presupposition, because it allows the dismissal of all embarrassing parallel texts, not only by previous and contemporary Platonist and Neoplatonist authors,[329] but also by Hierocles himself, because he allegedly writes sometimes as a philosopher and sometimes as a man of letters, and it is obviously Mr. Aujoulat alone who decides, on the basis of mysterious criteria known to him alone, which passages are scientific and which literary.[330] The most serious point, however, is that he not only lowers Hierocles to the rank of a rhetor or a sophist, but that he even presents him as stupid: indeed, Hierocles is, it is alleged, incapable of realizing that if he uses the technical vocabulary or technical schemes current not only in surrounding Neoplatonism, but also throughout the many-centuries-old tradition of number mysticism, he will not be understood by anybody, since he gives these terms another meaning without pointing this out, at least by a word. If Hierocles had desired that, in the typical scheme of number mysticism he reproduces, one should, contrary to tradition, see the ontologically superior principle no longer in the monad, but in the tetrad, it would have been urgently necessary to explain this, for no one except Mr. Aujoulat could have guessed it. He should have said explicitly that for him, the fact that the tetrad is engendered predisposes it to be the first principle. In order to do this, he would have had to attempt the impossible, for one does

---

[329] This is, moreover, what he has already done with the help of another argument: since, according to him, Origen did not recognize a first principle that was *one*—which is false, as we have demonstrated above (pp. 87–88)—, and since all other Platonists except Hierocles recognized it, all parallel texts are excluded. For instance, on p. 419 he writes in a reproving tone: "In this regard she does not fail to rely on citations from Iamblichus, Syrianus, and Macrobius, all of whom were subject to the influence of Plotinus."

[330] At p. 424 of his article, Mr. Aujoulat writes: "I therefore see in Hierocles a philosopher who is punctilious on certain points of doctrine, but above all practical, rebellious to transcendental speculations, and a writer who does not disdain literary effects, even in a passage which appears 'scientific.' I have been very aware of the difficulties engendered by his sometimes reticent attitude with regard to a Neoplatonism which one could qualify as orthodox, whereas Mme Hadot considers Hierocles as above all a Neoplatonic philosopher of the strict observance, using all the expressions and recipes of traditional arithmology in a strictly literal way." I regret to say that I have not noted in Hierocles' work a single passage that reveals his reticence with regard to surrounding Neoplatonism. Nor did I ever allow myself to say that Hierocles was a Neoplatonist of the strict observance, because I have no idea what is meant by that. However, I have demonstrated that, in those of texts which remain, he does not depart in any way from surrounding Neoplatonism; that is, he positions himself somewhere between Iamblichus and Proclus. For a supplementary survey of Iamblichean elements in Hierocles' thought, cf. D. J. O'Meara (1989), pp. 112–118.

not have to be a philosopher, but merely possess common sense, to know that what is engendered is posterior to that which has engendered it. Nevertheless, Mr. Aujoulat believes Hierocles is capable of having thought the contrary.

Next,[331] concerning the phrase "for the monad, as principle of all number, contains within itself the powers of all, whereas the hebdomad, as motherless and virginal, has the value of the monad in a secondary [sc. derivative] way . . . ," Mr. Aujoulat criticizes my way of translating *deuterôs* by "in a secondary way." First, I refer to my quotation from Hierocles on page 89, where *deuterôs* has exactly the same meaning. That this adverb cannot, as Mr. Aujoulat would have it, signify that the hebdomad possesses the merit of the monad on an equal basis and not on one of inferiority, is made obvious by the context. Hierocles describes the hebdomad as being virginal and motherless, a description that evokes the myth according to which Athena burst forth from the head of Zeus without having been engendered by a mother. The hebdomad is, moreover, often identified with Athena in texts concerning number mysticism.[332] The hebdomad thus does have a father—the monad—but not in the sense that it is engendered by it in the proper sense of the term. A text[333] from the *Theologoumena arithmeticae*, summarizing the *Arithmetical Introduction* of Nicomachus of Gerasa, shows that the monad does not produce any other number, although it is the cause of them all. In this context, the attribute "engendered" means that a number is constituted by multiplication, like the numbers four (two times two), six (two times three), eight (two times four), nine (three times three), and ten (two times five). Thus, the hebdomad does indeed have a cause, and this is what distinguishes it from the monad, but it was not engendered, as is the case for Athena, who was not engendered by the seed of her Father Zeus, but burst forth from his head.[334] Yet what brings the hebdomad even closer to the monad is the fact that it is not only unengendered (although it is caused), but neither does it engender (that is, constitute by multiplication) another number within the decad, which is not the case for any other number within the decad, except for the monad, which does not engender either. Nevertheless, since the hebdomad is caused—for it has a father, the monad—it is necessarily inferior to the monad, which is unengendered in the proper sense, and it therefore possesses the merit of the monad in a secondary way. Nicomachus of Gerasa makes the hebdomad the providence (*pronoia*) of the

---

[331] P. 420 of Mr. Aujoulat's article.
[332] Cf. the references given above, n. 283.
[333] Cf. [Iamblichus], *Theol. arithm.*, p. 1, 1, 8 de Falco.
[334] The dyad, the triad, and the pentad are not engendered either.

demiurgic god;[335] Proclus compares it to the soul, first of the demiurge's works.[336] By reserving a privileged place within the decad for the hebdomad, Philo thus maintains the spirit of texts on number mysticism, but he never elevates it to the position of first god, contrary to what Mr. Aujoulat believes.[337]

The privilege of the tetrad, by contrast, consists in the fact that it is the only number within the decad that is both engendered (two times two = four) and engendering (two times four = eight), and if, as Hierocles says, it unites within itself both the powers of the engendered numbers and those of the engendering numbers, it nevertheless does not unite within itself the powers of either the monad or the hebdomad, which are neither engendered nor engendering. Only the monad contains within it the powers of all the numbers. If we take the text "as it is," we thus see once again that the tetrad cannot have a higher ontological rank than the monad.

That the demiurge-tetrad is not the supreme god in Hierocles' ontological hierarchy is therefore not a gratuitous hypothesis, which one is free to accept or to reject—unless one wishes to deny what is obvious—, but it is a fact—as is proved by the text from Hierocles that we have studied—and this fact ruins Mr. Aujoulat's basic hypothesis, from which all the details of his book derive.

We thus observe that Hierocles, with regard to his doctrine of the demiurge and the latter's position within the development of Neoplatonic philosophy, is situated somewhere between Iamblichus and Proclus. We have also noted the fact that this doctrine, as well as that of the soul, presupposes a system already richly diversified with regard to its hierarchy of ontological levels, which must have resembled that of Iamblichus. Yet why, this being the case, did Hierocles mention the ontological levels above the demiurge so briefly, and by way of allusions?

To this question, I shall make the following very brief reply: of the

---

[335] *Apud* [Iamblichus], *Theol. arithm.*, p. 57, 21ff.

[336] Proclus, *In Tim.*, II, p. 203, 4–6 Diehl: "For if the demiurgic intellect is a monad, and if the soul is first to proceed outside the intellect, it has the relation of a hebdomad to it; for the hebdomad comes from the father, and is motherless."

[337] Pp. 422–423. Initially, I had wanted to devote a note to the analysis of the text from Philo reproduced by Mr. Aujoulat, which can only be done by comparing it with the parallel text of Johannes Lydus, for these two texts complete one another. F. E. Robbins ([1921]: p. 101) has demonstrated beyond the least doubt that these two texts go back to the same source. Yet this would lead us too far afield, so I will report only one detail therefrom. The text of Johannes Lydus (*De mens.*, II, 12, p. 33, 8–34, 3) informs us about the identity, in the quotation from Philolaus reported by both authors, of this "rector and leader of all things, one (Mr. Aujoulat has forgotten to translate *heis*), always existent, stable (*monimos*), immobile, identical with himself and different from the others," of whose stability the immobility of the hebdomad is the image (*eikôn*): it is Apollo, identified with the transcendent One.

seven books of Hierocles' *On Providence,* Photius has preserved only extracts, the totality of which does not exceed twenty pages in the Budé edition. The fact that Photius, in his extracts, does not mention any principle ontologically superior to the demiurge, does not at all prove that Hierocles himself had not spoken of one. On the other hand, as far as his commentary on the *Carmen aureum* is concerned, Hierocles had two reasons not to speak of his theological system in it in a detailed way. In the first place, the highest-placed god in the *Carmen aureum* is Zeus, in his role as leader of the gods of the cult, and that Zeus was never located above the hypostasis of the intellect by any of the contemporary Neoplatonic systems. Interpreting the *Carmen aureum,* Hierocles therefore did not feel inclined to speak of a higher ontological entity. Yet I see the main reason in the fact that the commentary on the *Carmen aureum* was addressed to beginners in philosophy,[338] since the *Carmen aureum* itself was, according to Hierocles, only a summary of basic Pythagorean dogmas (τῶν κεφαλαιωδεστέρων δογμάτων ἐπιτομή) and an elementary pedagogical course (παιδευτικὴ στοιχείωσις)[339]—and it would have been out of place, from a pedagogical point of view, to confront them with all the details of a complex Neoplatonic system. This fact has also been pointed out by Neil Linley[340] in the preface to an Arabic commentary on the *Golden Verses* attributed to Proclus: "The impression given throughout the commentary of Hierocles is that it was composed specifically as a tool for beginners, using the Pythagorean poem as a text upon which to base a preparatory ethical treatise and avoiding questions of Theology and of Philosophy." At the end of his commentary,[341] Hierocles speaks of the methodological restrictions he had thought necessary to impose upon himself:

> Such has been our exegesis of the *Golden Verses.* It contains a summary, modest glimpse of the teachings of the Pythagoreans. Indeed, it did not seem that it was permitted to maintain in my explanations the brevity of the *Golden Verses* themselves (for in this way many things which had been excellently prescribed would have remained obscure), nor to extend them to the full amplitude of the whole of philosophy—this would have been too great a task for the present discourse. Instead, it seemed to me desirable to impose upon my explanations a measure such that it might be apt to give the meaning of the *Verses,* and, with regard to their interpretation, to develop of

[338] Cf., on Hierocles and Simplicius, I. Hadot, 1978, pp. 160–164; reprinted in I. Hadot 2001, pp. xcii–xcvii.
[339] Hierocles, *In Carmen aureum,* XXVII, 11, p. 122, 1–5 Köhler.
[340] N. Linley, 1984, p. x.
[341] Hierocles, *In Carmen aureum,* XXVII, 10–11, p. 121, 19–122, 5 Köhler.

the general dogmas (ἐκ τῶν καθόλου δογμάτων) only that which is suitable to an exegesis of these verses. For the poem is nothing other than a perfect sketch of philosophy and an epitome of its basic dogmas, and an elementary pedagogical course, written by those who have already started out upon the divine path, for those who come after them. . . .

CHAPTER IV

Hierocles' Philosophical Ideas
on Providence

Let us now consider Hierocles' doctrine on providence. Here again, after noticing a number of analogies between this theory and that professed by Simplicius in his commentary on the *Manual*, Praechter[342] wished to recognize doctrinal characteristics proper to the school of Alexandria, which he thought were due to Christian influence. In the first place, he thought Hierocles takes up a position proper to Middle Platonism, according to which *Heimarmenê* consists only in the fact that our actions, which are freely chosen, necessarily have quite determinate consequences.[343] However, he thought, Hierocles replaces the necessity (ἀνάγκη) of these consequences, which was repugnant to the Christians,[344] by the coercive and educative action of the divinity, who recompenses our good and bad actions by their consequences, with a view to our moral progress. If this is accepted, divine justice, which sometimes seems debatable, could be justified, if we consider more generally that it recompenses actions committed in a previous life. According to Praechter, then, Hierocles—in opposition, one is to understand, to the Neoplatonists of the school of Athens—replaces Platonic *Anankê* by the idea of a coercive education willed by God. But this is completely false. Quite to the contrary, it is precisely this idea of a divine education that we find in Proclus and in the Neoplatonists who came after him. There was, moreover, no substitution: *Anankê*, or at least a kind of Anankê,[345] is identical to *Heimarmenê*;[346] which, as a re-

---

[342] Praechter, "Hierokles," col. 1482.

[343] Praechter cites Albinus (*i.e.*, Alcinous), *Didascal.*, 26 (179, 9), p. 51 Whittaker as an example.

[344] According to Nemesius, *De natura hominis*, 38 (306), p. 110 Morani.

[345] On the two *Anankai*, cf. Proclus, *In Remp.*, vol. II, p. 205, 27ff. Kroll. Cf. *In Tim.*, vol. III, p. 274, 14 Diehl.

[346] Cf. Proclus, *De prov.*, 13, 13, p. 120 Boese (trans. Moerbeke): "Ad hec etiam et Plato, ut estimo, respiciens dixit mixtam quidem huius mundi consistentiam ex intellectu et necessitate, intellectu principante necessitati [*Tim.*, 48a1–2] corporum, motivam causam *necessitatem* vocans, quam et in aliis *fatum* appellavit. . . ."

sult of the influence it exerts on man, is interpreted as a means of education. I can only explain Praechter's mistake by the fact that he did not take into consideration Proclus' *Tria opuscula,* which, in his day, were known only in the Latin translation by Moerbeke. If he had studied these three little works attentively, two of which deal especially with questions related to providence, and the third of which deals with the origin of evil, he would have been able to note that everything he thought was a particularity of Hierocles' doctrine on providence is found equally in Proclus. Let us add that, in the tone of the *Tria opuscula,* he would have found a general interpretative problem analogous to the one set forth for us by those of Hierocles' works that have come down to us. In these books, for instance in the second treatise, entitled *On Providence,* Proclus uses extremely simple philosophical language. Instead of displaying before the treatise's addressee, the mathematician Theodorus, the entire complicated hierarchy of the multiple hypostases of his system, Proclus keeps to what is essential, and mentions only the three principal hypostases: the Good or the One, the *Noûs,* and the souls, most often speaking only of God, without distinguishing between the first two hypostases. Upon seeing this, Praechter would perhaps have been more prudent in his judgment on Hierocles' philosophical system. It is true that this simple pedagogical precaution, which Proclus takes with regard to an audience without philosophical training, has been interpreted in a peculiar way by certain scholars. Such simplicity of language can, it is maintained, be explained by the fact that the *Tria opuscula* were written by Proclus in his youth, when he was close to the philosophy of Plotinus. But this hypothesis was refuted by H. Boese.[347] We are thus in the presence of a case analogous to that of Hierocles: an author's silence on the subject of the complex hierarchy of hypostases does not imply the absence or the ignorance of this hierarchy in the author's thought. We may also note that D. Amand,[348] in his book on *Fatalism and Freedom in Greek Antiquity,* makes no mention of these three treatises by Proclus, however incredible this may seem, since two of them concern the subject of his book directly. It is thus not surprising that the author should end up with completely false conclusions concerning Hierocles and Proclus.

The continuation of our investigations will lead us to a wholly other judgment than Praechter. We shall see that the Neoplatonic doctrine on providence was already fixed, in its broad outlines, at the beginning of Neoplatonism; that it owed a great deal to Middle Platonism; and that,

[347] Boese, 1960, pp. ix–x.
[348] D. Amand, 1945.

as a whole, it underwent a development analogous to the overall ontology of Neoplatonism. We shall also see that the place that Hierocles occupies within the evolution of the Neoplatonic doctrine on providence corresponds to that which he occupies within the overall evolution of Neoplatonism; that is, he is situated between Iamblichus and Proclus.

I therefore give the continuation of the text by Photius cited above,[349] and start by recalling the last phrase partially commented upon:

> [B]ut the god who is their creator and father reigns as king over them all, and his paternal royalty (πατρονομικὴ βασιλεία)[350] is providence (πρόνοια), which decrees to each kind what is suitable to it; and the justice (δίκη) that follows upon it is called *Heimarmenê* (εἰμαρμένη). For this is not the thoughtless necessity (ἀνάγκη) of the casters of horoscopes, nor the constraint (βία) of the Stoics, nor, as Alexander of Aphrodisias thinks, is it identical with the Platonic nature of bodies, nor is it that lot (γένεσις) which is altered by incantations and sacrifices, as some think, but it is god's justice-dealing activity, concerning those things that occur in accordance with the decree of providence, and corrects the things that are up to us in order and sequence (τάξει καὶ εἱρμῷ), with regard to the freely-chosen hypotheses of our voluntary acts.

1. The Definition of Providence

The preceding text from Hierocles thus distinguishes *Heimarmenê* from providence, and gives a definition of these two entities, that enables us to see the subordination of *Heimarmenê* to providence. First of all, let us consider this definition of providence, as well as its historical background, more closely. We note that Hierocles defines providence as "that which attributes to each kind what is suitable to it." Such a definition is found

---

[349] Hierocles, in Photius, *Library*, cod. 251, p. 461b19ff. Bekker, vol. VII, p. 192 Henry; cf. above, chap. 3, sec. 5, n. 107. Cf. the parallel text from codex 214, p. 172a41 Bekker, vol. III, p. 127 Henry, cited above, p. 30.

[350] πατρονομικὴν βασιλείαν *AM*: πατρωνυμικὴν βασιλείαν *A²*. Each of these two readings gives an excellent sense. For the meaning of the first reading ("paternal royalty"), cf. above, p. 58; for the meaning of the second reading, cf. below, p. 102, the remarks on the etymology of the word *pronoia*. For my part, I doubt Henry's affirmation that the corrections of *A²* could have been carried out without the help of a manuscript, and merely on the basis of a good overall education (Henry, vol. I, p. xxx). In the present instance, it is not at all easy to see the need for a correction; and if it was one, it will have been the work of a specialist in Neoplatonist philosophy.

in Proclus.[351] Besides such definitions, the Neoplatonists liked to give an etymological definition of the word *pro-noia*. Thus, according to Plotinus,[352] providence is intelligence prior to all things (πρόνοια = νοῦς πρὸ πάντων), whereas for Proclus and the Neoplatonists who came after him, providence is in the strict sense an activity prior to the intellect: πρόνοια = ἐνέργεια πρὸ τοῦ νοῦ.[353] In the texts from Hierocles that have been preserved, we find no trace of etymological definitions. However, if we adopt the reading πατρωνυμικήν of the anonymous eleventh-century corrector, which, joined to βασιλείαν means "royalty which derives its name from the father," we could consider this formula as proof of the fact that Hierocles makes πρόνοια derive from the demiurge-*Noûs,* and this would seem, at first glance, to indicate that he was closer to Plotinus' definition.[354] Clearly, the position occupied by providence within the divine hierarchy changes according to the etymological doctrine one adopts; the first one identifies it with the *Noûs,* while the second gives providence a rank higher than the *Noûs.* In any case, Hierocles' affirmation that the royalty of the demiurge is providence is also reconcilable with the second etymological interpretation, as is shown by the following text from Proclus:[355]

---

[351] Cf. Proclus, *De decem dubit.,* 33, 1, p. 55 Boese: πρῶτον οὖν λέγωμεν ὅτι, τῆς προνοίας ἑκάστοις . . . τὰ προσήκοντα νεμούσης . . . Cf. Proclus, *In Tim.,* I, p. 415, 15–18 Diehl, trans. based on Festugière, 1966–1968, 2:290: "And this is what true Providence is: the communication of the Good to all things, and the return of all things towards that which communicates . . . [t]he communicator giving to all the gift which he gives in accordance with each being's capacity for this gift."

[352] Cf. Plotinus, *Enn.,* VI, 8, 17, 9: "If we wish to call this state of things 'providence' this word must be understood in the sense that before this whole, there is an intellect at rest, from which and in conformity with which this whole exists. If, then, the intellect is before all things . . ."

[353] Cf. Proclus, *El. Theol.,* prop. 134, p. 118, 25ff. Dodds: "Thus, in so far as it exercises pro-vidence, since pro-vidence consists in a pre-noetic activity, the intellect is a god." Cf. Proclus, *De. prov.,* 7, 1–14 apud Isaacum (p. 113 Boese): ". . . providence, which completely reveals pre-noetic activity, which it is necessary to attribute only to the Good, since it is more divine than the intellect, since the intellect also desires the Good with all things and before all things." Cf. *De decem dubit.,* 4, 3, p. 6 Boese.

[354] Cf. Calcidius, *In Tim.,* cap. 176, p. 204, 9ff. Waszink, where we also find a connection between *noûs* and *pronoia.* In the sentence preceding the quotation, Calcidius was saying that all things are in the first instance governed by the first god, who is the supreme good and is above intelligence, and he continues: "Deinde a providentia, quae est post illum summun secundae eminentiae, quem noyn Graeci vocant; est autem intellegibilis essentia aemulae bonitatis propter indefessam ad summum deum conversionem, estque ei ex illo bonitatis haustus, quo tam ipsa ornatur quam cetera quae ipso auctore honestantur. Hanc igitur dei voluntatem, tamquam sapientem tutelam rerum omnium, providentiam homines vocant, non, ut plerique aestimant, ideo dictam, quia praecurrit in videndo atque intellegendo proventus futuros, sed quia proprium divinae mentis intellegere, qui est proprius mentis actus." Cf. the commentary on this passage by J. den Boeft, 1970. A previous state of Platonic doctrine, very close to Stoicism, is perhaps reflected in Philo (*De provid.* I, 45; 33), where providence is assimilated to the World Soul.

"[I]f the Demiurge is Intellect, and at the same time Providence, in so far as within it there is something superior even to the Intellect, it is precisely that it has received the name of 'Providence' because of the activity which transcends the Intellect."

2. *The Definition of the Function of* Heimarmenê

Let us now move on to the examination of the definition of *Heimarmenê*, and its doctrinal background. The continuation of our text first describes *Heimarmenê* as the justice (δίκη) that accompanies providence, and as god's justice-dealing activity. Clearly, Hierocles is inspired here by the image of *Dikê* accompanying Zeus (= demiurge-providence). This image is taken from Plato's *Laws*,[356] where it is said that

> *Dikê*, who always accompanies Zeus, punishes all breaches of the divine law.

This Platonic passage is itself probably the reflection of an Orphic myth, for it does seem that the old story (παλαιὸς λόγος) to which Plato refers in this context is an Orphic text. Be that as it may, for the Neoplatonists the identity between Plato's *Dikê* and that of the Orphic myths was a fact. Thus, in his commentary on the *Timaeus*, Proclus connects the text from the *Laws* with fragment 158 of the *Orphica:*

> There followed him *Dikê,* who punishes severely.[357]

Hierocles himself is probably alluding to an Orphic text when he says that *Dikê* keeps watch over human affairs.[358] P. Boyancé[359] compares

---

[355] Proclus, *In Tim.,* I, p. 415, 20ff. Diehl, trans. based on Festugière, 1966–1968, 2:290.

[356] Plato, *Laws,* IV, 716a2: τῷ δὲ ἀεὶ συνέπεται Δίκη τῶν ἀπολειπομένων τοῦ θείου νόμου τιμωρός. Hierocles, in Photius, *Library,* cod. 214, p. 172b3 Bekker, vol. III, p. 127 Henry, maintains the composite verb συνέπεσθαι from the Platonic text.

[357] Proclus, *In Tim.,* vol. III, p. 232, 32: Τῷ δὲ Δίκη πολύποινος ἐφέσπετο. See below, n. 368. Cf. Hermias, *In Phaedr.,* p. 154, 13 ff. Couvreur: in this text, *dikaiosunê* is identical with Dikê mentioned *ibid.,* pp. 162, 9; 170, 13.

[358] Hierocles, *In Carmen aureum,* XI, p. 50, 1 Köhler: δίκην ἐφορᾶν τὰ ἀνθρώπινα τιθεμένους. In Neoplatonic texts, we cannot always decide whether δίκη is personified or not; in other words, whether or not the word should be capitalized. This is unimportant, but we should be aware that a relation to divine Justice at least underlies the thought. Compare the text by Hierocles we have just quoted with Pseudo-Demosthenes, *Contra Aristogit.,* I, 11: when judging, we must respect "inexorable and grave *Dikê,* whom Orpheus, while teaching us the most holy mysteries, says is seated beside the throne of Zeus, and watches over all the actions of men."

[359] P. Boyancé, 1967, pp. 173–178.

Orphic Hymn no. 62, addressed to *Dikê*, with texts from Philo and Plato: the role of *Dikê* as an avenger (τιμωρός) appears both in the Orphic hymn and in Philo and Plato,[360] as well, I might add, as in Proclus,[361] Damascius, and Simplicius.[362] In our context, we must pay particular attention to a text from Philo, cited by Boyancé, in which the author relieves God of all punitive activity. He is the cause only of good things, and does not produce anything evil; and it is *Dikê* who must take upon herself the responsibility for punitive actions.[363] Here we see the appearance of a distinction analogous to the one Hierocles establishes between the providence that essentially distributes and preserves goods and *Heimarmenê-Dikê*, which corrects the faults committed.[364] In the same article, as well as in another, entitled "Xénocrate et les Orphiques,"[365] Boyancé emphasizes the importance for Neoplatonic exegesis of the figure of *Dikê* of a second text from the *Laws*.[366] Here Plato starts from a verse by Homer: "This is the *Dikê* of the gods who hold Olympus" (*Odyssey*, XIX, 43).

The Neoplatonists used the two texts from the *Laws* that mention *Dikê*, comparing them with the speech by the demiurge to the recent gods in the *Timaeus*,[367] in order to associate *Dikê* with the recent or encosmic gods.[368] What is more, the functions of *Dikê*, as Plato describes them in

[360] P. Boyancé, 1967, p. 175.

[361] Proclus, *In Remp.*, vol. II, p. 294, 9f. Kroll; cf. *ibid.*, p. 145, 3.

[362] Cf. following note.

[363] Philo, *De decalogo*, § 177, pp. 128ff. (trans. based on Nikiprowetzky, p. 129): "He [*scil.* God] thus did not think it right to issue his decrees together with punishment [*scil.* in case of disobedience], not because he accords impunity to the workers of iniquity, but because he knew that Justice, who sits beside him and watches over human affairs, would not remain inactive, since by her nature she hates evil, but would assume the task of punishing transgressors as her own duty." Cf. *Leg. Alleg.*, § 177 (= SVF III, 116, p. 26 von Arnim). Cf. Pseudo-Plutarch, *De fato*, 573f1ff., where *Heimarmenê* is used analogously, to relieve providence of the responsibility for punishments. The same theme appears in Simplicius, *In Ench Epict.*, XXXV 45ff., I. Hadot 1996: ἡ θεία δίκη τὸ τιμωρὸν εἶδος τῆς δικαιώσεως . . . ἐπάγει. Cf. Damascius, *Vita Isid.*, 189, p. 258, 4–9 Zintzen = fr. 126A Athanassiadi.

[364] Cf. for instance in Photius, *Library*, cod. 251, p. 464a16ff. Bekker, vol. VII, p. 199 Henry: "Thus, the preliminary distribution of goods, and the conservation of the properties appropriate to the nature of each thing, are the proper work of pure providence, whereas the correction of dispositions contrary to nature and the punishment of faults are incumbent upon that providence which is active in matter, and which utilizes chance (τύχη) and opportunity (καιρός)." This providence active in matter is *Heimarmenê*.

[365] P. Boyancé, 1948.

[366] Plato, *Laws*, X, 904e4.

[367] Plato, *Tim.*, 41c.

[368] Proclus, *In Tim.*, vol. III, p. 232, 29 Diehl (trans. based on Festugière, 1966–1968, 5:96): "Plato is right to associate 'Justice' (Δίκη) with the encosmic gods, for she is the companion of Zeus, as is affirmed by Orpheus, when he says [fr. 158]: 'There followed him *Dikê*, who punishes severely,' and the Athenian Stranger [*Laws*, IV, 716a2]: 'always, he is accompanied by *Dikê*,' who is established with the encosmic gods, and who directs

these two texts from the *Laws,* are absolutely identical to those Hierocles attributes to *Heimarmenê:* at the time of the reincarnations of human souls, *Dikê* assigns to each soul, in accordance with what it has deserved in its previous life, a determinate place in the various regions of the *cosmos,* and during each individual life, she keeps watch over the conduct of each person.[369] The text from Hierocles we are now commenting seems, moreover, to be an interpretation of the second text from Plato's *Laws,* for the demiurge appears in Plato in the image of a king (904a6). In addition, the text suggests the identification of *Dikê* and *Heimarmenê.* Here Plato describes (904c6f.) the rewards and punishments human souls undergo, as a function of their moral attitudes, in accordance with the law and the order of *Heimarmenê,* by the Homeric verse:

this is the *Dikê* of the gods who hold Olympus.

Thus, Hierocles follows Plato by failing to make any apparent distinction between *Dikê* and *Heimarmenê.* Can we conclude from this

---

the universe together with them, according to their [*scil.,* that of the individual soul's] merit (κατ' ἀξίαν). For from the midst of the sphere of the Sun, she makes her providence shine forth in all directions, and causes the dissemination of the distribution of its goods." Cf. also Proclus, *In Remp.,* vol. II, p. 144, 17–145, 19 Kroll, trans. based on Festugière, 1970, 3: pp. 89ff.: "The Judges' decision is a multiform sentence, divided as a function of the souls that share in it. For just as the Judges are particularized with regard to *Dikê,* which is the unique judicial Monad, which distributes to all according to their merit (κατ' ἀξίαν)—to gods, demons, immortal souls, mortal natures, and bodies—for nothing may fall outside of universal Justice—so souls too receive their judgement in divided ways, so that some souls obtain certain measures, others, other ones; whereas the Judges have the same views, and act in accordance with one mind, and fulfill the entire will of *Dikê* with regard to souls. For *Dikê* presides even over the gods, and she guards the value (ἀξία) of each thing in the Universe, and the demiurgic limit. This is why Orpheus [fr. 158 Kern] says that, when Zeus is preparing to assign to the Titans their encosmic lots, he is followed by *Dikê:* 'There followed him *Dikê,* the severely punishing helpmate.' For if she is a helpmate who punishes severely, if she shares the government of all things with the Demiurge of the All, she rules over the gods; she shares supervision with the demons; she passes judgement on souls, and in general this judgement extends to all of them; and we are told that, <according to> the sentence of the gods, the just souls are disseminated throughout in better resting-places, <the unjust in worse ones>. Besides this, the Judges pronounce their sentence in so far as they have judicial power over the souls, and thus they imitate universal Justice, attributing different measures to different souls, as we have said. And although the mind of the judges is one, the diversity of souls judged makes the judgments multiform: for different souls have different value (ἀξία), and the vote is different with regard to different souls.—Such, then, is the meaning of the arbitral sentence, which, since souls are many, assigns to them many judicial measures, and since they are various, assigns them varied measures, in accordance nevertheless with the one mind of the judges, which strains towards the same divine Monad, *Dikê.*" Cf. Hermias, *In Phaedr.,* p. 170, 11–14 Couvreur.

[369] Cf. also Proclus, *In Remp.,* vol. II, p. 144, 17ff. Kroll, cited in the preceding note.

that he saw no difference between these two entities from the point of view of their essence? Nothing could be less certain, as is shown by the example of the late Neoplatonists. In Proclus too, the functions of *Dikê* and of *Heimarmenê* appear to be strictly parallel—both of them embrace all the encosmic laws[370]—but there is nevertheless a difference in essence between the two.[371] For Proclus, whereas *Dikê* is an encosmic goddess, who is consequently situated within the class of rational souls, *Heimarmenê* is assimilated to the Nature of the All, which, although it is "a nature imbued with the divine," rather than merely plain Nature, corresponds to a lower ontological echelon than the hypostasis of rational souls.[372] This hierarchization of *Dikê* and of *Heimarmenê* perhaps corresponds to a final effort to reconcile all the disparate elements which, over time, made their entry into Platonism: thus, it may not yet have been carried out by the Neoplatonists in Hierocles' time. As in the

---

[370] For *Dikê*, cf. the text from Proclus' *Commentary on the Republic* cited above. n. 368; and for *Heimarmenê* cf. Proclus, *In Tim.*, vol. III, p. 274, 15 Diehl (trans. based on Festugière, 1966–1968, 5:151): "And if I must say what I believe, Plato places one after the other as the causes of order, these three, Adrasteia, Anankê, and Heimarmenê, the intellective, the hypercosmic, and the encosmic. After all, the Demiurge, as Orpheus says [fr. 162 K.], is brought up by Adrasteia, unites with Anankê, and engenders Heimarmenê. And just as Adrasteia is the one who embraces divine decrees, and who brings together all kinds of laws, so also Heimarmenê is the one who embraces all encosmic laws, which laws the Demiurge now engraves in the souls, so that they may conduct themselves in accordance with the Universe, and determine what is appropriate for them, in accordance with their various choices of lives."

[371] See the texts cited n. 368 and the following note. The Platonists distinguish between the function (ἐνέργεια) and the essence (οὐσία) of *Heimarmenê*; cf. Pseudo-Plutarch, *De fato,* 1, 568c; Calcidius, *In Tim.,* cap. 144–145, p. 182, 5–183, 6 Waszink.

[372] Cf. Proclus, *In Remp.,* vol. II, p. 356, 3–357, 27 Kroll (trans. based on Festugière, 1970, 3:313–314), especially p. 357, 10ff.: "That the rest is true, *viz., that [Heimarmenê]* is the Nature of the All, we may conclude from the following considerations. . . ."; and *In Tim.,* vol. III, p. 273, 19ff. Diehl (trans. based on Festugière, 1966–1968, 5:150): "But only Plato saw its true essence, he who called it Nature, but Nature dependent on the Demiurge. How, indeed, could the Demiurge 'reveal Nature,' unless he possessed its principle within himself? How can he 'state the fatal laws' (*heimarmenous nomous*) after having 'revealed the Nature of the All,' unless he has brought Nature into existence as the unique maintenance of these laws?" But since Nature is dependent on the Demiurge, she is "Nature imbued with the divine, filled with divine, intellective, and psychic illuminations. For to *Heimarmenê* there pertain both the order (τάξις) of the gods called *Moiregetes,* and the higher kinds; these too give powers which issue from themselves to the unique life of *Heimarmenê*" (= Proclus, *In Tim.,* vol. III, p. 272, 26ff. Diehl, trans. based on Festugière, 5:149). Thus, the functions of the recent gods—that is, of the encosmic gods like *Dikê*—are nevertheless somehow included within *Heimarmenê,* and Proclus admits that the "motley and multiform appearance" of *Heimarmenê* has always made its classification difficult: "This is why the Ancients . . . have been induced now to one opinion, now to another; some call it 'Goddess,' because of the way it is imbued with the divine; some 'Demon' because of the efficacy and diversity of its productive activity; others 'Intellect,' because a certain imparting of Intellect descends to its level; others 'Order,' in so far as it embraces invisibly all that is ordered by it" (Proclus, *In Tim.,* vol. III, p. 273, 13ff. Diehl, trans. based on Festugière, 5:150).

case of providence, the Hieroclean formulation we are interpreting does not furnish any information on the essence of the entities in question, nor does it necessarily mean that Hierocles really considered *Dikê* and *Heimarmenê* to be identical. We have already alluded several times to the extraordinary fluidity of vocabulary which their system allows the Neoplatonists. Since each ontological level is illuminated by the one superior to it, so that each hypostasis contains within itself, in the form of an image and in a weakened way, the functions of the one before it, it would be completely legitimate for a Neoplatonist occasionally to confuse *Dikê* and *Heimarmenê,* or to designate them by a single term, even if they are not situated on the same ontological level.

Through the internal logic of the Neoplatonic system, the notion of *Heimarmenê* underwent an evolution that was the converse of that of the notion of providence. Providence was placed ever higher in the ontological hierarchy, and *Heimarmenê* ever lower. To illustrate this development, we offer a brief account of a few elements going back to old Platonism. We know that Iamblichus identified *Heimarmenê* and nature,[373] and, since he clearly considered nature as the inseparable (ἀχώριστος) principle of the *cosmos,* which for him was probably situated on the level of the vegetative soul, we cannot doubt that, for him, too, *Heimarmenê* did not belong to the same ontological level as the rational souls. In Calcidius, Pseudo-Plutarch, and Nemesius we encounter a doctrine that identifies the essence of *Heimarmenê* with the World Soul.[374] If the distinction between the three classes of different essences

---

[373] Compare Iamblichus, *Letter to Macedonius,* in Stobaeus, *Eclog.,* II, 8, 43, p. 173, 5ff. Wachsmuth: "The substance of the soul, taken in itself, is an immaterial substance, incorporeal, utterly unengendered and incorruptible, having being and life by itself, being completely moved by itself, the principle of nature and of all movements. In so far as it is such, then, the soul also contains within itself a life that determines itself, and that does not depend on anything. And in so far as it communicates itself to engendered things, and submits to the overall movement of the universe, to this very degree it is subject to the power of *Heimarmenê,* and it is the slave of the necessities of nature," with Iamblichus, *Letter to Sopater,* in Stobaeus, *Eclog.,* I, 5, 18, p. 81, 8 Wachsmuth: "The essence of *Heimarmenê* is entirely within nature; I call nature the non-separated cause of the world, which envelops in a non-separated way the totality of the causes of generation." Cf. also Hermias, *In Phaedr.,* p. 200, 29 Couvreur.

[374] Calcidius, *In Tim.,* cap. 144–145, p. 182, 5–183, 6 Waszink: "Fatum ergo iuxta Platonem dupliciter intellegitur et dicitur, unum, cum substantiam eius animo intuemur, alterum, cum ex his quae agit et esse id et cuius modi vim habeat recognoscimur. . . . At vero in substantia positum fatum mundi anima est, tripertita, in aplanem sphaeram inque eam quae putatur erratica et in sublunarem tertiam." These three spheres are then assimilated to Atropos, Clotho, and Lachesis, the three Parcae. Cf. Pseudo-Plutarch, *De fato,* 1, 568c–d: *Heimarmenê* is said and is conceived in two ways: one is act, and the other essence . . ."; *ibid.,* 2, 568e: "*Heimarmenê,* taken in its essence, seems to be entirely the Soul of the world, divided into three parts: the sphere of fixed stars, that which is considered as errant, and the third, which is sublunary, situated around the earth." Cf. also Nemesius, *De natura hominis,* 38, (303), p. 109, 10–12 Morani. This inter-

(rational souls, irrational souls, and vegetative souls) was already known at this time, such an identification would mean that *Heimarmenê* was considered as being on the level of the rational souls. Otherwise, *Heimarmenê* would simply be the soul, which includes within the same essence different aspects of rational soul, irrational soul, and of nature or vegetative soul. We know, for instance, that Atticus and Alcinous did not yet recognize these differentiations. For Atticus, the World Soul and nature are one and the same, and he reproached Aristotle with having introduced a useless distinction between soul and nature.[375] A text like Plato, *Laws,* 892c2, which carries out a concrete assimilation between nature and soul, may have been at the base of such a conception. Alcinous, for his part, sees in nature one of the two aspects of the World Soul, the other one being its intelligence.[376] It is approximately this state of Platonic doctrine that is reflected by the *Chaldaean Oracles,* as was shown by Hans Lewy.[377] To *Hecate,* their personification of the World Soul, they attributed the following three functions: as *Psykhê,* she animates all of creation; as *Physis* (or *Anankê*), she keeps watch over the stars' regular movement; as *Heimarmenê,* she reigns over men, through the intermediary of her demons. Thus, we find the equation World Soul = nature = *Heimarmenê.*

As far as *Dikê* is concerned, taken either in its essence or in its relation with *Heimarmenê,* I do not know of any text, for the period going from Atticus-Alcinous as far as Iamblichus, that alludes to it. Yet it is interesting to note, with regard to the first generation of Platonists, that a fragment of Xenocrates attests the identification of the Soul of the All with *Dikê:* here, *Dikê,* as the Soul of the All, is opposed to Zeus, who reigns over the sky, whereas she reigns over the lower part of the world.[378]

---

pretation, especially with regard to the three Parcae, seems to be based on *Epinomis,* 982c1–5. Cf. also Cicero, *Acad.* I, 7, 29 (based on Antiochus of Ascalon; trans. H. Rackham in the Loeb Classical Library): ". . . and this force they say is the soul of the world, and it is also perfect in intelligence and wisdom, which they entitle God, and is a sort of 'providence,' knowing the things that fall within its province, governing especially the heavenly bodies, and then those things on earth that concern mankind, and this force they also sometimes call Necessity, because nothing can happen otherwise than has been ordained by it under a 'quasi-fated and unchangeable concatenation of everlasting order.'"

[375] Cf. Atticus, in Eusebius, *Praep. Evang.,* XV, 12, 1–4, p. 375, 7ff.

[376] Alcinous, *Didasc.,* 10, (164, 40–165, 4), p. 23 Whitakker.

[377] H. Lewy, 1978, chap. vi, 9: *The Cosmic Soul,* pp. 355–358.

[378] Xenocrates, fr. 15 Heinze (= Stobaeus, *Eclog.,* I, I, 29, p. 36, 6ff. Wachsmuth), cited with the correction of P. Boyancé, who capitalizes Δίκη: "Xenocrates the Chalcedonian, son of Agathenor: the monad and the dyad are gods; the first, being of masculine sex, occupies the rank of a father, reigning as a king in the heavens . . . but the second, being of feminine sex and occupying the rank of mother of the gods, he calls *Dikê;* she governs the part beneath the heavens, and for him she is the Soul of the world."

3. Some Negative Definitions of the Essence of "Heimarmenê"

All the definitions of *Heimarmenê* we find in Photius, as well as those we encounter in the commentary on the *Carmen aureum,* refer exclusively to its function, and they seek to specify the limits of the power it exercises on human beings. Nevertheless, we may find some indications on the essence of *Heimarmenê* in the series of negations our text contains, which define what it is not: It is neither the constraint of the Stoics, nor nature as defined by Alexander of Aphrodisias. What Hierocles implies by protesting in this way against Alexander's definition becomes more clear by means of a parallel text from Proclus:[379]

> [W]e say that we must not define *Heimarmenê* as the particular natural disposition (τὴν μερικὴν φύσιν), as some Peripatetics, like Alexander, will have it; for such a natural disposition is without strength and not eternal, whereas, in accordance with the common notions, we assume that the power of *Heimarmenê* is something omnipotent and fixed; nor as the order of the cosmic revolutions ... [f]or the cause of order is one thing, and order is something absolutely different ...

In his treatise *De fato,* Alexander[380] identified in principle fatality and nature—(εἰμαρμένη = φύσις). Yet this definition needed to be made more precise; that which happens "in conformity with nature" does not happen "necessarily" (ἐξ ἀνάγκης), for within what habitually occurs in conformity with nature we may encounter products that are "contrary to nature" (παρὰ φύσιν). Such products would thus also be "contrary to fatality" (παρὰ τὴν εἰμαρμένην). It must therefore be specified that the nature that is identical with fatality is each individual's own nature (οἰκεία φύσις): the cause of what happens most often to natural constitutions and dispositions as a consequence of their actions and of their modes of life, or the cause of what happens fatally in the development of individual life. Proclus translates this into Platonic language: μερικὴ φύσις (the nature peculiar to each one), and Hierocles identifies his nature with the "Platonic nature of bodies." For Hierocles, there could be no question of allowing this assimilation of fatality to individual nature, probably for the same reasons as Proclus: individual nature is too weak, and it is not eternal.

---

[379] Proclus, *In Tim.,* III, p. 272, 5f. Diehl, trans. based on that of Festugière, 1966–1968, 5:148.

[380] Alexander of Aphrodisias, *De fato,* 6, (169, 28–170, 9), p. 8f. Thillet. The texts have been collected by Festugière, 1966–1968, 5:148, n. 2.

Nor, for Hierocles, is *Heimarmenê* the so-called constraint of the Stoics.[381] In Calcidius, we find a rather well-developed refutation[382] of the Stoic thesis from a Platonic point of view. It may be supposed that this kind of argumentation still remained more or less the same in the Neoplatonists of the fifth and sixth centuries. Calcidius proceeds as follows. First, according to Plato, providence and *Heimarmenê* are not, as Chrysippus would have it, two names that denote the same reality, namely, the divine will. Instead, *Heimarmenê* is subordinate to providence. Second, Plato does not admit that all events are fixed in advance by providence and *Heimarmenê*. According to Plato, there are things that pertain to providence alone, others that result from *Heimarmenê*, others that depend on our free will or on chance (fortuna = τύχη); and still others that occur spontaneously (casu = αὐτομάτως).[383] What must be explained, therefore, is first of all the mutual implication of providence and *Heimarmenê*, and then the relation between *Heimarmenê* and free will. For it is the interplay of these complex relations that allows Platonic *Heimarmenê* no longer to possess the supposedly constraining character of Stoic *Heimarmenê*.

4. The Relations Between Providence and Heimarmenê

The last phrase from the text by Hierocles on which we are now commenting[384] provides us with a succinct account of these relations, which we must elaborate:

> *Heimarmenê* is god's justice-dealing activity, concerning those things that occur in accordance with the decree of providence, and it corrects the things that are up to us in order and sequence, with regard to the freely-chosen hypotheses of our voluntary acts.

Here and in the preceding phrase, *Heimarmenê* appears as a function subordinate to providence. The doctrine according to which *Heimarmenê* is a part of providence, that the former is contained within the lat-

---

[381] The Neoplatonists' anti-Stoic polemic attributes to Stoicism the doctrine according to which fatality is absolutely constraining, and therefore free will cannot exist. In fact, however, as is shown by the texts from Chrysippus cited by Aulus Gellius (*Noctes Atticae,* VII [VI], 1 and 2), and by Cicero (*De fato,* XVIII, 41), the Stoics tried to leave the field open for man's free will just as much as the Neoplatonists. On this point, cf. B. Inwood, 1985, pp. 66–91.

[382] Calcidius, *In Tim.,* cap. 144, p. 183, 6 Waszink.

[383] On the place of contingence, cf. below, pp. 114–118.

[384] Cf. the end of the text cited p. 101 = Hierocles, in Photius, *Library,* cod. 251, p. 461b28–31 Bekker, vol. vii, p. 192 Henry.

ter, and that everything that takes place through *Heimarmenê* has providence as its first cause, is common to Hierocles and all the other Neoplatonists.[385] It is hard to say when this doctrine originated. It seems to be sketched in the *Chaldaean Oracles,* and appears for the first time, so far as I know, in Pseudo-Plutarch.[386] Since *Heimarmenê* is included by providence, Hierocles can also speak, as Plotinus had already done, of two providences, the second of which exerts its influence upon the lower domain.[387] The former is pure providence, the latter is none other than *Heimarmenê,* or providence that exerts its influence in matter (πρόνοια ἔνυλος), and that utilizes chance (τύχη) and opportunity (καιρός).[388] The function of the former is essentially to distribute goods and to conserve the properties appropriate to the nature of each individual, whereas the latter corrects the dispositions that are contrary

[385] Hierocles, in Photius, *Library,* cod. 251, p. 462b30ff. Bekker, vol. VII, p. 195 Henry: "so that *Heimarmenê* is a part of total providence, which part is adapted to the souls of men, in order to judge them." Cf. Proclus, *In Tim.,* III, p. 273, 9–12 Diehl; *De prov.,* 3, 3ff., pp. 110ff. Boese: "Providentiam et fatum non hac differre qua scripsisti, hoc quidem connexam consequentiam, hanc autem necessitate huius causam, sed ambo quidem causas mundi et eorum que in mundo fiunt esse, preexistere autem providentiam fato, et omnia quidem quecumque fiunt secundum fatum multo prius a providentia fieri; contrarium autem non iam verum esse: summa enim totorum a providentia recta esse diviniora fato." Cf. Boethius, *Consol. philosoph.,* IV, prose 6, 14: "Quo fit, ut omnia, quae fato subsunt, providentiae quoque subiecta sint, cui ipsum etiam subiacet fatum. . . ." Cf. Calcidius, *In Tim.,* cap. 143, p. 181, 20ff. Waszink: "Igitur iuxta Platonem praecedit providentia, sequitur fatum; ait enim *deum post mundi constitutionem divisisse animas stellarum numero pares singulasque singulis comparasse universique mundi monstrasse naturam atque universam fatorum seriem revelasse.* Horum enim quae prima sunt providentiam indicant, secunda leges fatales, proptereaque iuxta Platonem praenascitur providentia; ideoque fatum quidem dicimus ex providentia fore, non tamen providentiam ex fato." Cf. Pseudo-Plutarch, *De fato,* 9, 573b: "And *Heimarmenê* acts entirely according to providence, but providence does not, by any means, act according to *Heimarmenê.*" Cf. Iamblichus, *Letter to Macedonius,* in Stobaeus, *Eclog.,* II, 8, 45, p. 174, 1ff. Wachsmuth: "Secondary causes are attached to antecedent causes, and the multitude found within generation, to essence, which is undivided; and in this way all that belongs to *Heimarmenê* is linked to antecedent providence. As far as its essence is concerned, *Heimarmenê* is therefore interwoven (ἐπιπλέκεται) with providence, and *Heimarmenê* exists by virtue of the fact that providence exists, and it exists through it and in conjunction with it." Cf. Olympiodorus, *In Gorg.,* p. 198, 9 Westerink: ". . . *Heimarmenê* depends on providence."

[386] On *Heimarmenê* in the *Chaldaean Oracles,* cf. O. Geudtner, 1971, pp. 30–34. For Pseudo-Plutarch, cf. the citation in the preceding note.

[387] Cf. *Enn.,* III, 3, 4, 11ff: "And these first principles are the providence above, the other providence derives from the one above, like a second rational order linked to the first, and it is from both that the whole complex, and the whole of providence, derive."

[388] Hierocles, in Photius, *Library,* cod. 251, p. 464a16ff. Bekker, vol. VII, p. 199 Henry. On πρόνοια ἔνυλος cf. Sallustios, *De diis et mundo,* 9, 4, p. 13ff. Rochefort: ". . . and the incorporeal providence of the gods towards bodies and souls is as I have said. But corporeal providence, which resides in bodies, is different from the first, and is called 'Heimarmenê,' because of the fact that the sequence of events (εἱρμός) appears more evidently in bodies."

to nature, and corrects our faults. The distinction between a pure providence and a justice-dealing providence exerting its influence within matter shows us that Hierocles, like Proclus, attributes to providence jurisdiction over the entirety of intelligible and sensible things, whereas the realm of *Heimarmenê* is limited to sensible things.[389] And since *Heimarmenê* is included within providence, it is also possible to speak only of one single providence. Thus, in his treatise *De decem dubitationibus*, Proclus distinguishes only rarely between providence and *Heimarmenê*, but in general deals with both under the name of providence, whereas in the treatise *De providentia et fato*, he always distinguishes *Heimarmenê* from providence, and subordinates the former to the latter. Hierocles, at the same time as he strongly emphasizes this intimate link between providence and *Heimarmenê*, speaks quite often of a providential *Heimarmenê* (προνοητικὴ εἱμαρμένη).[390]

According to another point of view, that of participation, Proclus is even aware of more than two providences, at different ontological levels. This is another necessary consequence of the Neoplatonic system. Starting from original providence, which functions as a cause, there are several providences that derive from this cause, and are placed successively each on a level lower than the preceding one. Among others, there is the providence of the encosmic gods, and the providence of the demons. At the last level come human souls, which are still able to exercise a certain providence, albeit very limited, upon themselves, animals, and plants.[391] Original providence makes beings on the immediately lower level participate in it, and it is primarily to them that its activity extends; yet through mediation it extends down to the last degree. As far as human souls are concerned, it is the demons that exercise the providence closest to them; because it exerts its influence

---

[389] Cf. the quotation from Sallustios in the preceding note. Cf. Proclus, *De prov.*, 14, 1ff., p. 121 Boese: "You must therefore recognize two kinds, one which is intelligible, and the other sensible, and for these two kinds there are two realms: one above, which belongs to providence, and extends over intelligible things and sensible things; and one below, which extends over sensible things." The same distinction between providence and *Heimarmenê*, which rules over the bodies and the lives that are indissolubly linked to it, is at the origin of Simplicius' exposition on the evils of this world as elements of divine therapy (*In Ench. Epict.*, XIV 59–272 Hadot [1996] = XIV 75–348 Hadot [2001a]).

[390] Cf., for instance, Hierocles, in Photius, *Library*, cod. 251, p. 464a41 Bekker, vol. VII, p. 200 Henry; p. 465a19ff. Bekker, vol. VII, p. 202 Henry; p. 465b36ff. Bekker, vol. VII, p. 204 Henry. Boethius expresses the essential unity of providence and of *Heimarmenê* as follows: "It is she [*sc.* divine intelligence], who, having retired into the citadel of her simplicity, assigns a multiform order to phenomena. When we consider this order from the point of view of the very purity of the divine intelligence, we call it providence, but with regard to the facts to which it gives rise and which it regulates, the Ancients call it *Heimarmenê* [*fatum*]" (= *Consol. philosoph.*, IV, prose 6, 8).

[391] On the providence of gods and demons, cf. Proclus, *De decem dubit.*, 16, 3ff. (p. 28f. Boese); for human providence, cf. 15, 14; 18, 1–22 (pp. 27; 33 Boese).

within matter, this providence is a part of *Heimarmenê*.[392] Thus, the Neoplatonists can equally well speak of one unique providence, or of several partial providences, as they can of providence and of *Heimarmenê*. In all three cases, these are three particular aspects of the same system, which, rather than excluding one another, mutually imply one another.[393]

Hierocles calls *Heimarmenê* "the justice-dealing activity of god." In Neoplatonists like Simplicius, who, as a result of the progressive diversification of hypostases, distinguish between *Dikê* and *Heimarmenê*, it may happen that it is *Dikê* who is called "the punitive form of divine justice-dealing activity."[394] *Dikê* thus seems to be intercalated between providence and *Heimarmenê*. Yet we must always remember that *Dikê* and *Heimarmenê* are mere aspects of providence, which may, according to the laws inherent in the Neoplatonic system, sometimes be confused with providence, and sometimes be distinguished from it,

---

[392] Cf. Hierocles, in Photius, *Library,* cod. 251, p. 462a29ff. Bekker, vol. VII, p. 194 Henry.

[393] The definition of the relations of *Heimarmenê* with providence or providences has caused difficulties right from the beginning: cf. the text from Proclus cited p. 106, n. 372, 3rd quotation. Cf. also the treatise *De fato* by the Pseudo-Plutarch. After enumerating three providences (572f–573a), that of the first god, who corresponds to the demiurge of the *Timaeus,* that of the secondary astral gods, and that of the demons, he speaks of the place occupied by *Heimarmenê,* which is, for him, the Soul of the All, with regard to these three providences: the first providence engenders *Heimarmenê* and somehow includes it within itself; the second providence was co-engendered with *Heimarmenê,* and completely coincides with it; the third was engendered after *Heimarmenê,* and is included within it in the same way as τύχη and what is ἐφ' ἡμῖν. A little further on, however, he admits that it would be even more clear if we also said that the second providence is included within *Heimarmenê,* or else, even more briefly, that everything that has become is included within *Heimarmenê,* if the essence of *Heimarmenê* has been correctly defined by saying that it is the Soul of the All (*De fato,* 574b–d; 568e). For Pseudo-Plutarch, the difference between the second and third providences and *Heimarmenê* consists essentially in the fact that these providences are primarily distributive of goods, whereas *Heimarmenê,* like Philo's *Dikê* (cf. n. 363), is the cause of sanctions that are experienced as evils (*De fato,* 9, 573f). Ultimately, however, these are only two aspects of one and the same thing, the unity of which is imposed by the definition of *Heimarmenê* as the Soul of the All.

[394] Following Proclus, Simplicius distinguishes between *Pronoia, Dikê,* and *Heimarmenê*. This is clear from the following considerations. On the one hand, Simplicius speaks of the "medical art" of providence (*In Ench. Epict.,* XIV 191–193 Hadot [1996] = XIV 243–245 Hadot [2001a]) or of "the god's medical art" (XIV 269–273 [1996] = XIV 345ff. [2001a]) which aims to cure sick souls—that is, souls that have become bad—by punishments. On the other hand, he designates *Dikê* or "divine *Dikê*" as she who cures souls of evil (cf. Plato, *Gorgias,* 478d6–7) and as she who produces the punitive form of justice-dealing action (XXXV 451; 652f.; 690–693 Hadot [1996]). Thus we can see that it is *Dikê* who applies the medical art of providence (cf. Proclus, *De decem dubit.,* 51, 19ff., p. 81 Boese, cited p. 119, n. 411, and Damascius, *Vita Isidori,* 189 p. 258, 4–9 Zintzen = fr. 126A Athanassiadi). Finally, Simplicius distinguishes *Dikê* from *Heimarmenê* by giving the latter a function that is even more purely executive, and almost mechanical (*In Ench. Epict.,* I 384–387; 391–394 Hadot [1996] = I 485–491; 494–499 Hadot [2001a]).

according to a hierarchical order. This has no effect upon the substance of the question.

A bit further on, Hierocles defines *Heimarmenê* as the divine will (θεία βούλησις), the law of god's justice (νόμος τῆς τοῦ θεοῦ δίκης), and elsewhere as divine judgement (κρίσις θεία).[395] It is simultaneously the law decreed by the demiurge and the executive of this law. It was an old habit of the Platonists to call fatality a law, the demiurge-*Noûs* the legislator. We find parallel expressions in pseudo-Plutarch, Porphyry, and Calcidius.[396] Ultimately, they are based on *Timaeus*, 41c2, where the demiurge announces the "fatal laws" (νόμους τοὺς εἱμαρμένους) to the souls.

5. Heimarmenê, *Contingency, Free Will*

The character of this law is hypothetical, as is the case for every law.[397] It only fixes general rules of the following kind: "If you do this, you will

---

[395] Hierocles calls *Heimarmenê* θεία βούλησις καὶ νόμος τῆς τοῦ θεοῦ δίκης (Photius, *Library,* cod. 251, p. 462b2ff. Bekker, vol. VII, p. 194 Henry), θεία κρίσις (p. 465b30 Bekker, vol. VII, p. 204 Henry; *In Carmen aur.,* XI, p. 44, 18 Köhler), κρίσις θεοῦ (*In Carmen aureum,* X, p. 45, 8–9 Köhler); κρίσις προνοίας (*In Carmen aureum,* XI, p. 51, 12 Köhler and in Photius, *Library,* cod. 251, p. 463a37 Bekker, vol. VII, p. 197 Henry). As I have said, it is not rare for the Neoplatonists to distinguish, for instance, the activities of the demiurge or the first god by attributing to them an independent existence. Thus Calcidius says of providence, which for him is the *Noûs,* that it is the will of the supreme god (cf. the quotation p. 102 n. 354). Cf. also Pseudo-Plutarch, *De fato,* 9, 572f: "For the highest and primary providence is the thought or the will of the first god . . ." Stoicism had tried to understand the multitude of traditional Greek gods as different aspects of one and the same god; a tendency that is also reflected in the pseudo-Aristotelian *De mundo,* where the one god Zeus is simultaneously *Anankê, Heimarmenê, Nemesis, Adrasteia,* etc. (401b8–22). With Neoplatonism, we again witness a development in the direction of a more and more pronounced diversification. Since, however, all these Neoplatonic divinities are emanations of a supreme entity, Stoic monism is, in a sense, maintained.

[396] For instance, Porphyry, *On What Depends on Us,* in Stobaeus, *Eclog.,* II, 8, 42, p. 169, 3ff. Wachsmuth = fr. 271, 20–22 Smith: "He chooses to believe that *Heimarmenê* is such; that is, that it resembles the prescriptions of the laws, since it is itself a law. . . ." Pseudo-Plutarch, *De fato,* 1, 568d–e: "If someone wished to describe these things, by transposing them into more customary terms, he would say, in the style of the *Phaedrus,* that *Heimarmenê* is an inviolable divine reason, resulting from a cause without hindrances, and, in the style of the *Timaeus,* that it is a law in conformity with the nature of the All, according to which all that happens unfolds." Calcidius, *In Tim.,* cap. 177, p. 206, 1–2; cap. 180, p. 208, 14–15; cap. 189, p. 213, 7 Waszink. For the demiurge-intellect called νομοθέτης: Plotinus, *Enn.,* V, 9, 5, 28; Numenius, fr. 13 des Places; Hierocles, *In Carmen aureum,* XI, p. 48, 9 Köhler: ὁ θεὸς νομοθέτης ὢν ἅμα καὶ δικαστής. . . . Calcidius, *In Tim.,* cap. 188, p. 212, 24 Waszink.

[397] Cf. also I. Hadot, 2001, the Appendix on "La destinée des âmes: Fatalité (εἱμαρμένη), Providence (πρόνοια), pouvoir de détermination ou libre arbitre (τὸ ἐφ' ἡμῖν, τὸ αὐτεξούσιον)," pp. CXXIX–CLXII.

have such-and-such a punishment or reward," but it does not order "Do this!" and it is constraining only with regard to the consequences of our voluntary actions.[398] It is up to our free will to make a choice; however, the consequences of this choice no longer belong to our free will, but will be imposed upon us. The choice we have made is thus the preliminary condition for the functioning of *Heimarmenê*. It precedes the necessary sequence of inevitable consequences that follows our choice, and in which *Heimarmenê* consists. This is the meaning of the brief phrase from Hierocles we cited earlier: "It corrects what we do, as a function of the freely-chosen hypotheses which are our acts." In the *De fato* of Pseudo-Plutarch, we find a rather elaborate exposition of the doctrine that *Heimarmenê* functions ἐξ ὑποθέσεως.[399]

The origin of the distinction between absolute necessity, which applies only to eternal beings, and a conditional necessity (ἐξ ὑποθέσεως), which exercises its influence upon all the beings subject to becoming, goes back to Aristotle.[400] When applied to *Heimarmenê*, this formulation does not seem to be attested in the later Neoplatonists; yet with regard to its substance, this doctrine is omnipresent in them, as the rest of our investigation will show.

Fatality does not strike mankind blindly, but acts in accordance with merit. It is simultaneously the result of man's free choice and of the providence of the demiurge, so that, as Hierocles says, once we have freely chosen what we want,[401] we must often, as a consequence of this choice, undergo what we do not want. In Proclus, we find the same interweaving between providence, *Heimarmenê*, and man's free will, ob-

---

[398] The comparison of *Heimarmenê* with civil law is found in Porphyry, *On What Depends on Us*, in Stobaeus, *Eclog.*, II, 8, 42, p. 169, 3–10 Wachsmuth, and Pseudo-Plutarch, *De fato*, 4, 569d. Cf. also Hierocles, *In Carmen aureum*, XI, p. 45, 25ff. Köhler.

[399] Pseudo-Plutarch, *De fato*, 4–5, especially 5, 570a: "After this, we must learn what the 'by hypothesis' is, and that *Heimarmenê* is also of this nature. We have called 'by hypothesis' that which is not established in itself, but comes close to (πρός) something else which is truly taken as a hypothesis, all which things signify consecution (ἀκολουθίαν)." In the Greek text, I adopt πρός, the reading of the manuscripts, against πως, which is a conjecture by Wyttenbach, and I read ὑποθέντι instead of ὑποτεθέν. Cf. also Calcidius, *In Tim.*, cap. 150, p. 186, 13–22 Waszink; Nemesius, chap. 38, and on these three texts, the commentary by J. Den Boeft, 1970, pp. 25–27. Cf. Hierocles, in Photius, *Library*, cod. 251, p. 462b26ff. Bekker, vol. VII, p. 195 Henry, and p. 464a23 Bekker, vol. VII, p. 199 Henry: ἐξ ὑποθέσεως τῆς τῶν προβεβιωμένων ἀξίας (cf. below, p. 122, n. 427).

[400] Cf. Aristotle, *De part. animal.*, 639b20–23.

[401] Hierocles, in Photius, *Library*, cod. 251, 463b4 Bekker, vol. VII, p. 197 Henry: "And that is *Heimarmenê*, which leads us now in one direction, now in another: an interweaving and meeting of free human choice and divine judgment, so that, once we have chosen what we want in virtue of the freedom of our choice, we often undergo what we do not want, because of the judgment which inevitably follows."

tained thanks to a learned combination of several texts from Plato, as he shows us clearly.[402] Punishments, which are the consequence of the actions or intentions which it was in our power to commit or not to commit, are themselves situated within the domain of things that are not in our power, like the body and external possessions.[403] They are thus manifested as illnesses, or as the loss of possessions, or in other forms. For we must recall[404] that *Heimarmenê* exercises its influence within matter, and has no power over the rational soul itself,[405] by

[402] Cf. Proclus, *In Rem. publ.*, II, p. 357, 28ff. Kroll, trans. based on that by Festugière, 1970, 3:315: "That these two—free will and *Heimarmenê*—are mutually coordinated, and that their interweaving is due to Providence, you could grasp from what has been said in the tenth book of the *Laws* (904a6–d3). To demonstrate that neither *Heimarmenê* nor Providence constrains free will, Plato says the following—I shall summarize the passage: '*When our King had seen that all our actions proceed from a soul, and that they contain a great deal of virtue and a great deal of vice*'—for this is the *proprium* of free will—'*he thought up a disposition in which each part was placed in such a way that it would bring about the triumph of virtue and defeat of vice*'—for this is the *proprium* of Providence, to utilise all things, as far as possible, with a view to the good— . . . '*everything was thus thought up with a view to this: which place shall fall to the share of the being who becomes qualified in a given way? As far as the production of a given quality is concerned, he left the causes to the will of each one of us: for it is according to how he desires and according to the state of his soul that each one of us, on almost every occasion, goes in a specific direction and becomes such-and-such.*' By these words, Plato saves above all the soul's freedom of choice and free will—for the quality of life depends on our will—since, in this passage, he called the faculty of choice 'will' (904c1). Since free will is such, hear how he coordinates it with *Heimarmenê*: '*Thus, all beings that participate in a soul change, since they possess within themselves the cause of their change*'—once again, he said this because of free will—; '*and*,' he adds, '*while changing, each of us is borne along in conformity with the order and the law of Heimarmenê.*' He says, moreover, how each one is borne along, and that he goes to the place which is due to him: '*If they change only slightly in their moral character, then their horizontal movement in space is less; if they have degenerated more seriously, they are swept into the abyss and the places called 'below,' all that is called by the name of Hades and other such names, which are so greatly feared.*' In this way, then, we do not escape *Heimarmenê*, but we are borne along in conformity with its laws, by the changes which take place in our lives—of which changes moreover, we remain the masters—towards ever different places, either more holy or more punitive, or again intermediate between the two."

[403] Hierocles, in Photius, *Library*, cod. 251, p. 465a20ff. Bekker, vol. VII, p. 202 Henry: "[I]t [*scil.* providential *Heimarmenê*] is what educates us in that which depends on us, thanks to trials that do not depend on us"; and p. 465b30ff. Bekker, vol. VII, p. 204 Henry: ". . . *Heimarmenê* . . . which is the judgement of God in order to give us, in what does not depend on us, what we deserve in exchange for what depends on us." Cf. Simplicius, *In Ench. Epict.*, XIV 143–148 Hadot (1996) = XIV 182–188 Hadot (2001a).

[404] Cf. above, pp. 111ff.

[405] For Iamblichus, cf. *De myst.*, VIII, 6 (269, 1), p. 199 des Places, and the quotation from the *Letter to Macedonius*, p. 107, n. 373. Cf. Proclus, *De prov.*, 20, 1ff., p. 129 Boese: "<in sum, then, let us say that> the rational and intellectual soul, if it is moved in any way in conformity with nature, becomes external to bodies and sensations, <so that> it necessarily possesses an essence separated from these things. . . . [I]t is obvious that, since it acts according to nature, it is too excellent to be led by *Heimarmenê*." The thesis according to which the rational soul is subject to *Heimarmenê* only when it is too closely united to the body seems already to be present in the *Chaldaean Oracles*; cf. H. Lewy, 1978, p. 265, n. 21; F. W. Cremer, 1969, 83.

which man is defined,[406] and which, by essence, is moved by itself (αὐτοκίνητος). It exercises power on the soul only if the latter is too closely united to matter; that is, if it allows itself to sympathize with the body and thus, in a way, becomes moved by something else (ἑτεροκίνητος).[407] This is an essential doctrinal element, which we find in all the late Neoplatonists.

> We suffer in our bodies and in external things, says Hierocles, what has been decreed by that justice that watches over us. For it is the aggravation and the respite that occur in the things around us,[408] as well as their multiple modifications, that instruct the soul's free will to act in a healthy manner, which happens fairly quickly if it greets the trials which happen to it with generosity. If, however, its behavior in the face of these trials is impudent and senseless, this will happen only after numerous and long detours. For it is then that it

---

[406] Cf. Hierocles, *In Carmen aureum*, XIII, p. 60, 10–13 Köhler: "You were the rational soul; you will therefore, if you think carefully about it, not have to put up with what causes damage to you, you who are a rational essence. For you *are* the rational soul, whereas the body *is yours*, and external things belong only to the body." This is clearly a reminiscence of Plato's *First Alcibiades* (131b–c), but, like Proclus, Hermias, Olympiodorus, Simplicius, and Damascius, Hierocles too understands the "soul" of the Platonic text in the sense of "rational" soul. For Hermias, cf. above, p. 35, n. 125. Cf. Olympiodorus, *In Alcib.*, 4, 6–14, p. 7 and 203, 20ff., p. 128 Westerink; *In Gorg.*, p. 6, 1–6 Westerink, etc.; Simplicius, *In Ench. Epict.*, I 26ff. Hadot (1996) = I 35 Hadot (2001a), etc.

[407] In what remains of Hierocles, we do not find an exposition of the difference between the essence that moves itself (αὐτοκίνητος οὐσία) and things that are moved by another (ἑτεροκίνητα). In the moral context of his commentary on the *Carmen aureum*, Hierocles speaks several times of man's "free choice moved by itself" (αὐτοκίνητος προαίρεσις); for instance X, p. 41, 12ff. Köhler: "How indeed, if there is a providence and if our soul, which on the one hand is indestructible by essence, and which on the other hand tends by a free choice moved by itself towards virtue or towards vice …", and he speaks of the αὐτοκίνητος διάθεσις at Photius, *Library*, cod. 251, p. 463b17–24 Bekker, vol. VII, p. 198 Henry. These texts show that he too was clearly aware of this distinction. It is therefore quite legitimate, in order to explain the limits of the power of *Heimarmenê*, to quote two texts from Proclus that are based on these distinctions: Proclus, *De prov.*, 10, 12ff., p. 117 Boese: "<It is obvious that> the things that are … woven together by *Heimarmenê* are moved by something else, and are corporiform …", and 13, 10ff., p. 121 Boese: "And, in turn, the things that fall under providence do not all have need of *Heimarmenê* as well, but the intelligibles transcend *Heimarmenê* …" Cf. the long exposition by Simplicius, *In Ench. Epict.*, XIV 59–204 Hadot (1996) = XIV 75–260 Hadot (2001a). Cf. also Proclus, *De prov.*, 22, 1ff., p. 130 Boese: "Hanc igitur et talem preiaciens vitam anima non erit eorum que ducuntur a fato. Si autem velit corpora plasmare et corporalibus bonis vocatis intendat et honores persequatur et potentatus et divitias, idem patitur vinculato philosopho et in navem ingresso: et enim iste servit moventibus navem ventis, et si conculcet aliquis nautarum ipsum et iniurietur aliquis vinculantium. Valere igitur dicentes hiis ad que alligamur, et virtutis valorem speculabimur et fatum, non in nos aliquid operans, sed in ea que circa nos (οὐκ εἰς ἡμᾶς τι δρῶσαν, ἀλλ᾽ εἰς τὰ περὶ ἡμᾶς)." Cf. also Boethius, *Consol. Philosoph.* IV, prose 6, 14–17.

[408] τὰ περὶ ἡμᾶς; cf. the last quotation from Proclus in the preceding note.

incurs punishments for its thoughtlessness; nevertheless, it is still led, through its sufferings, towards its duty.[409]

As Hierocles explains at length in his commentary on verses 67–69 of the *Carmen aureum,* the soul's duty is clearly to remember its origin and its essence, and to extricate itself from all sympathy with material things; that is, with its body and with external possessions.[410] Providence, *Dikê,* or *Heimarmenê* thus act like a doctor toward his patients: just as the latter cures bodies by the administration of medical treatments and remedies, so *Heimarmenê* cures souls by appropriate measures. The use of this analogy is once again common to all the Neoplatonists.[411]

6. *The Relations Between* Heimarmenê *and Demons*

In the previous section, we have seen Hierocles use the comparison of *Heimarmenê* to a doctor and his use of medical science. He now adds a third term to his analogy, that of judges:

> The judgment of the judges who keep watch over us resembles medical science.[412]

He thus assimilates these judges to *Heimarmenê.* Other texts from the summary by Photius will reveal to us who these judges are.

> "We must," says Hierocles, "account for our acts down here to the beings who have been allotted the middle domain, for they are our

---

[409] Hierocles, in Photius, *Library,* cod. 251, p. 463a19–31 Bekker, vol. VII, p. 196f. Henry.

[410] Cf. Simplicius, *In Ench. Epict.,* XIV 188ff. Hadot (1996) = XIV 239ff. Hadot (2001a). Cf. also Hierocles, *In Carmen aureum,* X, p. 36, 24ff. Köhler: "Down here below, then, what depends on us has a very great power, which consists in the possibility of judging well of what does not depend on us, and thus not to destroy the virtue of self-determination by attachment to what does not depend on us."

[411] Cf. Hierocles, in Photius, *Library,* cod. 251, p. 464a20ff. Bekker, vol. VII, p. 199 Henry: "[F]or it is not according to a pre-established design that divine judgment brings misfortune to some of us, and to others attributes happiness, but it bases itself on the merits of our previous life, since the judgment of the judges who keep watch over us resembles medical science, which takes charge of those who have fallen ill by their own fault, and which, at the appropriate moment, prescribes everything that will be advantageous to those who must be treated." Cf. Hierocles, *In Carmen aureum,* XIV, p. 65, 16ff. Köhler. Cf. Proclus, *De decem dubit.,* 51, 19ff., p. 81 Boese: "It is obvious that the cure of souls that is called 'justice' (δίκη) is the most artistic of all medical arts." Cf. Plato, *Gorgias,* 478d6–7: "Justice becomes the art of curing evil." Cf. Simplicius, *In Ench. Epict.,* the references cited above, n. 394.

[412] Cf. preceding note.

guardians and they watch over us. All their activity with regard to us is called *Heimarmenê,* and it arranges our affairs according to the laws of justice."[413]

That the "beings who have been allotted the middle domain" are the demons, is confirmed by the following text:[414]

> "The soul," says Hierocles, "whose impulse towards any choice whatsoever is not without incurring sanctions, is judged worthy of being guided by the superior kind that is closest to it, and it always finds the justice, the purification, or the punishment that its disposition deserves. The choice depends on it, but what results from this choice is determined by the judgment of providence, which sanctions the soul's dispositions according to its merits. And thus it is said that we choose, and at the same time obtain by lot, one and the same form of life."

The "superior kind" closest to the rational human soul is thus the intermediate class of souls—that is, the class of demons—which, in accordance with a long tradition, is closely associated with *Heimarmenê.*[415] The last phrase of the second quotation alludes to the famous edict of Lachesis in the myth of Er, which announces the drawing of lots and the choices of forms of life and of their demons for the souls destined for a new incorporation:

> Ephemeral souls! This is the beginning of another death-bearing cycle for the mortal race. No demon shall obtain you by lot, but you shall choose a demon. Let he who has drawn the first lot be the first to choose a form of life, to which he will be linked by necessity. Virtue has no master; and it is by honoring or failing to honor it to a greater or lesser degree that each shall have his share of it. Responsibility falls upon him who chooses; but god is not responsible.[416]

A bit further on, Plato adds:[417]

> In any case, when all the souls had chosen their form of life, maintaining the rank that they had drawn by lot, they advanced in order

[413] Hierocles, in Photius, *Library,* cod. 251, p. 462a29ff. Bekker, vol. VII, p. 194 Henry.
[414] Hierocles, in Photius, *Library,* cod. 251, p. 463a32ff. Bekker, vol. VII, p. 197 Henry.
[415] Cf. above, p. 112 and n. 391.
[416] Plato, *Republic,* X, 617d6ff.
[417] *Ibid.,* X, 620d6ff. 417.

before Lachesis; she gave to each one as a companion the demon he
had chosen, as guardian of his form of life, and fulfiller of the things
that have been chosen.

As we have seen,[418] Hierocles clearly alludes to these guardian
demons. In the following text, however, Hierocles' formulations are
even closer to the text of Plato:

> As for us, it is by the verdict of our judges the demons, that we ob-
> tain by lot, in accordance with what we have deserved in the course
> of our previous existences, a life in which everything is included:
> race, city, father, mother, moment of birth, bodily qualities, upsets
> and blows of fortune that are appropriate to the life [which one has
> chosen][419], mode and time of our death; and the guardian of all these
> things and fulfiller is the demon who has obtained us by lot.[420]

In this last text, the "demon chosen by the soul" mentioned in the
myth of Er is assimilated to the "demon who has obtained us by lot"
alluded to in the *Phaedo*.[421] Plotinus had already tried to reconcile these
two contradictory texts,[422] whereas Proclus, probably basing himself on
them, had distinguished two groups of demons who watch over souls.[423]

---

[418] Cf. the text cited pp. 118–119, and the reference at n. 411–412.

[419] These are the circumstances that are proper to the form of life one has chosen. If,
for instance, one chooses prior to incarnation the life of a soldier, one must live a soldier's life and put up with all that characterizes it: cf. Porphyry, fr. 270 Smith.

[420] Hierocles, in Photius, *Library,* cod. 251, p. 466a21ff. Bekker, vol. VII, p. 205
Henry.

[421] Compare Hierocles in Photius, *Library,* p. 466a26ff. Bekker, vol. VII, p. 205
Henry: "And the demon who has been allotted to us is the guardian and executor of all
these things", with Plato, *Republic,* X, 620d8ff.: "Lachesis gave to each person the demon he had chosen, so that it should serve as a guardian in life, and make him fulfill the
destiny he had chosen"; and Plato, *Phaedo,* 107d5ff.: "It is also said that each person's
demon, who has received a given living individual by lot, takes on the responsibility of
leading him, once he has died, to a certain place...."

[422] Cf. Plotinus' treatise entitled *"On the Demon Who Has Received Us by Lot"*
(= *Enn.,* III, 4).

[423] Cf. Proclus, *In Rem. publ.,* vol. II, p. 271, 13 Kroll, trans. based on that by Festugière, 1970, 3:229ff.: ". . . For at the same time as it chooses a life, the soul is at any
rate united with an overseer of that life. For in the ordered whole of all things there is
nothing that is without a principle, <not> life nor allotment nor ascent nor descent; but
each thing has been given over to its proper authorities. And as Plato himself said in the
Laws (X, 903b), the providence of the All reaches the utmost division, subdividing itself and generating providences from one another: the more particular from the more
universal, and the more demonic from the more divine. Thus, there are also demonic
overseers of lives linked to generation, who act as guardians of the souls who live their
lives in these ways. They are accustomed to call them 'angelic,' contrasting them with

The attribution of the function of judges to the demons is based on the myth of the *Gorgias*. As is well known, this myth is centered around the *post-mortem* judgment of souls, and the need for every soul to undergo punishments for the faults it has committed during life on earth. The fundamental Neoplatonic law, also stated by Hierocles,[424] according to which each class of beings produces the class of beings which comes immediately after it in the hierarchy, and exercises providence over it, brings it about that the function of judges with regard to us falls to the lot of the class of demons, which is the closest class of souls, situated immediately above human souls.

In the Neoplatonic interpretation of the myth of Er, we always encounter the same learned combination and reconciliation of Providence–*Heimarmenê* with human free will that Hierocles formulated in his definition of *Heimarmenê*, and that inspires the three passages mentioned concerning the role of demons with regard to us. The following text by Proclus gives us an excellent example:[425]

> The lot is thus twofold, one prior to choice, and the other posterior. One is the sum total of the types of existence, and of this lot each type is a part, and the other is the sum total of the accidental elements which the Cosmos assigns as direct consequences to a given type. Each of these two lots comes from the All, but the soul's choice intervenes between the two, and thus, on the one hand, the autonomous movement of free will is maintained; and on the other the rules of Justice are preserved, which assign to souls the recompense due to them. . . .[426]

---

the divine demons that precede them, and which attach the souls' original being (ὕπαρξις) to the gods who lead them. And it seems to me that it is they that the Prophet has in mind when he says to the souls: 'No demon will obtain you by lot,' thereby manifesting the difference between these demons linked to generation and to destiny, and our overseers who pertain to the essence; for it is they that truly obtain souls by lot. . . . [B]ut the demons linked to destiny rule over them throughout a specific form of life, the choice of which is up to the souls. In the case of the former, we were ruled, in order that we should subsist; in the case of the latter, we chose to live in such-and-such a way, in order that we might be ruled. . . . Thus, even if we are the allotted portions of that demon, it is no longer true that he receives us by lot; for before our choice we are not under his jurisdiction. Once we have chosen the life ruled by him, however, we come under his rule. . . ."

[424] Hierocles, in Photius, *Library,* cod. 251, p. 461b18ff. Bekker, vol. VII, p. 192 Henry.

[425] Proclus, *In Rem. publ.,* vol. II, p. 264, 8ff. Kroll, trans. based on that by Festugière, 1970, 3:222ff.

[426] Cf. Simplicius, *In Ench. Epict.,* I 394ff. Hadot (1996) = I 499ff. Hadot (2001a).

The technical terms προβιοτή and προβιοῦν that the Neoplatonists, and Hierocles himself, often use in this context, appear for the first time, as far as I know, in Porphyry.[427]

7. The Limits of Free Will

If *Heimarmenê* exerts its influence on the external and physical conditions of our life—that is, if the demons ensure the complete accomplishment of all the elements included in the lot that *Heimarmenê* assigns to us as a consequence of our choice—it is therefore *Heimarmenê* that settles almost all the external details of our life. Our free will must therefore have no influence upon such details, except in those cases when we have the impression that we can choose between several possibilities. This is affirmed by Hierocles, as well as by Proclus and Simplicius:

> "Our power of determination," says Hierocles, "is not such that it can, by its voluntary movements, change all that is and all that becomes. For if it were, according to each individual another world would have been produced, and another organization of life, since we do not all want the same thing, but, if they were active and creators of essence, the dispositions of each person would turn all things upside down, and they would be modified by the rapid changes of human choices. This is why it is appropriate that the power of human free will, mobile and ephemeral, is completely incapable of producing or modifying anything without some cooperation coming from outside. . . . It [*scil.* human choice] has no power over anything other than itself, and over the possibility of improving or degrading itself by its behavior; it can only judge that which is, and greet what happens; and thus it acquires virtue or vice, through the good or bad dispositions it manifests in its own activities. Indeed, the power of determination reveals that the only thing that depends on us is to transform ourselves as we please, without the body in which we are clothed, nor external things falling within the domain of this power of determination."[428]

---

[427] Cf. Porphyry, *On What Depends on Us,* in Stobaeus, *Eclog.,* II, 8, 39, p. 163, 21 Wachsmuth = fr. 268, 6; 271, 17 Smith: ἐκ τῶν προβεβιωμένων, and *ibid.,* p. 168, 25: προβιοτή. See also Porphyry, *Ad Gaurum,* XI, p. 50, 1 Kalbfleisch: προβιοτή. Compare Hierocles in Photius, p. 464a23 Bekker, vol. VII, p. 199 Henry: ἐξ ὑποθέσεως τῆς τῶν προβεβιωμένων ἀξίας.

[428] Hierocles, in Photius, *Library,* cod. 251, p. 465a40ff. Bekker, vol. VII, p. 203 Henry.

This is exactly what Simplicius explains at length in his exposition on "What depends on us," and what Proclus also affirms.[429] Yet this, I repeat, does not mean that *Heimarmenê* settles absolutely all the external details of our lives. In particular, we always have the possibility of a true choice when we have the impression, which is by no means illusory, that we are faced by an alternative. The faculty of choice and deliberation has not been given to us in vain.[430] With regard to the results of our actions in the area of external things, they depend to a large extent on our cooperation and the effort we make, although we are not the only masters of these actions.[431] Besides, the practice of oracles and of the hieratic art proves the existence of the contingent.[432]

8. Conclusions

Basing myself on parallel texts, mostly taken from Proclus and cited above all in the notes, I hope to have been able to demonstrate that Hierocles' doctrine on providence and *Heimarmenê*, with regard to those of its elements that we can still grasp, coincides with those of the late Neoplatonists. The thesis of K. Praechter, according to which "Hierocles scarcely goes beyond pre-Plotinian Platonism"[433] and, in contrast to the Athenian Neoplatonists, had undergone Christian influence, therefore loses its credibility; and all the erudite hypotheses constructed thereupon collapse along with it.[434] However, this result of our research does not authorize us to affirm that Hierocles' doctrine on providence, which the state of his work allows us to know only insufficiently, was, in all its details, the same as that of Simplicius, for example, who does not entirely set forth his complete doctrine on this subject either. We are, however, in a position to say that if changes did occur between Hierocles and Simplicius, as is probable, in view of the overall development of Neoplatonism, they can concern only minor details in the supplementary subdivisions of the hierarchy. In its broad outlines—that is to say, with regard to the subordination of *Heimarmenê*

---

[429] Cf. Proclus, *De prov.*, 35, 1–5, p. 145 Boese: "Ubi igitur hic le in nobis, quando quod fit connectitur cum periodo mundi, et rursum quando ex illa solummodo efficitur? Ubi autem alibi dicemus quam in nostris interius electionibus et impetibus? Horum enim solorum nos domini; hiis autem que extra factis cum aliis et pluribus et potentioribus." Cf. Simplicius, *In Ench. Epict.*, I 1ff. Hadot (1996) = I 1ff. Hadot (2001a).

[430] Cf. Proclus, *De prov.*, 36, 1–13, pp. 145–147 Boese.

[431] Cf. Simplicius, *In Ench. Epict.*, I 482–490 Hadot (1996) = I 610–624 Hadot (2001a); cf. Proclus, *De prov.*, 36, pp. 145–147; 55, 5–8, p. 164 Boese.

[432] Cf. Proclus, *De prov.*, 37–39, pp. 146–149 Boese.

[433] Ueberweg-Praechter, 1926, p. 641.

[434] For example, Th. Kobusch, 1976; N. Aujoulat, 1986.

to providence, the compatibility of divine providence with contingency and free will,[435] the function of *Heimarmenê* as renderer of justice for our acts, accomplished both in this life and in a previous life, the Neoplatonic doctrine of providence remained unchanged from Porphyry down to Damascius and Simplicius.

Our research on Hierocles has therefore shown that the fragments known to us of Hierocles' doctrine are characteristic and integral parts of that Neoplatonism that is called "Athenian." In the preceding chapters, we have seen this with regard to the history of philosophy and the notions of matter and the demiurge. In the present chapter, we have been able to confirm that the features of Hierocles' doctrine on Providence, alleged to be archaic, Middle Platonist, or "Christian," are found in Iamblichus or Proclus. The result of our research is thus that we must not doubt Hierocles' affirmation when he declares that his own philosophical views received their orientation from Plutarch of Athens, who, we might add, had undergone the influence of Iamblichus.[436] We therefore note that neither Hierocles nor Simplicius may be claimed as witness of the doctrinal originality of Neoplatonism as taught at Alexandria. I will go still farther: such a doctrinal originality never existed.[437] How, moreover, could it have existed, given that the same philosophers studied and taught both in Athens and in Alexandria, maintaining a constant exchange of ideas between them? We need only read the Introduction by Saffrey and Westerink to their edition of Proclus' *Platonic Theology*[438] and the *Life of Isidorus* by Damascius in order to be struck by the continuous coming and going that took place between the two schools. It is true that local political conditions may sometimes have menaced the freedom of instruction at Alexandria, as was also the case at Athens, which Proclus was once forced to flee;[439] yet this fact did not place the philosophical orientation of the school in jeopardy. It was chance that brought it about that we possess almost exclusively commentaries on the writings of Plato from the Athenian school, and commentaries on Aristotle from the Alexandrian school. Yet in both places the explanation of both authors was practiced, in conformity with the order of studies. The differences that have been discerned between these Platonic and Aristotelian commentaries are due

---

[435] On the position of the Neoplatonists, which they themselves considered intermediate between that of the Peripatetics and that of the Stoics, see the excellent article by F. Brunner, 1976. However, the Neoplatonists' opinion with regard to the Stoics is not justified: cf. p. 110 and n. 381.

[436] Cf. above, pp. 11ff.

[437] Cf. I. Hadot 1990, pp. 177–182 of the conclusion; *Eadem* 1991; *Eadem* 2001a, pp. XLV–C; K. Verrycken 1990.

[438] *Proclus, Théologie platonicienne,* vol. I, pp. xxvi–liv.

[439] Marinus, *Vita Procli,* XV.

to a large extent to the internal demands of the subject dealt with, and not to divergences in philosophical tendencies. Perhaps, as a result of mutual polemics, there was an influence from Christianity on Neoplatonism—I shall leave this question to be decided by others[440]—but if this were the case, neither Simplicius nor Hierocles underwent it to a more noticeable extent than, for instance, Proclus or Damascius. The doctrinal evolution of Neoplatonism took place homogeneously.

[440] For a negative judgment on this subject, cf. P. Hadot, 1972, pp. 109ff.

Bibliography

al-Šahrastānī, *De sectis* (= *Livre des religions et des sectes* [Kitāb al-milal wa-l-mihal]), translated with introduction and notes by D. Gimaret, J. Jolivet and G. Monnot. Leuven-Paris 1986.

Amand, D., *Fatalisme et liberté dans l'Antiquité grecque*. Louvain 1945.

Andresen, C., *Logos und Nomos. Die Polemik des Celsos wider das Christentum*. Berlin 1955.

Athanassiadi, Polymnia, *Damascius, The Philosophical history*, text with trans. and notes by P. A., Oxford 1999.

Aujoulat, Noël, *Le Néo-platonisme alexandrin. Hiéroclès d'Alexandrie. Filiations intellectuelles et spirituelles d'un néo-platonicien du Vᵉ siècle*. Leiden 1986.

———, "Le démiurge chez Hiéroclès d'Alexandrie: en réponse à l'article de Mme Hadot (R.E.G. 1990, pp. 241–262)," *REG* 106 (1993), pp. 400–429.

Badawî, A., *Plotinus apud Arabes*. Cairo 1955.

Beatrice, P. F., "Porphyry's Judgement on Origen", in R. J. Daly, ed., *Origeniana Quinta*. Papers of the 5th International Origen Congress, Boston College, 14–18 August 1989 (= Bibliotheca Ephemeridum Theologicarum Lovaniensium 105), Leuven 1992, pp. 351–367.

Bernard, H., *Hermeias von Alexandrien, Kommentar zu Platos "Phaidros"* (= Philosophische Untersuchungen, 1). Tübingen 1997.

Beutler, R., "Plutarchos von Athen," *RE* 21 (1951): 962–75.

Boeft. J. den, *Calcidius on fate: his doctrine and sources* (Philosophia antiqua, 18). Leiden 1970.

Boese, Helmut, ed., *Proclus, Tria opuscula: De providentia, libertate, malo: Latine Guilelmo de Moerbeka vertente; et Graece ex Isaacii Sebastocratoris aliorumque scriptis collecta* (= Quellen und Studien zur Geschichte der Philosophie, 1). Berolini 1960.

Boyancé, Pierre, "Xénocrate et les Orphiques," *Revue des Études Anciennes* 50(1948): 218–31.

———, "Echo des exégèses de la mythologie grecque chez Philon," in: *Philon d'Alexandrie: Lyon, 11–15 septembre 1966* (Colloques nationaux du Centre national de la recherche scientifique), Paris 1967, 169–186.

Brunner, F., "Providence et liberté," *Revue de Théologie et de Philosophie* 26(1976): 12–24.

Burkert, Walter, *Weisheit und Wissenschaft—Studien zu Pythagoras, Philolaos und Platon* (= Erlanger Beiträge zur Sprach- und Kunstwissenschaft, 10) Nurenberg 1962.

———, trans., *Lore and Science in Ancient Pythagoreanism*, Cambridge, Mass. 1972.

Couvreur, Paul, ed., *Hermias, In Platonis Phaedrum scholia, ad fidem codicis Parisini 1810 denuo collati edidit et apparatu critico ornavit Paul Couvreur.* Novae huius libri impressioni indicem verborum epilogumque addidit Clemens Zintzen, Hildesheim-New York, 1971.

Deuse, Werner, "Der Demiurg bei Porphyrios und Jamblich," in: *Die Philosophie des Neuplatonismus* ([ed. Cl. Zintzen] = Wege der Forschung, 436). Darmstadt 1977, 238–78.

———, *Untersuchungen zur mittelplatonischen und neuplatonischen Seelenlehre* (= Akademie der Wissenschaften und der Literatur, Mainz, Abhandlungen der Geistes- und Sozialwissenschaftlichen Klasse, Einzelveröffentlichung, 3). Wiesbaden 1983.

———, Review of J. F. Finamore 1985, *Gnomon* 59(1987): 409.

Dillon, John M., *Iamblichi Chalcidensis in Platonis dialogos commentariorum fragmenta,* ed. with trans. and commentary by J. M. D. (= Philosophia Antiqua, 23). Leiden 1973.

Dodds, Eric Robert, *Proclus, The Elements of Theology,* a revised text with trans., Introduction, and Commentary by E. R. D., 2nd ed. with addenda and corrections. Oxford 1963 (1st ed. 1933).

Dörrie, Heinrich, "Der Platoniker Eudoros von Alexandreia," *Hermes* 79(1944): 25–39.

———, *Porphyrios' "Symmikta Zetemata": Ihre Stellung in System und Geschichte des Neuplatonismus nebst einem Kommentar zu den Fragmenten* (= Zetemata Heft, 20). München 1959.

Dörrie, Heinrich and M. Baltes, eds., *Der Platonismus in der Antike:* Grundlagen-System-Entwicklung. 4, Die philosophische Lehre des Platonismus: einige grundlegende Axiome, platonische Physik (im antiken Verständnis). 1, Bausteine 101–24: Text, Übersetzung, Kommentar/Heinrich Dörrie, Matthias Baltes. Stuttgart-Bad Cannstatt 1996.

———, *Der Platonismus in der Antike:* Grundlagen-System-Entwicklung. 5, Die philosophische Lehre des Platonismus: platonische Physik (im antiken Verständnis). 2, Bausteine 125–50: Text, Übersetzung, Kommentar/Heinrich Dörrie, Matthias Baltes. Stuttgart-Bad Cannstatt 1998.

Évrard, Étienne, "Le maître de Plutarque d'Athènes et les origines du néoplatonisme alexandrin," *L'Antiquité Classique* 29(1960): 391–406.

Finamore, J. F., *Iamblichus and the Theory of the Vehicle of the Soul* (= American Classical Studies, 14). Chico 1985.

Festugière, A.-J., *La révélation d'Hermès Trismégiste.* I: *L'Astrologie et les sciences occultes.* Paris 1944. II: *Le dieu cosmique.* Paris 1949. III: *Les doctrines de l'âme.* Paris 1953. IV: *Le dieu inconnu et la gnose.* Paris 1954.

———, *Proclus, Commentaire sur le Timée* (Bibliothèque des Textes philosophiques). Paris Vol. 1: 1966; II: 1967; III: (with assistance from Ch. Mugler) 1967; IV: 1968; V: 1968.

———, "L'ordre de lecture des dialogues de Platon aux Vᵉ–VIᵉ siècles," *Museum Helveticum* 26(1969): 281–96, reprinted in *Études de philosophie grecque.* Paris 1971, 535–50.

———, *Proclus, Commentaire sur la République* (Bibliothèque des Textes philosophiques), 3 vols., Paris 1970.

Geudtner, Otto, *Die Seelenlehre der chaldäischen Orakel* (= Beiträge zur Klassischen Philologie, Band 35). Meisenheim am Glan 1971.

Hadot, I., *Le problème du néoplatonisme alexandrin. Hiéroclès et Simplicius*. Paris 1978.

———, "Ist die Lehre des Hierokles vom Demiurgen christlich beeinflußt?" in: *Kerygma und Logos, Festschrift für Carl Andresen*. Göttingen 1979, 258–71.

———, (= 1990a), *Simplicius, Commentaire sur les Catégories, traduction commentée sous la direction de Ilsetraut Hadot, Directeur de Recherche au C.N.R.S.* Fascicule I: *Introduction, première partie* (1–9, 3 *Kalbfleisch, Traduction de Ph. Hoffmann (avec la collaboration de I. et P. Hadot), Commentaire et notes à la traduction par I. Hadot avec des appendices de P. Hadot et J.-P. Mahé* (= Philosophia Antiqua, 50). Leiden/New York/København/Köln 1990.

———, (= 1990b), "Le démiurge comme principe dérivé dans le système ontologique d'Hiéroclès," *Revue des Études Grecques* 103 (1990): 241–62.

———, "The Role of the Commentaries on Aristotle in the Teaching of Philosophy according to the Prefaces of the Neoplatonic Commentaries on the *Categories*," in: *Aristotle in the Later Tradition*, ed. H. J. Blumenthal and H. Robinson (= *Oxford Studies in Ancient Philosophy. Supplementary Volume* 1991). Oxford 1991, 175–89.

———, "À propos de la place ontologique du démiurge dans le système philosophique d'Hiéroclès le néoplatonicien," *REG* 106(1993): 430–59.

———, *Simplicius, Commentaire sur le Manuel d'Épictète, Introduction et édition critique par Ilsetraut Hadot* (= Philosophia antiqua, 66). Leiden/New York/Köln 1996.

———, "Le commentaire philosophique continu dans l'Antiquité," *Antiquité Tardive* 5(1997): 169–76.

———, "Hiéroclès d'Alexandrie," *DPhA* 3(2000): 692–94.

———, (2001a), *Simplicius, Commentaire sur le "Manuel" d'Épictète. 1*, Chapters I–XXIX; texte établi et traduit par Ilsetraut Hadot (= Collection des universités de France. Série grecque, 411). Paris 2001.

———, (2001b), "Les aspects sociaux et institutionnels des sciences et de la médecine dans l'Antiquité tardive," *Antiquité Tardive* 6(1998): 223–50. Italian translation in *Storia della Scienza*, vol. I: *La Scienza Antica*. 2001, 999–1014.

———, "Die Stellung des Neuplatonikers Simplikios zum Verhältnis der Philosophie zu Religion und Theurgie," in: *Metaphysik und Religion: zur Signatur des spätantiken Denkens*, ed. T. Kobusch & M. Erler. München-Leipzig 2002, 323–42.

———, "Simplicius or Priscianus? On the author of the commentary on Aristotle's *De anima* (CAG XI): A methodological study," *Mnemosyne 55*, 2 (2002): pp. 159–199.

Hadot, Pierre, *Porphyre et Victorinus*, 2 vols. Paris 1968.

———, "Fürstenspiegel," *Reallexikon für Antike und Christentum* 8(1970): Lief. 60, 555–632.

————, "La fin du paganisme," *Histoire des religions,* vol. II. Paris 1972.

————, "'Porphyre et Victorinus': Questions et hypothèses," *Res Orientales* 9(1996): 117–25.

————, cf. P. Henry-P. Hadot.

Hager, F. P., "Die Materie und das Böse im antiken Platonismus," *Museum Helveticum* 19(1962): 73–103.

Hägg, T., *Photius als Vermittler antiker Literatur.* Uppsala 1975.

Henry, R., *Photius, Bibliotheca,* edition and trans. by R. Henry, vol. I–VII, Paris (Collection des Universités de France) 1959–1974.

Henry, P., and Hadot, P., Marius Victorinus, Traités Théologiques sur la Trinité, text by P. Henry, trans. and notes by P. Hadot, vol. I–II, Paris 1960 (Editions du Cerf).

Hoffmann, Philippe, "Damascius," *DPhA* 2(1994): 541–93.

Inwood, Brad, *Ethics and Human Action in Early Stoicism.* Oxford 1985.

Kobusch, Theo, *Studien zur Philosophie des Hierokles von Alexandrien. Untersuchungen zum christlichen Neuplatonismus* (= Epimeleia 27). München 1976.

Köhler, Friedrich Wilhelm, *Textgeschichte von Hierokles' Kommentar zum Carmen aureum der Pythagoreer.* Diss. Mainz, Münster 1965.

————, ed., *Hieroclis in aureum Pythagoreorum carmen commentarius,* Stuttgart (Teubner) 1974.

Linley, Neil, ed., *Ibn at-Tayyib: Proclus' Commentary on the Pythagorean Golden Verses, Arabic text and trans.* (= Arethusa Monographs, 10–11). Buffalo 1984.

Lewy, Hans, *Chaldaean Oracles and theurgy. Mysticism, magic and Platonism in the later Roman empire,* new edition by M. Tardieu, with a contribution by P. Hadot, Paris 1978.

Merlan, Ph., "Zwei Untersuchungen zu Alexander von Aphrodisias", *Philologus,* 113 (1969), pp. 85–91.

O'Meara, Dominic J., *Pythagoras revived: Mathematics and Philosophy in Late Antiquity.* Oxford 1989.

Pépin, Jean, *Théologie cosmique et théologie chrétienne.* Paris 1964.

Pinès, Shlomo, "Les textes arabes dits plotiniens et le courant 'porphyrien' dans le néoplatonisme grec," in: *Le néoplatonisme: Royaumont, 9–13 juin 1969.* Paris 1971, 303–13.

Praechter, Karl, "Hierokles 18," *RE* 8(1913): 1479–87.

Robbins, F. E., "The tradition of Greek arithmology," *Classical Philology* 16(1921).

Saffrey, H. D., and L. G. Westerink, *Proclus, Théologie platonicienne,* text established and translated by H. D. S. and L. G. W. (Collection des Universités de France), 6 vols. Paris 1968–1997.

Schweighäuser, Johann, *Epicteteae philosophiae monumenta,* hrsg. von J. S., 5 vols. in 3. Leipzig 1799–1800. Reprinted Hildesheim, New York 1977.

Schwyzer, H.-R., "Proklos über den Platoniker Origenes," in: *Proclus et son influence. Actes du colloque de Neuchâtel, juin 1985,* ed. G. Boss and G. Seel, with an introduction by F. H. Brunner. Zürich 1987.

Segonds, Alain, "Ainéas de Gaza," *DPhA* 1(Paris 1989, 1994²), 82–87.

Steel, Carlos G., *The Changing Self. A Study on the Soul in later Neoplatonism: Iamblichus, Damascius and Priscianus* (= Verhandelingen van der Koninklijke Akademie voor Wetenschapen, Letteren en Schone Kunst van Belgie. Kl. Lett., 40, n° 85), Brussels 1978.

Taormina, Daniela, *Plutarco di Atene: l'Uno, l'anima, le forme, saggio introduttivo, fonti, traduzione e commento* (= Symbolon, 8). Catania-Rome 1989.

Tardieu, Michel, "Recherches sur la formation de l'Apocalypse de Zostrien et les sources de Marius Victorinus," *Res Orientales* 9(1996): 7–114.

———, cf. Lewy, Hans.

Theiler, Willy, *Porphyrios und Augustin*. Halle 1933. Reprinted in *Forschungen zum Neuplatonismus*, Berlin 1966.

———, "Ammonios, der Lehrer des Origenes", in *Forschungen zum Neuplatonismus*, Berlin 1966, p. 1–45.

Tresmontant, Claude, *La Métaphysique du christianisme et la naissance de la philosophie chrétienne*. Paris 1961.

Überweg, F. and K. Praechter, *Grundriss der Geschichte der Philosophie des Altertums*. Berlin 1920 (12th ed. 1926).

Van Liefferinge, Carine, *La théurgie. Des Oracles Chaldaïques à Proclus* (= Kernos Supplément, 9). Liège 1999.

Van Winden, J. M. C., *Calcidius on matter*. Leiden 1965.²

Verrycken, Koenraad, "The Metaphysics of Ammonius son of Hermeias," in: *Aristotle Transformed, the ancient commentators and their influence*, ed. R. Sorabji. London 1990, 199–231.

Von Albrecht, Michael, *Iamblichos, Pythagoras*. Zurich 1985.²

Waszink, J. H., "Observations on Tertullian's treatise against Hermogenes," *Vigiliae Christainae* 9(1955): 129–47.

———, "Bermerkungen zum Einfluss des Platonismus im frühen Christentum," *VChr.* 19(1965): 129–62.

Wolfson, H. A., *Philo: Foundations of religious philosophy in Judaism, Christianity and Islam*. Cambridge, Mass. 1962.³

Zambon, Marco, *Porphyre et le moyen-platonisme* (= Histoire des doctrines de l'Antiquité classique, 27). Paris 2002.

Zintzen, Cl.: cf. Couvreur, Paul.

———, ed., Damascii vitae Isidori reliquiae. Hildesheim 1967.

———, ed., cf. Deuse, Werner.

Zum Brunn, E., *Le dilemme de l'être et du néant chez Saint Augustin*. Paris 1969.

Indexes

a) Index of names and notions

133

b) Index of texts cited